The Cat in the Mysteries of Religion and Magic

AUTHOR'S NOTE

PLEASE note that there is an exhaustive bibliography of authorities consulted at the conclusion of each chapter, so that it is possible for the student to confirm every statement, whilst the ordinary reader is not annoyed by constant footnotes.

My thanks are due to Mr. H. C. Brooke, the well-known cat fancier and first editor of *Cat Gossip*, for permission to include some of his valuable literary and artistic contributions to the subject.

SACRIFICE OF AN INTRUDER IN THE SHRINE OF BAST
Original drawing by H. C. Brooke.

The Cat in Magic, Mythology, and Religion

M. OLDFIELD HOWEY

BRACKEN BOOKS
LONDON

Previously published as The Cat in the Mysteries of Religion
and Magic by
Rider & Co., London

This edition published 1989 by Bracken Books
an imprint of Bestseller Publications Ltd.
Princess House, 50 Eastcastle Street
London W1N 7AP, England

ISBN 1 85170 271 7

Printed and bound in GDR

CONTENTS

CONTENTS

LIST OF ILLUSTRATIONS

LIST OF ILLUSTRATIONS

The Cat in the Mysteries of Religion and Magic

INTRODUCTION

"MAN created God in His own image," was the dictum of Voltaire, but the Gods have not always been visualised by man in human form. In comparatively early stages of religious evolution it became apparent to the devotee that man as man could not adequately symbolise or personify the conception of divinity innate within him. Among primitive peoples life is intimately interwoven with religion, and every concrete object of perception is recognised as an idea and manifestation of the Creator God, and therefore as a claimant for man's awful reverence. Beasts, birds, fish, reptiles, and even insects, plants, and stones, and monstrous forms of imaginative fantasy, have all been seen by poet primitives as images of attributes of the Infinite.

Thus a fundamental equality of all things animate or inanimate was first accepted ; but profounder study proved that certain forms presented such many-sided facets that they outshone all lesser lights, and in themselves conveyed to their observer something of the all-inclusiveness of the Divine. One of such symbols is found in the Serpent, as I have endeavoured to prove in a former volume, but another most outstanding example of a *multum in parvo* emblem that, because of its essential appropriateness, has persisted millenniums beyond the age in which it took birth, is the subject of this present study, the Cat. The Cat, like the Serpent, conveys, though necessarily imperfectly, the thought that God is All. Such a stupendous conception involves the examination of many totally distinct, and even apparently antagonistic aspects which can only be unified by that single thought. Therefore my readers must pardon any lack of sequence that may obtrude itself in this study. The Cat is the symbol of Good and of Evil, of Light and of Darkness, of Christ and of Satan, of Religion and of Black Magic, of Sun and of Moon, of Father, Mother, and Son. It will repay our investigation because of the vastness of the vistas upon which it opens rifts in the veil. The subjects to which the Cat Symbol introduces us are themselves so tremendous that scarcely one of them could be exhausted by a lifetime's exclusive devotion, so of course no claim of completeness is made for this work. But absolutely inadequate as it must be in relation to its theme, I believe it still contains much that will be found of absorbing interest both to the general reader and to the student of Life's mysteries.

M. O. H.

THE CAT IN THE MYSTERIES OF RELIGION AND MAGIC

CHAPTER I

BAST

AT the head of the deities of ancient Egypt to whom the cat was specially sacred stood the great goddess Bast, or Ubastet—also known as Bubastis and Pasht—the second member of the Triad of Memphis, and the loved and constant companion of Ra himself. She appears to have been originally a foreign deity, but, in very early times became identified with the female counterparts of the Sun-gods, Ptah, Ra, Osiris, and Tem. We may see in her a personification of certain aspects of Isis, who, as the moon, or the Cat that represented the moon, was specially adored in the city named after Bubastis—Aboo-Pasht, the City of Pasht. Here the worship of Bast dates from a remote antiquity, and the Cat was held in such reverence as her symbol by its citizens, that deep mourning followed the death of the sacred animal.

Bubastis was situated east of the Delta, at a short distance from the Pelusiac branch of the Nile, and lofty mounds named Tel Basta still mark its site. It is referred to in Ezekiel xxx. 17, as Pi-beseth (margin, Pubastum), and seems to have been then a city of some importance. The prophet foretells its downfall, saying its young men shall fall by the sword, and it shall go into captivity.

BAST WITH SISTRUM AND SACRED CATS

By courtesy of the British Museum.

It is not known where the greater number of the numerous statues of Bast now in the British Museum came from, but some were brought from Thebes, and some probably once graced the Temple of Bubastis. Many of them bear the name of Amunothph III, and it is difficult to understand why this monarch of the Theban line made so many statues in honour of a goddess who more especially belonged to Lower Egypt. Sharpe suggests it is partly explained " by the title used within the second oval of his name, where he calls himself ' Ruler of the city of Mendes.' " However this may be, great honour was accorded to Bast in the Upper Country; and at Thebes, as at Heliopolis, she held a conspicuous position among the contemplar deities. She is mentioned in the Pyramid Texts,* but only occasionally figures in the Book of the Dead.

Herodotus has bequeathed to us a vivid description of the shrine of the goddess as " standing on an island completely surrounded by water except at the entrance passage. Two separate canals conduct from the Nile to the entrance, and diverging to the right and left surround the Temple." These were about 100 feet broad and their banks were planted with trees. The remains of the once magnificent building show it to have been about 500 feet long. It was built of the finest red granite, and encompassed by a sacred enclosure about 600 feet square, beyond which was a larger enclosure, 900 by 1200 feet, containing a canal, a grove of trees, and a lake. "The vestibule," continues Herodotus, " is sixty feet high, and is ornamented with handsome figures, six cubits in height. The temple stands in the centre of the city, and in walking round the place you look down upon it from every side, because the foundations of the houses having been elevated, and the temple still remaining on its original level, the sacred enclosure is encompassed by a wall, on which a great number of figures are sculptured, and within it is a grove, planted round the cella of the temple, with trees of a considerable height. In the cella is the statue of the goddess. The sacred enclosure is a stadium (600 feet) in length by the same in breadth. The street which corresponds with the entrance of the temple crosses the public square, goes to the east, and leads to the Temple of Mercury."

One of the principal festivals of the Egyptians was that celebrated at Bubastis, in honour of Bast, in the months of April and May. Herodotus (II, 59, 60) considers that the Egyptians took more interest in this than in any of the numerous fêtes which were annually held in their country, and he has handed down to us an account of the ceremonial observed on the pilgrimage to

* Texts of the Pyramid of Pipi.

Bubastis. The celebrants "go by water," he says, "and numerous boats are crowded with persons of both sexes. During the voyage several women strike the *crotala*; some men play the flute; the rest singing and clapping their hands. As they pass by a town they draw the boat into the bank. Some of the women still singing, and playing the *crotala*; others calling out as long as they are able, uttering reproaches against the people of the town, who begin to dance, whilst the former pull up their clothes before them in a scoffing manner. The same performance is repeated at every town they pass upon the river. Arrived at Bast, they celebrate the festival of Diana, sacrificing a great number of victims, and on that occasion a greater consumption of wine takes place than during the whole of the year; for, according to the accounts of the people themselves, no less than 700,000 persons of both sexes are present, besides children."

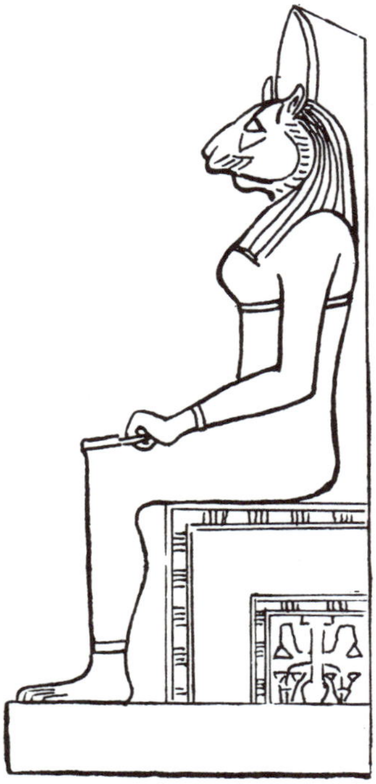

COLOSSAL FIGURE OF BAST WITH LION-HEAD
Now in the British Museum.

Although the name Bast implies "the tearer," or "the render," yet, in contradistinction to the fierce Sekhmet, goddess of war, who represented the destructive powers of the solar orb, Bast typified its kindly fertilizing heat. She was considered as embodying the beneficent portion of the elemental fire, and as the bringer of good fortune. She was also known as "the lady of Sept," i.e. of the star Sothis. Bast is a counterpart of the joyous Hathor, like her delighting in music and the dance. We may recognise her by the sistrum of the dancing women adorned with the heads or figures of cats, which she holds in her hand, and by the ægis, or by the basket supported on her arm. But occasionally she is represented without these attributes, and then it is difficult to know whether we are viewing the Cat's head of the kindly Bast, or the lion's head of the mighty and terrible Sekhmet. Bast herself is often represented as lion-headed, and occasionally the demonstrative sign following her name is a lion instead of a cat, though the latter was her particular emblem. Some of the black basalt figures in the British

Museum are of Bast as a lion-headed goddess, and it is probable that these are of the earliest date, since Bast only appears with the head of a cat at a later period, and then principally in small votive bronzes.

Finding wolf and jackal were both dedicated to Anubis, we may easily admit lion and cat to have been alike emblems of Sekhmet and Bast. Originally Bast seems to have been represented with the head of a lion (not of a lioness, for the mane is indicated) in allusion to the arsenothelic, or male and female nature which was hers. The Egyptians appear to have regarded these feline animals as interchangeable from the standpoint of symbology. But in the bronze figures the Cat's head is distinct. They sometimes represent her with the sistrum in her right hand, and in her left, the head of a lion surmounted by a disk and asp ; but such bronzes are of later date, and so can less be depended upon as a true mirror of the goddess's attributes than the sculptures of the ancient monuments. Probably the lions, which Ælian states were kept in the courts of the Temple of the Sun, were dedicated to Bast. It is as a lion-headed woman that Bast is represented in the colossal seated figure in sienite which is now in the British Museum (No. 57).* It is clothed in a tight-fitting dress, the feet side by side, the hands resting on the knees, the left hand holding the ankh, the symbol of life, and the right hand open. On the sides of the seat is an inscription in honour of " the priest, the Son of the Sun, the good king of Upper Egypt, Lord of battles, Amunothph III, beloved by Pasht." This statue is 5 feet 2 inches high from the feet to the top of the head, exclusive of the base on which it rests and the crowning solar disk.

Another colossal statue of Bast bears a cat's head. This is six feet high, exclusive of the disk and the base. Sharpe gives its number as 517. It immortalises the name of Shishank, the earliest Egyptian king personally mentioned in the Hebrew scriptures. He reigned at Bubastis, which was the chief city in that part of Egypt where the Jews dwelt, both during the life of Moses and afterwards. But Shishank made himself master of Thebes, and was king of all Egypt. He fought against Rehoboam, king of Judah, about 956 B.C., as recorded in 1 Kings xiv. 25, where we are told that " he took away the treasures of the house of the Lord, and the treasures of the king's house ; he even took away all." The Kingdom of Judah is enumerated among the conquered nations listed on the walls of the Temple of Karnak. It seems to have been as the Tearer and Render that Shishank honoured Bast.

* Sharpe, p. 44.

BAST WITH KITTENS HOLDING A SEKHMET ÆGIS

From the British Museum, No. 37641.

CAT SACRED TO BAST: HER HEAD CROWNED BY A SERPENT

From the British Museum, No. 11556.

Another aspect of Bast is symbolised in the striking exhibit in the British Museum (listed by Sharpe as No. 105), showing the forehead and ears of a colossal cat-headed goddess with a large head-dress formed by a ring of sacred asps, each crowned by a sun. This gives us an idea of the reverence in which Bast was held by her worshippers, and clearly exemplifies her dual nature, embracing both sun and moon, and all that was symbolised by them to the Egyptian mystic, especially the essential unity of the light proceeding from them both. As the Cat sees in the darkness, so the Sun which journeyed into the underworld at night saw through its gloom. Bast was the representative of the Moon, because that planet was considered as the Sun-god's eye during the hours of darkness. For as the moon reflects the light of the solar orb, so the Cat's phosphorescent eyes were held to mirror the sun's rays when it was otherwise invisible to man. Bast as the Cat-moon held the Sun in her eye during the night, keeping watch with the light he bestowed upon her, whilst her paws gripped, and bruised and pierced the head of his deadly enemy, the serpent of darkness. Thus she justified her title of the Tearer or Render, and proved that it was not incompatible with love.

Later Egyptian theology seems to have produced little original thought, but to have spent its powers in reconstructing and resuscitating the old. It lost its pristine purity, and conceptions which owed their origin to magic were admitted into religion. Because the gods had often been symbolised as birds, a bird-shape was given to the great gods of each nome. Bast was represented as a cat-headed hawk in this corrupted theology. Perhaps the metaphor was intended to emphasise her identity with Isis, for that goddess hovered over the dead body of Osiris in the form of a sparrow-hawk, and caused breath to enter into his lifeless form by the fanning of her wings, so that the dead god entered upon a new existence as king of the underworld. It was whilst Isis thus restored life to her lord that she became pregnant, and, later, gave birth to the hawk-headed Horus.

The Vulture which represented Mut (the World-Mother and great female counterpart of Amen-Ra), also appears in connection with Bast where the latter is considered as a member of the Egyptian Trinity that is recognised by the composite name of Sekhmet-Bast-Ra. This figure well illustrates the extraordinarily complicated nature of the goddess, for it depicts a man-headed woman with wings springing from her arms. And the symbolism is further complicated by two vultures growing from her neck, and lions' claws that arm her feet.

It is impossible not to recognise this deity in Diana Triformis and Tergemina, who, by virtue of her three different offices is known as Luna in the Heavens, Diana on Earth, and Hecate in Hell. Symbologists employed various means of typifying these paradoxical aspects of the Great Mother. Porphyry sees her with the triple forms of bull, and dog, and lion united. Other writers said she had the head of a horse on the right side, of a dog on the left, and of a human being in the centre. Virgil refers to:

> "Threefold Hecate with her hundred names,
> And three Dianas: . . ."

And Claudian says:

> "Behold, far off, the Goddess Hecate
> In threefold shape advances."

In her aspect as Hecate this deity seems to have been enough to terrify the bravest. According to Tooke, "They say that she was excessive tall, her Head was covered with frightful Snakes instead of Hair, and her Feet were like Serpents." But he also points out that her name suggests the Moon's action in darting her rays or arrows long distances and "according to the Opinion of some, she is called Triformis because the Moon hath three several Phases."

As Bast was sometimes identified with Mut, so we find Diana occasionally coalesced with Venus. Thus Servius, in his commentary on Virgil (2. *Æneid*), says that the men sacrificed to Venus under the name of Luna, in women's clothes, and the women in men's clothes, and the Roman historian, Spartianus, has a similar allusion (*Imp. Caracal*).

Wilkinson has pointed out that we must admit the identity of Diana with Venus, for otherwise she could not rank among the eight great deities, but only with those of the third and even fourth order, and this is belied by the exalted character she bears in the temples of Thebes. He thinks it possible that Horus the Elder, or Aroeris, who was the brother of Osiris, and like him represented the Sun, has been confused with Horus, the son of Osiris, identified with the Grecian Apollo, whose sister was Diana. But he warns us not to push such analogies too far. The younger Horus had no sister, and Bast could not have been the sister of the elder Horus.

Herodotus, who travelled in Egypt about 450 B.C., endeavoured to point out the identity of the Egyptian and Grecian gods, but apparently found the origin of Bast even then obscure. He considered her to be the daughter of Osiris (or Bacchus) and Isis, and to be one with the Greek Diana. A rock temple dedicated to Bast, which bears the name *Speos Artemidos* (The Cave of

Artemis, i.e. Diana), shows that this was the accepted opinion in Egypt during the Greek period ; and by the Greeks at Sais and Alexandria she was sometimes called Diana and sometimes Minerva. This is the origin of the Alexandrian proverbial description of two things very unlike, by saying they bore the same amount of resemblance to one another as a cat to Minerva. The Greek myth related by Ovid, in which Diana assumes the form of a cat to escape from Typho (*Met.* v. 330), further confirms the conclusion arrived at by Herodotus.

BIBLIOGRAPHY

"Egyptian Antiquities in the British Museum," pp. 12, 44–7. By Samuel Sharpe. Pub. by John Russell Smith, London, 1862.

"Symbolism." By Gerald Massey.

"The Ancient Egyptians." By Sir J. Gardner Wilkinson, D.C.L., F.R.S., F.R.G.S. Pub. by John Murray, London, 1878.

"The Secret Doctrine," Vol. I, pp. 323, 416. By H. P. Blavatsky. Pub. by the Theosophical Publishing Company, London, 1888.

"A Handbook of Egyptian Religion." By Adolph Erman. Trans. by R. Griffith. Pub. by Constable & Co., London, 1907.

"Among the Primitive Bakongo," p. 160. By John H. Weeks. Pub. by Seeley, Service & Co., Ltd., London, 1914.

"Myths of Ancient Egypt." By Lewis Spence. Pub. by George G. Harrap, London, 1922.

"Egyptian Mythology," p. 150. By W. Max Muller, Ph.D. Pub. by George G. Harrap, London.

CHAPTER II

SEKHMET

THE dread Sekhmet, the cat- or lioness-headed goddess of Egypt, who personified the fierce consuming fire of the scorching sun, was the feminine counterpart of Ptah—the title by which the Sun-god Ra was known at Memphis. The temples of Ptah, Sekhmet, Bast, Hathor, Osiris, and Seker were all placed in this city, and it seems probable that this proximity was not accidental, but intended to prompt the recognition of the essential unity of all these deities.

To aid us in comprehending the nature of Sekhmet, let us glance for a moment at the multiform character of her spouse Ptah. As we do so, we realise how dear to the heart of the Egyptian mystic was the doctrine of the Encircled Serpent, or—in the terms of the metaphor we are now considering—the Coiled Cat. The Deity was All, and Unity embraced Plurality. The name Ptah is said to signify the "Opener," because this god personified the rising sun, and threw wide the gates of day. But we find him continually fused with other divinities, and sometimes even with those whom we should normally expect to see represented as his deadly foes. As Ptah-Seker, for example, he typifies the union of the Creative Principle with chaos and darkness, and is a form of Osiris as the dead Sun-god, or Sun in the night hours. In this character he is fitly represented by the Cat who traverses the night unseen.

We also find him as a member of the trinity, Ptah-Seker-Osiris, that about the XXIInd Dynasty had become merged in Osiris. As the Master-architect and demiurge who carried out the plans of Thoth and his helpers, together with Sekhmet his spouse, Ptah shared in the attributes of the Seven Wise Ones who came forth in the form of seven hawks from the pupil of the Eye of Ra. But his union with Sekhmet is more usually illustrative of the axiom that "extremes meet," for, in contrast to the creative activities of the benevolent Ptah, she represented the destructive force of solar heat, an aspect so much in evidence in Africa that it is impossible to entirely ignore it when contemplating the sun in that continent. Its rising is watched with dread and aversion by many African tribes who have learned to fear the strength of its burning rays, and carefully conceal themselves when it appears.

The solar cult originated with the hierarchy at Heliopolos, and all the feline goddesses of Egypt were representative of the varying degrees of the sun's intensity, from genial warmth to burning devastation. This accounts for many apparent paradoxes in the Egyptian pantheon, and for such descriptions as that of Isis-Hathor in a Philæ text: "Kindly is she as Bast, terrible is she as Sekhmet."

In a XIIth Dynasty tale Sekhmet is referred to as the awful goddess of plagues, but this is only one of her many aspects. She must be thought of as bearing the same relation to the kindly and beneficent Bast, as Nephthys, the consort of the evil Seth, bears to her sister Isis. The antagonism is more apparent than real. Essentially the two are one. Thus we find that though formerly the name of Bast was read as Pasht, some authorities go so far as to state that they consider the true reading to be Sekhmet. A further confirmation of the identity of the two goddesses is found in the fact that in the temple of Koptos, the Theban goddess, Mut, was at one time known as Bast, and at another time as Sekhmet of Memphis. In the sculptures various names are attached to the feline-headed goddesses, such as "Sekhmet, the great Merenptah," or beloved of Ptah, mistress of the heaven, and "Sekhmet, the great Urhek." Here also Sekhmet is connected with Mut, and is then styled "Mut dwelling in the abode of Ptah, mistress of Heaven, regent of Earth."

Instances occur where Mut is represented with the head of a cat or a lion, and Wilkinson tells us we may then think of her as having assumed the attributes of Bast or of Thriphis, since her own shape was that of a vulture.

It seems fairly evident that Sekhmet and Bast must originally have been one, or at least have had a common source, and developed from a sky-goddess such as Hathor, Nut, or Neith. The name Hathor signifies "House of Horus," and is an analogue for the sky, wherein the Sun-god Horus made his dwelling. She was also regarded as a Moon-goddess, and as such was often referred to as the "Eye of Ra," which was one of the titles of Sekhmet. Hathor was said to be the mother, wife, and daughter of Ra, and to the Egyptians represented ideal womanhood. She was described as "the lady of music and mistress of song, lady of leaping and mistress of wreathing garlands," and was a personification of the female principle.

In this aspect we recognise Bast, but when Hathor was the

instrument of the vengeance of Ra, we find her identified with the terrible Sekhmet, as Sekhmet-Hathor, slaying the human race, and wading exultantly in their blood till Ra himself had to deliver mankind from her hands by resorting to the stratagem of making her drunken, and so unable to continue the work of destruction.

The Syrian goddess Ashtoreth, known to the Egyptians as "Mistress of Horses" and "Lady of the Chariot," is also considered to be one of the forms of Hathor, or Sekhmet-Hathor: and her cult seems to have been introduced into Egypt during the Syrian campaign of Thothmes III. Like Bast and Sekhmet, she is depicted with the head of a lioness. She was the terrible and destructive goddess of war, and is mounted on a four-horsed chariot which she drives over the bodies of her fallen foes. A second Syrian deity, Getesh, or Gedesh, goddess of love and beauty, and the moon, was identified with the other aspect of Hathor in Egyptian thought. In her native country she was worshipped with somewhat licentious rites as a Nature goddess, and the Egyptians prayed to her for the gifts of life and health. She is regarded by some authorities as being the other aspect of Ashtoreth.

Though not lion-headed, she is represented in Egyptian art as standing upon a lion. She wears the sun and the moon on her head. Her figure is nude: in her right hand she grasps a mirror and lotus blooms, emblems of life, and in her left, two serpents, emblems of death, thus declaring the Gnostic and Manichæan doctrine of Antitheses.

At a later period we find her still more definitely identified with Hathor, and wearing the headdress of that goddess. In an inscription of the XVIIIth and XIXth Dynasties she is similarly described as "Lady of Heaven, mistress of all the gods, Eye of Ra, who has none like unto her."

This personification of the attributes of a single goddess in so many separate forms is confusing to a modern mind, but we must ever remember, as an old poet observed, that

> "Pluto, Proserpine, Ceres, Venus, Cupid,
> Triton, Nereus, Tethys, and Neptune,
> Hermes, Vulcan, Pan, Jupiter, Juno,
> Diana, and Apollo, are ONE GOD."

BIBLIOGRAPHY

" Celtic Researches," p. 297. By John Davies. Pub. about 1630.

" Egyptian Mythology," 2nd edition, p. 63. By Samuel Sharpe. Pub. by Carter & Co., London, 1896.

" Religion of the Ancient Egyptians." By A. Wiedemann. Pub. London, 1897.

" Myths and Legends of Ancient Egypt," p. 147. By Lewis Spence. Pub. by George G. Harrap & Co., London, 1922.

" The Book of the Dead." Trans. by Sir E. A. Wallis Budge, M.A., D.L., L.D. Pub. by Kegan Paul, Trench & Trübner, London, 1923.

CHAPTER III

THE SISTRUM

THE mystical musical instrument known as the Sistrum is of great interest and importance from a symbolical standpoint. Upon its apis the Sacred Cat is enthroned, as emblem of the moon, and the great goddess that planet represented. Perhaps no other instrument of music has been so generally associated with magic and religious ritual as has the ancient sistrum. But the Egyptians seem to have more especially dedicated it to Hathor (or Athor), the Egyptian Venus. This goddess was in reality but a popular personification of Isis in the rôle of the loving, protecting Mother of the living, and Guardian of the souls of the departed during their sojourn in the dreary Underworld. She is regularly identified with Isis in the inscriptions of the great Temple of Hathor at Denderah, although a smaller temple specially dedicated to Isis is within the same enclosure. Nowhere else do we find such prominence given to the sacred Sistrum as in this sanctuary of Hathor, so it is evident that it possessed a special significance in relation to this goddess; nor is it hard to guess what that may have been, since the Cat typifies and exemplifies the ideal Mother.

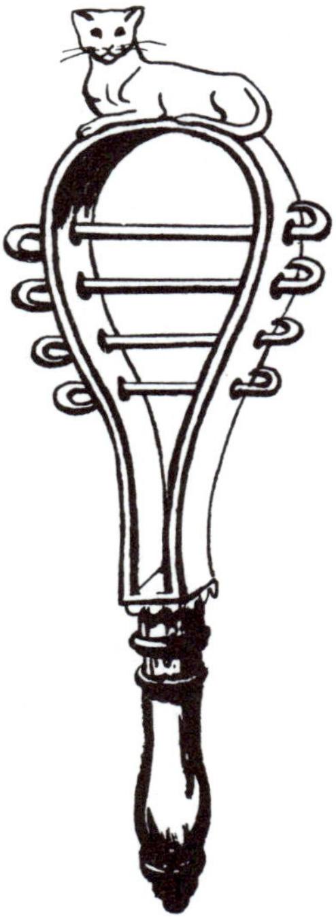

EXAMPLE OF ANCIENT SISTRUM WITH FIGURE OF SACRED CAT

It has been suggested that the form of the Sistrum was derived from that of the Ankh, the well-known symbol of life carried by every Egyptian deity. Or, conversely, that the Ankh was based on the Sistrum. The fruitfulness of the Cat accords with either theory. The erect oval is emblematic of the Female Principle of Nature regarded as the womb of Divine Manifestation, whilst the upright pillar of the handle symbolises the corresponding Male

Principle.. The Cat is the presiding Deity blessing the mystic union with fecundity and abundance.

We may compare this with the description and interpretation of the Sistrum bequeathed to us by Plutarch. He describes it as being " rounded above," and adds that " the loop holds the four bars which are shaken. Upon the bend of the Sistrum they often set the head of a cat with a human face ; below the four little bars, on one side is the face of Isis, on the other side that of Nephthys."

The Sistrum is the symbol of the world's harmony. The heads of Isis and Nephthys which adorn its handle signify birth and death. The shaking of the four bars within the circular apis represents the agitation of the four elements within the compass of the globe, by which all things are continually destroyed and reproduced, and further figures that all creatures must move in a fixed order as does the moon, whose orbit embraces all that is on earth.

To emphasise the lunar symbolism, the Cat is often represented with a crescent upon its head, but Plutarch would have us make no mistake. He points out that the Cat, from " its variety of colour, its activity in the night, and the peculiar circumstances attending its fecundicity " is the proper emblem of the moon.

In reference to this last matter, the Egyptians stated that the Cat brought forth at birth, first one, then two, afterwards three kittens, and so on, adding one at each later birth until she reached seven. So that she brought forth twenty-eight young altogether, corresponding to the several degrees of light which appear during the moon's revolutions. And Plutarch, who records this, comments that " Though such things may appear to carry an air of fiction with them, yet it may be depended upon, that the pupils of her eyes seem to fill up and to grow larger upon the full of the moon, and to decrease again, and diminish in their brightness on its waning."

When in use the Sistrum was held in the right hand (as illustration) and shaken, from which circumstance its name is derived (*aera repulsa manu.* Tibullus, I. 3, 24). Its most usual form is seen in the second drawing. It was really a kind of rattle, and generally consisted of a metal frame pierced by four brass or iron rods, which were either loose, or fitted with loose rings. Apuleius describes it as a bronze rattle, consisting of a narrow plate curved like a sword-belt through which rods were passed, that emitted a loud shrill sound. He seems to suggest that the shakes were in trios, thus making a sort of rude music. He says that the sistrums were sometimes of silver, or even of gold.

The Sistrum is said to have been also used in Egypt as a

military instrument for collecting the troops (Virgil, *Æneid* VIII, 696), but this does not imply a secularisation of it, as the Egyptians lived their religion and introduced it into every action. In this case it would probably be considered as an implement of Hathor or Isis in her warrior aspect personified by the terrible Sekhmet, for, like the Serpent, the Cat is a constant reminder that extremes meet, and that All is embraced by One. The Goddess inspires or destroys according to the angle from which she is contemplated. Mistress of the Heaven and Regent of the West, in her celestial character—she is the Eye of Ra, the Sun, and the solar deities Shu and Tefnut are her children ; but her terrestrial presentation may be that of the goddess of youth, and pleasure, and beauty ; like the Greek Aphrodite, the goddess of love, or may show us the cruel and destructive Sekhmet, whose counterpart was Bellona, goddess of war.

Sistra do not seem to have been entirely confined to Egypt. They were used in the Circle Dance of the Sebasian Mysteries, the origin of which is lost in the mists of antiquity, though they are thought to have been derived from the Mithraic Mysteries. The dance symbolised the motion of the Planets around the Sun. The Sistrum is said to be used to-day in Abyssinia and Nubia.

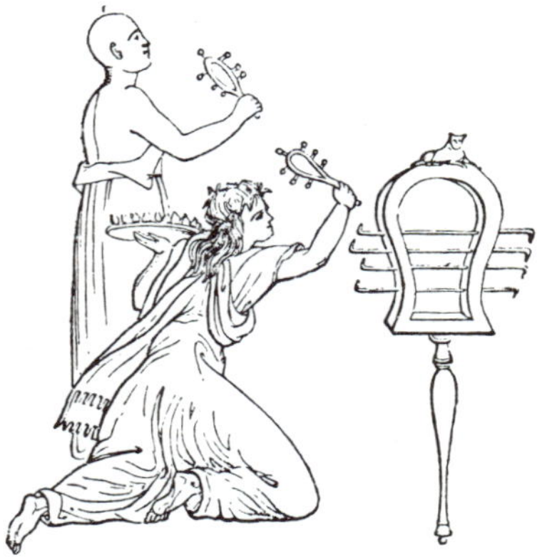

PRIEST AND DANCING WOMAN WITH SISTRA

The introduction of the worship of Isis into Italy shortly before the commencement of the Christian era made the Romans familiar with this instrument, and in two paintings found at Portici (at the foot of Vesuvius), a priest of Isis and a kneeling woman are represented as rattling it.

An analagous musical instrument used by the singing-girls of Japan is known as the Samisen, and its strings are made from cat-gut. Not so very long ago the geishas of Tokio subscribed for a Mass for the souls of the Cats whose lives had been brought to an untimely end in order to provide the material which was an integral part of the instrument. Such honour and recognition suggests that the connection of the Cat with the music of the geishas is not entirely a fortuitous one, but possibly owes its origin to the same conception as that which placed the Cat on the Sistrum of Isis.

BIBLIOGRAPHY

"Metamorphesos, sive de Asino Aureo," XI, 4. By Apuleius Saturninus.

"Metamorphoses." IX, 784. By Publius Ovidius Naso.

"Isis and Osiris." By Plutarch.

"Manners and Customs of the Ancient Egyptians." By Sir Gardner Wilkinson, F.R.S., M.R.S.L., etc. Pub. by John Murray, London, 1842.

"The Secret Doctrine," Vol. II, pp. 437, 483. By H. P. Blavatsky. Pub. by the Theosophical Publishing House, London, 1893.

CHAPTER IV

THE CAT AND THE SERPENT

THE Cat and the Serpent must be numbered among the most ancient glyphs of Egypt, and, in its original form, seems to have been identical with the symbol of the Virgin and the Dragon. Because the Cat is the emblem of the time-honoured ideal of Virgin-Motherhood, the Egyptian Great Mother Goddess, variously invoked as Isis, or Atet, or Mout, etc., as time and place might decree, was constantly represented as assuming feline form. Atet is said to have taken this shape when she conquered and slew the serpent of evil, and the myth gave rise to the Egyptian belief that cats possessed the power to heal those bitten by asps or other venomous creatures.

Like the other Great Mother Goddesses, Atet seems to have been eventually absorbed in the Great Mother Mout, "queen of the gods," who wears the double crown of Egypt. Her symbol was the lioness, and this animal was probably chosen that it might indicate her sovereignty over all other deities; since it is the head of the family to which the Cat—representative of so many deities—belongs.

The individuality of Atet having been obliterated by a greater than herself, her feat of slaying the serpent was attributed by later mythology to Ra, who personified the life-giving properties of the solar orb. It is certainly remarkable that Ra, like his predecessor, assumed the form of a cat in order to combat the evil power. The battlefield was in the Other World, for serpents were not only the foes of the living, but had to be counted among the enemies of the dead. The most formidable of these ghostly serpent antagonists was the monstrous Rerek, who had his abode in the deepest gloom of the Other World, and ever opposed the passage of Ra, and the host of glorious beings who accompanied him into the Kingdom of Day. Rerek had many forms, and was known by many names, but of all his metamorphoses the most terrible was when he appeared as Apap. He was immortal, so although Ra daily clove his head in twain, and his bones were crushed, and his body dismembered, and many other punishments inflicted on him by the gods, he always returned to life, and continued his evil doings.

During a solar eclipse a terrific battle would take place—a titanic combat between darkness and light, evil and good. Fear-

RA SLAYING APEP
From the Papyrus of Hu-Nefer.

ful of the issue, mankind breathlessly watched the peril of the Sun-god, shouting, and shaking the Sistrum to terrify the serpent foe. Suddenly the Celestial Cat would leap upon the deadly reptile with fiery eyes and bristling coat, and Apap would fly, bleeding and torn, to the depths of darkness. After the eclipse was thus ended, the veneration of the Egyptian people for the sacred animal was always intensified. At other times priestly interference might save the slayer of a cat from popular vengeance, but after an eclipse even the power of the priesthood could not rescue the guilty person, however high a position he might hold. The Sicilian historian, Diodorus, who travelled in Egypt during the first century B.C., recorded how a Roman soldier, stationed at Alexandria, slew a cat, and in consequence was seized and executed by the mob, notwithstanding his privileges as a Roman citizen, and the entreaties of King Ptolemy who feared the vengeance of Rome.

This incident is commented on in the following striking poem to a cat :

TEMPORA MUTANTUR

When Nile was young ; when Britain's savage hordes
Woad-stained, lurked beastlike in their woods and caves,
Whilst daily battling with the wolf and bear,
And mighty Urus : then, wast Thou divine !
'Fore Thee a priesthood, wise in ancient lore
Spread offerings rich and rare, and humbly bowed,
Whilst Temple girls paced in the votive dance,
With Utchat-Amulet of gold adorned,
Thou didst recline on Pharaoh's golden throne ;
And when Thy time upon this earth was o'er
—And mighty Pharaoh, too, must pass away,
*Ptah-Seker-Asar having called ye hence—
Then cunning workmen wrapped Thy slender form
In choicest swaddling-cloths, with spiçes rare,
And, jewel-decked, Thou shareds't the Pharaoh's tomb.
. . . . Egypt fell
On evil days : the Roman Eagles waved
Their threatening pinions o'er Nile's yellow sand—
'Gainst Thee the Roman raised an impious hand—
Not yet, not yet, was Egypt's spirit dead !
" The Roman slew a cat ! "—Athirst for blood—
Forgotten dread of Rome—the swarthy mob
Poured, howling vengeance, from each alley-way—
And the proud Roman knew the taste of death—
For he had slain a Cat ! . . . Far, far away
Are now those Pagan days ! O'er all our heads
Civilisation's blessings freely pour ;
O, Bast, look downward through the centuries,
And see Thy children ! Timorous through the streets
Some crouch, the sport of every ruffian lad ;
Cold-blooded torturers wrench their tender limbs
In name of Science : others meet their end
Choking and struggling in the deadly gas,
Whilst white-clad savants, smiling, book their throes,
And khaki soldiers, shuddering, stand aghast—
Yet scarce a soul lifts a protesting voice !
WE ARE NOT PAGANS, AS THOSE SONS OF NILE !
LET US GIVE THANKS WE ARE NOT SUCH AS THEY !

(*H. C. Brooke :* " Lines to an Abyssinian Cat," 1925.)

To return to our subject of the combat between the Cat of the Sun and the Serpent of Darkness ; we find it vividly described in the following lines, translated by Dr. Budge, from the papyrus of Nebseni (British Mus., No. 9900, sheet 14, 1, 16 ff.). Ra himself is speaking, and he says, " I am the Cat which fought (?) hard by the Persea tree (19) in Anni (Heliopolis), on the night when the foes of Neb-er-tcher were destroyed."

* The triune god of the resurrection.

FROM AN EGYPTIAN PAINTING ON THE COFFIN OF PA-KHAT-KHERT-HERU, INCENSE BEARER IN THE TEMPLE OF KHEN-SU AT THEBES
DATE ABOUT 900 B.C.

Now in the British Museum, No. 6666.

As the exact phrasing of the original of the sentence is admittedly somewhat obscure, I add a slightly different interpretation of the same lines by another authority, Samuel Birch. This version reads: "I am the Great Cat at the pool of the Persea, there in Heliopolis; the night of the battle made by the binders of the wicked, the day of strangling the enemies of the entire lord."

The vignette from the seventeenth chapter of the Ritual here reproduced, represents the Sun-god (variously known as the Great Máu, Ra, or Shu), in the form of a cat, slaying Apap (Apep, or Aphohis), the serpent of darkness. According to Karl Blind the Ritual was already ancient when, in the XIIth Dynasty, about 2500 B.C., or earlier, the gloss was added explaining that the Cat was the Sun-god himself who had adopted that form as his symbol.

Dr. Budge says that "the male cat is Ra," and "he is called 'Máu' by reason of the speech of the god Sa, [who said] concerning him: 'He is like [*máu*] unto that which he hath made'; thus his name became 'Máu';* or [as others say] it is the god Shu† who maketh over the possessions of Seb to Osiris."

Chapter XXXIII of "The Book of the Dead" is directed against Apap, here called Rerek, who was rendered powerless to harm the deceased if the latter pronounced the names of Seb and Shu. The deceased orders Rerek to stand, promising to give him to eat the rat, the abomination of Ra, and the bones of the "filthy cat." "Hail, thou serpent Rerek, advance not hither. Behold Seb and Shu. Stand still now, and thou shalt eat the rat which is an abominable thing unto Ra, and thou shalt crunch the bones of the filthy cat." Since the Cat is the emblem of Ra, and in that rôle is the Slayer of the serpent of darkness, it is difficult to explain the meaning of the text, unless we assume that the dead man hoped to disarm by flattery a foe against whom force could not prevail. Not only does he promise that the serpent shall devour the Sun Cat, but that it shall eat the rat on which the Cat feeds. The darkness shall swallow alike the Sun, and the grey clouds that are its prey.‡

* This is a very ancient pun on the words *máu* "cat" and *máu* "like." Possibly also, as Renouf suggests: "The cat, in Egyptian *Máu*, became the symbol of the Sun-god or Day, because the word *Máu* also means 'light'."

† Ra, the Father of the Gods, is said to have first created Shu, or Shoo, the wind-god, as a personification of himself. In this rôle he is "often represented in the Egyptian monuments seated and holding a cross, symbol of the four quarters, or the Elements, attached to a circle." (Blavatsky.)

Tefnut, the consort of Shu, like Mut, had the head of a lioness. She was named "The Spitter," because she sent the rain. Her title suggests another connection between the cat and the serpent, for it has often been remarked that the "spit" of the cat so perfectly imitates the hiss of the serpent as to suggest that it is a case of protective mimicry.

‡ See Chapter on the Cat and Mouse.

But possibly a more convincing explanation is that we are here up against one of those apparent paradoxes that are so numerous in Egyptian mythology. We must remember that the serpent not only represented evil and darkness slain by the Divine Cat of the Sun, but was also actually the symbol of the Sun-god himself, especially when the solar orb was personified as Ra-Tem, the setting sun entering the underworld of darkness; whilst the Cat, when considered as the representative of Sekhmet, the spouse of Ra, was the personification of destruction and chaos.* Read has pointed out that some passages in the *Book of Amduat* (or, the "Book of that which is in the Under-world") seem to suggest

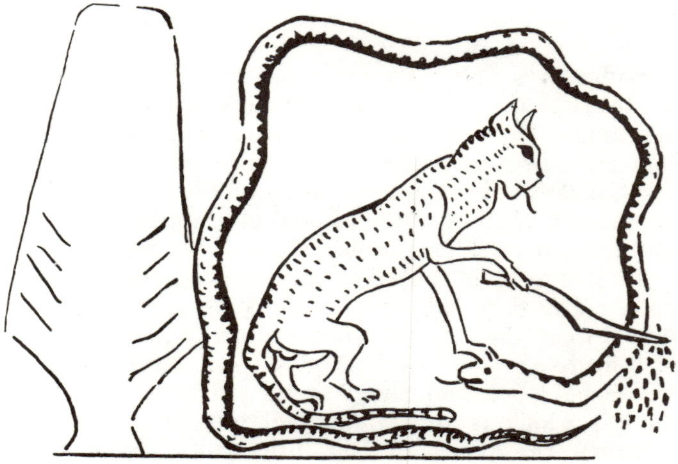

RA SLAYING APEP
From the "Book of the Dead."

that those who had not rendered due homage to Ra on earth shared after death in the punishment he inflicted upon Apep; and it would appear that the later Egyptians, at any rate, so understood the texts, for when they embraced Christianity their conceptions of Amenti were clearly transferred to the Hades of their new faith. In proof of this Sir Ernest Budge quotes as follows from the Gnostic work, *Pistis Sophia* ("Gods of the Egyptians"), Vol. I, p. 266:

"'Jesus tells the Virgin Mary: The outer darkness is a great serpent, the tail of which is in its mouth, and it is outside the whole world, and surroundeth the whole world; in it there are many places of punishment, and it containeth twelve halls wherein severe punishment is inflicted. In each hall is a governor,

* See Chapter on Sekhmet.

but the face of each governor differeth from that of his neighbour. . . . The governor of the second hall hath as his true face the face of a cat, and they call him in his place Kharakhar. . . . And in the eleventh hall there are many governors, and there are seven heads, each of them having as its true face the face of a cat ; and the greatest of them, who is over them, they call in his place Rokhar. . . . These twelve governors are in the serpent of outer darkness, and each of them hath a name according to the hour, and each of them changeth his face according to the hour.' "

In the above quotation we find cat-faced governors in charge of certain of the halls of punishment said to be within the body of the world encircling serpent of darkness. Cat and serpent are working in harmony to execute the vengeance of Ra.

These paradoxes of imagery were not accidental, or the result of confusion of thought as might appear to a casual reader, but are a constant feature in occult symbolism, and had a deep purpose. By thus portraying extremes in unity, the priestly initiator prepared the mind of the understanding aspirant for the reception of spiritual truths and mysteries otherwise unutterable. When we endeavour to interpret such sacred and ancient symbols it is essential that we take into account the context and environment in which they are found, and the fact that they almost invariably bear an esoteric as well as an exoteric significance.

For the purpose of comparison, we would ask our readers to recall the Norse myth, which relates how the God Thor was fooled by the giant's king, Utgard-Loki, during that deity's visit to Jotunheim. Thor was challenged to lift from the ground the cat that was the playfellow of the giant's children, but in spite of all his efforts was only able to raise one of its paws. Afterwards Utgard-Loki explained his failure by telling him that the seeming cat was in reality the Midgard serpent that encompasseth the earth. The Cat and the Serpent are merely two forms of the same allegory, both symbolically portraying the truth that God is All. Each alone represents the apparently dual and warring forces of Good and Evil.

Throughout mythology the idea underlying the symbol of the Coiled Cat (or Encircled Serpent) is emphasised and insisted upon. Of good beings, evil entities are born, and of evil good. From the beautiful the hideous comes forth, from the hideous the beautiful.

All natural phenomena confirm, and possibly gave rise to the allegory. Night is born of day, day of night, light of darkness, darkness of light, cold of heat, and heat of cold, life of death, and death of life. The cat in repose forms a circle, even as the serpent's head finds and bites its tail again. Thus it is the ideograph of Divinity in Nature, the Eternal, the Universal, the Complete. It is Om, the sacred Name, the prayer that exceeds all prayer and obviates words in realisation.

BIBLIOGRAPHY

"Archæologia: or Miscellaneous Tracts relating to Antiquity," Vol. VIII, pp. 174, 176. Pub. by the Society of Antiquaries of London, 1787.

"On the Origin and Growth of Religion as Illustrated by the Religion of Ancient Egypt," p. 237. By Peter le Page Renouf. Pub. about 1860.

"The Contemporary Review." Article by Karl Blind, October, 1881.

"The Secret Doctrine," Vol. II, p. 545. By H. P. Blavatsky. Pub. by the Theosophical Publishing Company, London, 1888.

"Egyptian Myth and Legend." By Donald A. Mackenzie. Gresham Publishing Company, London, 1913.

"The Book of the Dead," 2nd edition. An English translation of the "Theban Recension." By Sir E. A. Wallis Budge, M.A., Litt.D. Pub. by Kegan Paul, Trench, Trübner & Co., London, 1923.

Egyptian Religion and Ethics," pp. 139–41. By F. W. Read. Pub. by Watts & Co., London, 1925.

CHAPTER V

THE CAT AND THE RIDDLE OF ISIS

TO fully comprehend the tremendous powers which were anciently attributed to witches we must continually remember that they were originally the priestesses and votaries of the Moon-goddess Isis, Diana, or Luna, the Queen of Heaven, and Great Mother of all life. As such they claimed, and were credited with, power to wield the forces supposed to emanate from the planet over which their deity presided. These were numerous and far-reaching in their effects. The ancient alchemists taught that the human body was a microcosm, in which the heart represented the sun, and the moon the brain. Consequently the lunar orb was regarded as responsible for mental derangement, which belief is yet perpetuated in such words as lunacy and lunatic. Endless instances are recorded by physicians of all periods to prove that the insane become more violent when the moon is at the full. But the brain was not the only human organ to be affected by lunar changes. The very marrow of men's bones, and the weight of their bodies were said to suffer increase or diminution in sympathy with its modifications. In fact, hardly anything escaped the subtle influence of our satellite. The circulation of sap in trees, the quality of the vintage or the harvest corn were alike placed to its account. Therefore timber had to be felled, the juice of the grape expressed, and the harvest gathered, when the appearance of the moon indicated that the right time had arrived. Otherwise failure would follow. The influence of lunar motion upon the tides was observed long before it was explained, and gave countenance to the idea that the moon was responsible for weather conditions. It would be easy to fill a volume with accounts of the planet's supposed powers, so many directions were they believed to extend in. And all these varied potentialities were held to be within the control of witches and wizards, the degenerate and wicked survivors of Luna's once great hierarchy.

A CAT-EARED FIGURE HOLDING THE MOON, AND DENOTING THE WIZARD'S CONTROL

From an old print of 1868.

Shakespeare refers to this conception in " The Tempest " :

" A witch ; and one so strong
She could control the moon—make flows and ebbs,
And deal in her command* without her power."

That such occult forces might actually be seized upon, and controlled by human beings was a belief as widespread as it was ancient, and the student of religion will have no difficulty in tracing it to its source. Water is everywhere the symbol of the motherhood of God. Whether this be personified as Venus, or as Mary, the essential characteristics are the same. The Mother of the God of Love is the queen of the sea, and the patroness of sailors. Her colour is the ocean blue. The Power of God moves

* Or " with all her power." (See Corrector of folio of 1632.)

upon her waters, and is reflected therein, causing material phenomena to be manifested. Mary, or Mariah, in the Hebrew means "mirror." The name of Buddha's mother, Maya or illusion, conveys the same idea of unsubstantiality, and is perfectly symbolised by the seemingly actual forms imaged in the bosom of deep water which are not only unreal, but inverted. Many other examples might be given, but these will suffice. The sacred element was believed to be obedient to the priests and priestesses who served the goddess personifying both water and the moon that controlled its tides.

We have seen in other chapters how closely ancient peoples connected the Cat with the moon. So we shall not be surprised to find that witches specially favoured the feline form when they sought to raise a storm, and that sailors saw a disguised witch in every unknown cat. This is why the light breeze that ripples the water during a calm, and indicates a coming squall, is known to seamen as a Cat's Paw; and a frolicking cat is believed to foretell a gale, if not to be actually making one. It is common knowledge in Scotland that a cat scratching table or chair-legs is "raising wind," and the Rev. James Macdonald relates how he once "heard a Scotch matron order her daughter to 'drive out that beast: do ye no see she's making wind, and we'll no get a wisp o' hay hame the day gin she goes on.'"

In many languages the word cat is found with a nautical meaning attached to it. In English we have cat-block, cat-boat, cat-harping, cat-head, cat-rigged, cat-roller, cat-stopper, cat-tail, and other technical terms with the same prefix too numerous to name.

Even the ship itself was sometimes known as a cat. This was specifically so in the Norwegian type of vessel, and the flat-bottomed fire-boats employed by the English against the French in 1804. The "Cat" of Dick Whittington is sometimes said to have been a ship, and colliers and trading-boats are often so designated. We should probably not be far wrong in assuming that the idea of using the name of the sacred animal protectively was borrowed from Egyptian mythology, which, passing through Italy, permeated European thought and was employed in nautical nomenclature with the deliberate intention of invoking the assistance of Isis, and warning her priestesses from harming the vessel that had placed itself in her care. Where witches are credited with the destruction of sea-craft (as the annals of English law-courts gravely record was often the case), we may suppose that no such appeal had been made by the sailors to the Queen of the Deep, and that her votaries saw cause for anger in the too rude violation of the sanctified element. Some such religious or patriotic motive seems to have inspired the Witches of Mull, who, in the legend related by Dr. Macleod, are said to have assumed feline form in order to sink a hostile ship.

The Spanish king had sent a war vessel to the town with instructions that it was to avenge his daughter Viola, who had been murdered by Mrs. MacLean of Duart. But all the local witches took the shapes of cats and gathered together on the shrouds of the ill-fated ship in an effort to send her to the bottom. It so happened, however, that the captain also knew something of the art of magic, and was able to counteract their direful intent. So, seeing that they could not thus prevail, the witches enlisted the aid of the queen of Highland enchantresses, Great Garmal of Moy. She appeared on the top of the mast in the form of the largest cat ever seen, and she had only begun to sing one spell, when the vessel sank like a stone to the bottom.

A tale from the Isle of Skye related by the Rev. J. Gregorson Campbell has a peculiar interest, since it describes how a witch disguised as a cat, used a riddle for a boat, and so makes clear the Egyptian influence responsible for such stories.

"A witch who left home every night, was followed by her husband, who wondered what she could be about. She became a cat, and went in the name of the devil to sea in a sieve, with seven other cats. The husband upset the sieve by naming the Trinity, and the witches were drowned."

Reginald Scott tells us it was believed that witches "could sail in an eggshell, a cockle or mussel-shell, through and under the tempestuous seas." But their favourite vessel was certainly the riddle or sieve, which was one of the emblems of Isis, and as such is often depicted on Gnostic gems. It will be remembered that it was upon a riddle the goddess collected the scattered limbs of her husband Osiris, after he had been slain and dismembered by his enemy Set, known to the Greeks as Typhon.* The Christian Church, following her settled policy of placing the Gentile gods in Hell, transferred the Sieve of Isis to Satan, who, in his own person, she made representative of practically all the ancient deities other than Jehovah, whether they were male or female. An article so readily available, and with such a history as the ubiquitous riddle, was naturally regarded as a most favourable instrument for bearing the devotees of Satan—formerly the priestesses of Isis—upon the waters which were her sacred symbol, and even for raising the devil himself.

And when we refer to Satan's activities on the waters, we are reminded of another link between ancient cosmogony and the devil of Christian dualism. For in his familiar cognomen, "Old

* Cp. typhon, a whirlwind; typhoon, a hurricane.

Nick," we recognise the ocean and river god Nicksa, or Nixas, who possessed the attributes common to Neptune and Isis, and was formerly worshipped on the Baltic shores. Amid the terrible tempests that tore those gloomy seas, their presiding deity naturally loomed forth as an enemy to mankind, and was readily identified as the Prince of the Power of the Air, who led the witches and warlocks in their wild flights, and delegated to them the ruling of the storm.

The earliest ecclesiastical law in England, the *Liber Penitentialis* of St. Theodore (Archbishop of Canterbury 668–690), was directed against those who by invoking fiends (i.e. the ancient gods) cause storms.

"Si quis emissor tempestatis fuerit."

A RUINED TEMPLE OF ISIS
From an old engraving.

In the *Capitaluria* of Charlemagne, more than a hundred years later, the death penalty is decreed against such as by means of the devil disturb the air and excite tempests. And Pope Innocent VIII in his Bull (*Summis desiderantes affectibus*) of 1484 explicitly charges sorcerers with such practice.

Witches traded on these superstitions, and even went so far as to sell favourable winds to sailors. Summer, writing in 1600, records how in his times:

"In Ireland and in Denmark both,
Witches for gold will sell a man a wind,
Which in the corner of a napkin wrapp'd,
Shall blow him safe unto what coast he will."

("Last Will and Testament.")

It does not appear to have been essential for the witch or wizard to assume the form of a cat in order to raise a storm, since in many recorded cases a mortal cat was used for the purpose with equally effective results. Thus Polson tells us Highlanders used to draw a cat through the fire in order to raise the wind when they wished to affect the progress of a ship at sea.

Sometimes quite an elaborate ritual was followed to attain the desired result. For instance, when Satan wanted to shipwreck King James and Queen Anne on their voyage home from Denmark, he taught his following warlocks and witches to take a cat and christen it, and cast it into the sea, calling "Hola!" which, he said, would raise a storm. His advice was practically carried out by John Fian, *alias* Cunninghame, master of the School at Saltpans, Lothian. This gentleman was described by Agnes Sampson, whose own calling made her an authority on the subject, as "ever nearest to the devil, at his left elbock." Accordingly, in 1590, he was "fylit" in this connection, for the "chaissing of ane catt in Tranent; in the quhilk chaise, he was careit heich aboue the ground, with gryt swyftnes, and as lychtlie as the catt hir selff, ower ane heicher dyke, nor he was able to lay his hand to the heid off: And being inquyrit, to quhat effect he chaissit the samin? Ansuerit, that in ane conversatioune haldin at Brumhoillis, Sathan commandit all that were present, to tak cattis; lyke as he, for obedience to Sathan, chaissit the said catt, purpoiselie to be cassin in the sea, to raise windis for distructioune of schippis and boitis."

A scarce black-letter pamphlet, entitled "Newes from Scotland, declaring the damnable Life of Doctor Fian, a notable Sorcerer," describes him as "Register to the Devil, that sundrie times Preached at North-Baricke Kirke to a number of notorious Witches," and further discovers how "the said Doctor and Witches . . . pretended to Bewitch and Drowne his Majestie in the sea coming from Denmarke, with such other wonderful Matters as the like hath not bin heard at anie time."

According to the indictment on which John was tried and convicted, the devil appeared to him in the night "appareled all in blacke, with a white wande in his hande," and "demanded of him if hee would continue his faithfull service, according to his first oath and promise made to that effect, whome (as hee then said) he utterly renounced to his face, and said unto him in this manner 'Avoide, Satan, avoide—I utterly forsake thee.'" But this renunciation did not save John, and after appalling tortures had been inflicted on him by command of the zealous King James and his counsel, "hee was put into a carte, and being first strangled, he was immediately put into a great fire, being

SPHINX WITH CAT. XXIIND DYNASTY (About 950–650 B.C.)
Now in the British Museum, No. 11865.

readie provided for that purpose, and there burned in the Castle-hill of Edenbrough, on a Saterdaie, in the ende of Januarie last past, 1591."

An elaborate ritual for raising a tempest at sea by means of a cat is described in the confession of Agnes Sampson, "the wise wife of Keith," who belonged to the same coven as John Fian. According to Wright's "Newes from Scotland," "this aforesaide Agnis Sampson, which was the elder witch, was taken and brought to Haliriud-House, before the king's majestie, and sundry other of the nobilitie of Scotland, where she was straytly examined, but all the perswasions which the king's majestie used to hir, with the rest of his councell, might not provoke or induce her to confesse any thing, but stoode stiffely in the deniall of all that was layde to her charge ; whereupon they caused her to bee conveyed away unto prison, there to receive such torture as hath beene lately provided for witches in that country. . . . *Item.* The sayde Agnis Sampson was after brought againe before the king's majestie and his councell, and being examined of the meetings and detestable dealings of those witches, shee confessed that of Allhollon-Even, shee was accompanied, as well, with the persons aforesaid, as also with a great many other witches to the number of two hundreth, and that all they together went to sea, each one in a riddle, or cive, and went in the same very substantially, with flaggons of wine, making merrie and drinking by the way in the same riddles or cives, to the kirk of North-Barrick, in Lowthian, and that after they had landed, tooke handes on the lande, and daunced this reill, or short daunce, singing all with one voice :

> 'Commer, goe ye before, commer, goe ye ;
> Gif ye will not goe before, commer, let me.'

We are scarcely surprised to read that "these confessions made the king in a wonderfull admiration" ; but Agnes had many more marvels yet to relate, and poured them forth into his royal ears. "She confessed that at the time when his majestie was in Denmarke, shee being accompanied with the parties before specially named, tooke a cat and christened it, and afterwards bounde to each part of that cat the cheefest parte of a dead man and severall joyntes of his bodie ; and that in the night following, the saide cat was convayed into the middest of the sea by all these witches, sayling in their riddles or cives, as is aforesaid, and so left the saide cat right before the towne of Leith in Scotland ; this doone, there did arise such a tempest in the sea, as a greater hath not bene seene, which tempest was the cause of the perishing of a boat or vessell comming over from the towne of

Brunt Island to the towne of Leith, wherein was sundrie jewelles and rich giftes, which should have beene presented to the new queene of Scotland at her majesties coming to Leith.

" Againe it is confessed, that the said christened cat was the cause that the kinges majesties shippe, at his comming forth of Denmarke, had a contrarie winde to the rest of his shippes then being in his companie, which thing was most straunge and true, as the kinges majestie acknowledgeth ; for when the rest of the shippes had a faire and good winde, then was the winde contrarie and altogether against his majestie. And further, the sayde witch declared that his majestie had never come safely from the sea, if his faith had not prevayled above their intentions."

In the legal record of the witches' feat there is no mention of the sieves, but other details are supplied. The Coven of Prestonpans wrote a letter to the Leith Coven advising them to " mak the storm universall thro the sea. And within aucht dayes eftir the said Bill [letter] wes delyverit, the said Agnes Sampsoune, Jonet Campbell, Johnne Fean, Gelie Duncan, & Meg Dyn baptesit ane catt in the wobstaris hous, in maner following : Fyrst, Twa of thame held ane fingar, in the ane syd of the chimney cruik, & ane vther held ane vther fingar in the vther syd, the twa nebbis of the fingars meting togidder ; than thay patt the catt thryis throw the linkis of the cruik, & passit itt thryis under the chimnay. Thare-eftir, att Begie Toddis hous, thay knitt to the foure feit of the catt, foure jountis of men ; quhilk being done, the sayd Jonet fechit it to Leith ; & about mydnycht, sche & the twa Linkhop, & twa wyfeis callit Stobbeis, came to the Pierheid, & saying thir words, ' See that thair be na desait amangis ws ' ; & thay caist the catt in the see, sa far as thay mycht, quhilk swam owre & cam agane ; & thay that wer in the Panis, caist in ane vthir catt in the see att xj houris. Eftir quhilk, be thair sorcerie & inchantment, the boit perischit betuix Leith & Kinghorne."

Pitcairn I, 2, 237.

BIBLIOGRAPHY

" The Discoverie of Witchcraft." By Reginald Scott. Printed 1584.

" The Rare and Singular Work of Pomponius Mela, that excellent and worthy Cosmographer," Book III, Chapter 6. Trans. into English by Arthur Golding, Gentleman, London, 1590.

" Newes from Scotland, declaring the damnable Life of Doctor Fian, a notable Sorcerer, who was burned at Edenbrough in Januarie last, 1591. Pub. according to the Scottish Copie." Printed for William Wright.

"Letters on Demonology and Witchcraft," 2nd edition, pp. 302–4. By Sir Walter Scott, Bart. Pub. by John Murray, London, 1831.

"Criminal Trials," Vol. I, Part II, pp. 212, 218. By Robert Pitcairn. Pub. Edinburgh, 1833.

"Reminiscences of a Highland Parish." By Norman Macleod, D.D Pub. 1867.

"A Historical Account of the Belief in Witchcraft in Scotland," pp. 55 and 72. By Charles Kirkpatrick Sharpe, Esq. Pub. by Hamilton Adams & Co., London, 1884.

"Witchcraft and Second Sight in the Highlands and Islands of Scotland." By the Rev. J. Gregorson Campbell.

"Religion and Myth," p. 8. By the Rev. James Macdonald. Pub. by David Nutt, London, 1893.

"Myths and Legends of Japan," p. 264. By F. Hadland Davis. Pub. by George G. Harrap & Co., London, 1920.

"The Occult Review;" Article: "Horns of Elfland," p. 27. By Essex Smith. Pub. by Rider & Son, London, Jan., 1922.

CHAPTER VI

THE CAT IN CHALDEAN AND EGYPTIAN MAGISM

FROM the earliest ages to the present day the terror of the Great Unseen has haunted the lives of primitive peoples. The destructive forces of Nature and the many troubles of man have suggested that the course of events is governed by demons, or at best, by hostile deities. The spiritual foe is invisible, and cannot be fought by material means, so spiritual weapons must be devised, and the art of magic is evolved. The weapons of spell and incantation are formed, and adapted to meet the emergencies of every day, and since the protective formulæ soon become so numerous that only the most essential can be memorised by the ordinary man, the priest magician is called into being with specialised training and knowledge. Under his influence demonological religions sooner or later pass into dualistic form, and good as well as evil spirits are recognised. Then the gods arise from the darkness, and are invoked by the magician to aid him in his battle with the powers of inferno. The divine aid is granted and gladly accepted, but man, having tasted of power, will not be subservient even to a god, and devises new, and more scientific weapons to control the greater beings whose presence he now recognises.

The two principal sources of the scientific magic which occupied so prominent a position in ancient Greece and Rome, and reappeared in decadence in mediæval Britain, were Egypt and Chaldea. Therefore it will repay us to glance at the fundamental difference in doctrine which distinguished them, and to cast our eyes upon some of the links in the dual chain which bound them to the later witchcraft.

It was believed by the Akkadian Chaldean that by means of certain ritual and incantations man could command the demons, and even constrain the lesser deities to obey his will, and that the supernatural power necessary for the control of the spirits might be derived at his discretion from divine or diabolic sources. Indeed, he recognised that at the fountain-head good and evil were one, for in the fragmentary records that still preserve the ancient creed we see " odious demons, like Namtar, and propitious gods opposed to the demons like Nin-dar, both emanating from Mul-ge "* (Lenormant). When the Akkadian sought divine aid he applied to the priests who derived their power from the greater gods. This power was obtained by supplication, not compulsion, and was directed solely to beneficent ends. The remains of the sacred literature which we possess contain only the formulæ and incantations of divine magic. The diabolical aspect is severely condemned, but from this very condemnation we learn something of the terrors it held. Malevolent witches and wizards were numerous in ancient Chaldea, and figure largely on the tablets. It is interesting to see that they are there credited with similar potentialities and methods to those attributed to the daughters of Hecate in Christian England.

The Magic Magism of the ancient Medes was largely based on the Chaldaio-Assyrian religion, and helps us still further to understand the foundation on which mediæval witchcraft was built. For the Medians not only postulated two deities, representing the good and evil principles, as emanating from a common parent, Zarvana-akarana—but paid equal homage to them at the altars. Incantation and sorcery were greatly developed in this creed. A book attributed to the Magus Osthanes was circulated in Greece about the time of the Median wars, which, from what we know of it, seems to have taught, as the supreme secret of the caste of the Magi, invocation of the dead and the infernal spirits. The Magian priests spread over the whole of Persia, and it is because they were regarded as enchanters and magicians that the word magic acquired its present meaning.

Lenormant has pointed out the striking connection between Chaldean and Median Magism and Finnish mythology and magic. He expresses astonishment at finding so great a resemblance, " so many gods and spirits retaining the same character under different names, and such a perfect similarity between certain formulæ of incantations in spite of wide distance both in time and space which separates heathen Finland, which did not embrace Christianity until the Middle Ages, from purely Akkadian Chaldea, which was utterly annihilated fifteen centuries before the Christian era."

Finland can help us to penetrate the mists of time that obscure the magism of Chaldea. As in Akkadia, the priest of magic was distinguished sharply from the malevolent sorcerer who was thought of as abusing the supreme secrets and misusing them. An absolute power, for good or for evil, was thought to reside in incantations and magic rites. " The earth and the air, the

* The Akkadian counterpart of the Assyrian Bel.

visible and invisible regions, water and fire, were subject to the power of spells; they brought the dead back to torment the living; they even acted upon the most powerful gods, neutralised their influence, or exercised a sort of constraint over them."

In Finnish poetry describing hyperbolically the effects of these sorceries we meet with the Cat, and, as was so often the case in later witchcraft, it is the means of transportation. That it should be so regarded in occultism is certainly remarkable, since everything in ordinary life contradicts the possibility of employing the Cat as a beast of burden. Its small size alone negatives such an idea, and even if we imagine it suitably enlarged, its temperament and intense love of freedom would prove an insuperable obstacle But the explanation is that because of its supposed power of clairvoyance it represents the flight of thought.

The Finnish Kalevala describes the spells of Lemminkainen and what followed. He entered a house full of men talking freely, we read, and sang. "And the men were thrown into a sledge drawn by a discoloured cat; and the cat in its rapid course, bore them off to the extreme limits of Pohjola [the world of darkness and evil spirits], as far as the vast deserts of Lapland, where the horse's footstep no longer resounds, and the mare's foal finds no pasture. . . . Thus Lemminkainen mocked at young men, old men, and men in the prime of life, by means of his incantations."

Finnish mythology not only saw in evil spirits the cause of every kind of trouble, but personified the evil principle in its epic poetry as the giant Hiisi, with his wife and children, horses, cats and dogs, and servants, all deformed and wicked like himself. His cat, known as Hiiden-Kissa, seems to have been the least objectionable member of his household, for though she caused terror wherever she went, she forced thieves to confess their misdoings, and so served some good use.

The sorcerers held frequent intercourse with all these evil spirits and owed much of their power to them. But "the priests of magic brought about this communication entirely by means of a spiritual frenzy and sacred words," and exorcised the demons "by the power of their formulæ and by the help of the spiritual beings of the good principle; many of their incantations were destined thus to repulse the wicked demons, to break diabolic spells, and to invoke in this work the aid of the pure spirits" (Lenormant). "The Finnish incantations for exorcizing the demons of diseases were composed in exactly the same spirit, and founded upon the same data as the Accadian incantations destined for the like purpose. They were formulæ belonging to the same family, and they often showed a remarkable similarity of language ; the Egyptian incantations, on the contrary, having been composed by a people with very different ideas about the supernatural world, assumed quite another form " (Lenormant).

There is no trace in the Egyptian writings of belief in the elementary spirits that the Chaldeans attempted to propitiate, or exorcise, or control. The magic of the Egyptians had an entirely different basis, and developed from the doctrine of an Infinite One from whom proceeded a graded hierarchy of beings, each approaching nearer to earth than the last. According to this system it was possible for man by occult science and purgative ritual to rise towards Divinity, and become so identified with it as to obtain control of the powers of the lower emanations.

Magical spells and incantations formed no small part of Egyptian as of Chaldean liturgy, and in Egypt we shall find the key that will open a doorway on many dark passages of mediæval witchcraft, and flood them with unexpected light. Isis herself was the " witch-goddess " and derived a large part of her power from spells and incantations. Budge tells us that " her ' mouth was trained to perfection, and she made no mistake in pronouncing her spells.' "

The worship of sacred animals commenced in Egypt before the dawn of history, and survived for many thousands of years in conjunction with later creeds. It probably originated before the earliest civilization of which we have any relics, and it certainly occupied a prominent position in all the great centres and most of the nomes.

The cat of Bubastis, the ram of Thebes, the bulls of Memphis and Heliopolis, the hawk of Edfu, are the remains of faiths that were ancient when Bast and Amen, and Ptah and Horus, eclipsed them in the cities where they reigned so long. It is beyond doubt that they greatly modified the anthropomorphic ideal of the gods, which, it has been conjectured, was introduced by the Libyan race at the dawn of the prehistoric civilisation. With the fusion of the different races came the intermarriage of their respective ideals, resulting in the extraordinary animal-headed human figures of the gods, which, until the times of the Romans, were deeply venerated by the Egyptian people, as is proved by the multitude of amulets in the form of sacred animals which they have bequeathed to us.

Many most interesting examples are to be found in the fine collection of Egyptian amulets belonging to the University College, London, which has been so fully described by Flinders Petrie ; those which represent the *Uzat,* or Eye of Horus, in conjunction with cats, will illustrate the veneration accorded to the ancient feline deity. Petrie catalogues the following items :

"141c, green-blue glaze, flat back with 19 cats, and secondary *uzat* above the pupil*; 141d, blue and black glaze, with 13 cats; 141e, blue and black glaze, with 9 cats." He ascribes them to the XXIIIrd Dynasty, but beyond remarking that the *uzat* eyes of Horus represent the sun and the moon, does not attempt to explain the symbolism. No doubt the numbers of the cats had also a significance. We note that nine, so often connected with the Cat, figures among them. The *uzat* is further "associated with a group of seven goddesses whose names are found singly on the square eyes, or altogether on one eye." Among the seven are the cat-headed Bast and Sekhmet. These two deities are represented

A B

A. SEKHMET OR BASTET. PERIOD XVIII TO XXX

Blue glaze, faded; the dress suggests a male god, but the head is exactly like those of the goddesses.

B. CERTAINLY BASTET. SAME PERIOD

Bronze, holding sistrum, basket, and ægis.

From Professor Flinders Petrie's "Amulets." By kind permission of Messrs. Constable & Co.

on many amulets, and cannot always be distinguished from each other, which is not surprising when we remember that both were aspects of Isis.

The Egyptian placed great faith in the power of a living cat to protect him from all kinds of evil, natural or supernatural. But if he was so unfortunate as not to possess one of these animal amulets, he had resource to charms and spells and words of power, or in later times to invocation of the gods. Since any demon might annoy or injure him in his unprotected state, he

* See chapter-head, "The Clairvoyant Cat."

prayed to Ra, who in the form of a cat had destroyed the wicked Apep, to ward off the evil spirits; and he informed that deity of their misdeeds.

As he meditated on the pantheon of the gods, he was often led to make his appeal to a particular deity, by recalling some episode in the divine one's legendary past that formed a sympathetic link with his own problem. Thus, if he were stung by a scorpion, he would remember how the Cat-goddess, Bast, had had a similar misfortune during one of her journeyings, which might have proved fatal to her, had it not been for the incantation she had learned from Thoth, which instantly brought the Sun-god Ra to her aid.

The Egyptian would re-enact the drama of the Cat-goddess so soon as he was aware of the venomous sting, and cry out, "O Ra! Come to thy daughter! A scorpion has bitten her on her lonely road! Her cry reaches even to Heaven. The poison runs in her veins, and she applies her lips to it. But Ra has said, 'Fear not, fear not, my splendid daughter; see, I am with you. It is I who destroy the poison that is in all the limbs of this Cat.' He who thus repeated the correct formula, received the assistance of Ra, for the Sun-god was ever willing to save the Divine Cat over again, in the person of him, who by means of the incantation, put himself in her place."

The Egyptians considered spoken words as powerful weapons which could be wielded by the dead as strongly as by the living. Budge tells us that "The Kau, or Doubles, of the dead who had learned to utter words correctly, and who knew the proper tones to employ in uttering them, were in a position to go where they pleased and to do what they liked, for no god, spirit, fiend, or devil, and no inanimate object, could help obeying the commands which they uttered."

Therefore the Egyptian formulæ were directed not only to securing the good things of this life, but to making sure the safety and happiness of the disembodied soul. In the text of Unas, which was written towards the end of the Vth Dynasty, many such spells may be found, and several chapters of the Theban and Saite Books of the Dead consist wholly of spells and incantations. As the Nigritian protects himself with amulets hung around his person ere he will set forth on a journey, so, when the Egyptian departed this life, amulets were placed upon his embalmed body and his soul set forth on the unknown path fortified with incantations learnt on earth. Since the best results were thought to be effected by combining talisman and incantation, numerous small steles made of granite and basalt, and engraved with magical formulæ were made for the protection of both living and dead. Towards the close of the XXVIth Dynasty it became customary to use these as house talismans, and upon them was sculptured a figure of Horus the Child, who, thus invoked, was believed to protect the household. Many examples of this talisman may be found in European Museums. They are generally known as the "Cippi of Horus." The Cat incantation we have already quoted is engraved on the largest and most important of these Cippi, usually called the "Metternich Stele," which was dug up in Alexandria in 1828, and was made during the reign of Nectanebus I, between 378 B.C. and 360 B.C. Budge says: "This stele represented the power to protect man possessed by all the divine beings in the universe, and, however it was placed, it formed an impassable barrier to every spirit of evil, and to every venomous reptile." Either alone, or together with the Cat of flesh and blood, the stele protected the household from all ill.

For those who had passed on, a still simpler method of safety was sometimes provided. Every limb of the Cat contained the

BLUE-GLAZED PORCELAIN AMULET REPRESENTING CAT AND KITTENS SACRED TO BAST (ABOUT 600 B.C.)

Now in British Museum, No. 26239.

potentialities of a god or goddess, even if it were only represented by an effigy. The sacred cat is described as possessing "the head of Ra, the eyes of the Uræus, the nose of Thoth, the ears of Neb-er-tcher, the mouth of Tem, the neck of Neheb-ka, the breast of Thoth, the heart of Ra, the hands of the gods, the belly of

Osiris, the thighs of Menthu, the legs of Khensu, the feet of Amen-Horus, the haunches of Horus, the soles of the feet of Ra, and the bowels of Meh-urit " (Budge).

So small ivory wands ornamented with the head of a cat were buried with the beloved departed by his faithful friends. Thus was his soul enabled to successfully combat the scorpions of the Nether World, and pursue his perilous journey towards the Jalous Fields where dwelt the Dead.

In Chapter CXXV of the Book of the Dead, the deceased in his petition to the gods of the Underworld pleads his knowledge of a word of power.

" I am clean of mouth and clean of hands," he says ; " Therefore let it be said unto me, ' Come in peace ; come in peace ' (12), for I have heard that mighty word which the spiritual bodies (*sahu*)* spake unto the Cat (13) in the House of Hapt-re."

What the mystic word is we are not told. But it is recorded that the gods of their own volition sometimes gave to mankind the knowledge of their secret names by which they might be evoked.

Here the Cat would seem to be Isis in her feline form as Bast. The " mighty word " is, therefore, probably the secret name which she conjured from Ra on that occasion when, by means of a magical spell, she created a serpent whose bite caused him an agony she alone could cure. Ra had many names, but it was his hidden title that Isis sought, and finally forced from the suffering god. This name with all the supernatural powers its possession conferred passed from his breast to hers, still concealed from all other gods, even as it was from men. The legend of Ra and Isis was probably an effort to explain the newly accepted Chaldean doctrine that since even the gods were subject to law, it was possible for the man who gained knowledge of law to bend the higher beings to his will. Isis herself had shown the way. The Alexandrian writers say that the Egyptians claimed to be able to constrain the gods to obey their wishes, and manifest themselves to sight. The god could not resist the effect of their evocations and magic formulæ if he were called by his true name. " They not only called the god by name," says M. Maury, " but if he refused to appear they threatened him."

In the terrible ritual of the Taigherm (described in Chapter XVI) we may see the fruit of such impiety ; probably the same doctrine underlay many of the feline sacrifices called for in the practice of Black Magic. But when considering the motives of

* Budge says the ordinary reading is : " For I have heard the word which was spoken by the Ass with the Cat." This throws light on its meaning, as the Ass was a glyph of the Sun-god Ra.

these it must always be borne in mind that the gods and angels of an earlier religion are the demons of the creed that supersedes it, and suffer a progressive degradation in the popular conception which finally results in the formation of a third variation of magic, frankly diabolical. The magician, reared in the prejudiced outlook of the new creed, sees devils in the ancient gods; but evokes them by means of the ritual of the old religion, and sells his soul to obtain occult power from them. An example of such magic is provided in the religion of the Yezidis, or "Worshippers of Satan." Though fully recognising the Magian dualism, the sect pays homage only to the principle of evil.

Probably much of the magic of the Middle Ages was of this origin, and may be traced to an impious abuse of older theogonies. We propose to follow these decadent developments in the chapters dealing with the position of the Cat in witchcraft.

BIBLIOGRAPHY

"The Talmud. Treatise Berakoth." Folio 6.

"Masque of Queens." By Benjamin Jonson. Printed about 1600.

"The Magus, or Celestial Intelligencer." By Francis Barret, F.R.C, Printed for Lackington, Allen & Co., London, 1801.

"Chaldean Magic." By François Lenormant. Pub. by S. Bagster & Sons, London, 1877.

"A Handbook of Egyptian Religion." By Adolf Erman. Trans. by R. Griffith. Pub. by Constable & Co., London, 1907.

"The Liturgy of Funerary Offerings," p. 53. By E. A. Wallis Budge M.A., etc. Pub. by Kegan Paul, Trench, Trübner & Co., London, 1909.

"Legends of the Gods," pp. xlix, lxxiii. By E. A. Wallis Budge, M.A. etc. Pub. by Kegan Paul, Trench, Trübner & Co., London, 1912.

"The Natives of the Northern Territories of the Gold Coast," pp. 30, 93. By A. W. Cardinall. Pub. by George Routledge & Sons, London.

CHAPTER VII

FREYA AND HER CATS

THE ancient Scandinavian goddess of Love and Beauty known as Freya, was the daughter of the Waen-god Niorder, and the Earth-mother Nerthus, and was the sister of Freyer, or Fro, the god of sunshine, whilst her husband was Odur, the summer sun. She was blue-eyed and golden-haired.

> " The loveliest Goddess she in Heaven, by all
> Most honoured after Frea, Odin's wife."
>
> (" Balder Dead," *Matthew Arnold.*)

She has been identified with Venus, and to her worshippers she was pre-eminently the goddess of fruitful love. Therefore her car was appropriately drawn by the most affectionate and fecund of all domestic animals, the Cat, and it is significant that a pair of these creatures is employed. Her connections with the sun, of which the Cat was the symbol, should also be noted. As the goddess of Love and Beauty she blessed all lovers who sought her by prayer and sacrifice. Her temples were numerous, and maintained by her votaries until comparatively recent times, the last, which was in Magdeburg, Germany, being destroyed by Charlemagne.

Freya and her brother were so greatly honoured throughout Northern Europe that their names, in modified forms, are still used to address " master " and " mistress," and one day of the week, formerly held sacred to them, is yet known as Freytag, Freya's day, or Friday. This was regarded as the most appropriate day on which to marry, and the custom of wedding on Friday was only abandoned after Christian priests convinced the people that the day on which their Lord was slain must be an unfortunate one for commencing any enterprise ; but even so, they could not change its name, which reminds us of the gentle goddess of love, and her cats with their caressing, wooing ways, so suggestive of lovers.

> " Then came dark-bearded Niord, and after him
> Freyia, thin-robed, about her ankles slim
> The grey cats playing."
>
> (" Lovers of Gudrun," *William Morris.*)

Like the Cat, Freya, although so closely connected with love and beauty, was not merely a pleasure-loving, ease-seeking being, but when aroused, could don her armour and fight with the best. She often led the Valkyries to the battlefield, and when she headed their ranks was known as Valfreya, and claimed the right to choose half of the slain, leaving the other half as Odin's portion. The joys of the heaven to which she transported her chosen heroes were so intense that their wives and sisters often braved the horrors of battle to share with them the hope of being among the selected dead.

Freya was sometimes identified with Nerthus, her mother, who was the symbol of all-supporting Earth. Driving in her sacred chariot she adorned the land with verdure and blossom, caused the seeds to swell and sprout, and blessed the harvest. To those mortals who, with thoughtful kindness, placed a pan of milk in the cornfields for her cats' refreshment, she was specially gracious, and protected their crops from foul weather or other mishap.

But in Southern Germany she was known as Hel, or Holda, and, though still kindly, and beautiful, represented the winter season, covering the earth with her shining, icy armour to shield it from all harm in the months of trial. In this aspect she was not only the goddess of Life, but also of Death. But Death was not to her worshippers a ghastly, grinning skeleton, but a loving mother recalling her tired children to sleep in her bosom.

The Edda of the Scandinavians contains but few and scattered references to this once great goddess, but from it we may learn how Odin gave her power over the nine worlds, or, according to another version, over the ninth world.* Being goddess of both life and death, she was pictured half corpse-like, half life-like in colouring, much as was the Brahmanical goddess of Nature, Kali, the Mother. Originally, even in her darker aspect, she was no destructive power, but merely reigned over her abode in the lower world, and there received the spirits of the dead, when, after a long and weary journey, they arrived at Haljar. We may compare her with the Mater Terra of Italian mythology who nursed the tired dead in her gentle bosom. But materialism crept into these ideal conceptions, and made itself apparent in the symbols that expressed them. In German legends Hel became Mother Holle, a goddess of domestic arts, a spinner, weaver, and housekeeper. When snow fell, she was shaking her bed and making its feathers fly, when rain descended, she was washing the clothes, whilst long clouds showed that she was weaving.

* May we see an allusion to these nine worlds in the fabled nine lives of the cat ?

Christianity completed the degradation of Hel. The new creed acknowledged no goddess of death, but identified Hel with its own hideous place of punishment, transforming the deity into an abode. Freya herself, like almost all the ancient divinities, was branded as a demon, or witch, and banished to the mountain tops of the lands that had formerly held her sacred. She figures in mediæval German stories as old and wrinkled, insatiable and cruel. Her priestesses share her doom. No longer the beautiful daughters of the Mother of Life ; they are now deformed, withered, and wicked, fit offspring of Hell. But even so they are not unrecognisable, for the cats that once drew Freya's chariot have become the steeds on which the witches ride through the air, or their companions in daily life, which are said by the Christians to be attendant devils.

Notwithstanding this extraordinary change of religious outlook the witches still made love charms and potions, as befitted the servants of the goddess of Love, and not unfrequently some portion of the Cat's anatomy figured more or less prominently therein. Their weekly Sabbat assemblies were held on Freya's sacred day, and this was an additional cause of offence to the Christians, who connected that day inseparably with the tragedy of the Cross and observed it as a strict fast. We need not here recount how the priesthood of the new religion by torture and murder destroyed the last faithful followers of the older creed. So thoroughly did they carry out their work of extermination that its very tenets are obscure and doubtful to-day. But lingering Superstition still points her finger down the smoke-dimmed pathway, and here and there a distorted form is faintly discerned amid the gloom. One such has been noted by the Rev. R. Walsh, who, when travelling by water, found his messmates "were firmly persuaded of the ominous import of four things in a ship," the occurrence of which they considered as "inevitably connected with disastrous consequences—sailing from port on a Friday, having on board a black cat, and taking as a passenger either a pregnant woman or a clergyman." Mr. Walsh interested himself to enquire the reason for antipathies to such apparently harmless and inoffensive things, so unconnected with evil effects, and he was "generally informed that they were known to be unlucky ; but they could assign no reason except for the last, and that was that Satan, being 'the Prince of the Power of the Air,' had of course the direction of the winds, and as a clergyman is his greatest enemy, he always visits the crew who receive him with all the infliction of his elementary agents—calms, contrary winds, and storms."

The explanation, so far as it goes, is plausible enough, for the antagonism of Satan to a clergyman is understandable; but we should have expected the "Old Gentleman" to be rather pleased about the black cat which is so often introduced into magical ritual with an idea of propitiating him! Clearly, the reason is a deeper one. Those who embark on the mystic Water, Mother of Life, on the sacred name-day of its presiding deity (for Freya is one with Venus), carrying on board a woman who bears within her a concrete manifestation of the Life Principle personified by the goddess, or the animal sacred to Creation and Reproduction, or the priest consecrated to the service of the Divine Mother (whether she be named Mary, or Venus or Isis, is immaterial), have, consciously or unconsciously, invoked the Mysteries. Not only have they to combat with evil. Far more than mere negative goodness is required of them, and if they fail, retribution quickly follows their presumption. Prudence obviously forbids such tempting of the Unknown Power, and the sailor prefers not to tamper with the sacred symbols of the Great Mother on whose bosom his life is spent.

BIBLIOGRAPHY

"Notices of Brazil," Vol. I, p. 96. By the Rev. R. Walsh. Pub. 1830.

"Asgard and The Gods." Adapted from the work of Dr. W. Wagner. By M. W. Macdowall. Pub. by Swan Sonnenschein, le Bas & Lowrey, London, 1886.

"Myths of the Norsemen." By H. A. Guerber. Pub. by George G. Harrap & Co., London, 1909.

CHAPTER VIII

CHRIST AND THE CAT

IT is a remarkable fact that the Cat is never mentioned in the canonical books that compose the Bible, but we may suppose the omission to be partially explained by the intolerant hatred of the Jews for everything their Egyptian rulers and taskmasters had venerated as sacred. Or we may attribute it to the wandering life the peculiar people led so long, which made it impossible for them to know cats as household friends. But more probably some trait of their national character was responsible, for there is not a single instance recorded in the Bible of the Jews making a pet or companion of any animal, though the nations which surrounded them did so.

In the fragmentary teachings of Jesus which may be found in the four Gospels accepted by the Christian churches we have evidence that the Master recognised the Divine Life as innate in all creatures. Though men might so little realise the reverence due to the manifestations of God's thoughts that they slew and sold five sparrows for two farthings, yet not one of the small victims is forgotten before God, or falleth to the ground without the Father. It is unlikely that this was the only occasion on which Jesus emphasised the all-embracing love of the Creator, and its isolation is explained when we recall that innumerable gospels were suppressed as heretical by the Christian Church, and that even those now left to us, have, in the words of Wilberforce, been "considerably tampered with," and "correctores" actually appointed by ecclesiastical commissions "to correct the text of Scripture" in the interests of what was accepted as orthodoxy.

The hiatus we have noted in the records of the surviving gospels is bridged by a remarkable volume named "The Gospel of the Holy Twelve." Its contents were received in visions by the Rev. G. J. Ouseley, and it claims to be a translation of an early Christian document "preserved in one of the Buddhist monasteries in Thibet, where it was hidden by some of the Essene community for safety from the hands of corrupters."

As so many scriptures claim to have been originally communicated by inspiration, it would seem that the authority for

STUDIES BY LEONARDO DA VINCI FOR A VIRGIN AND CHILD WITH A KITTEN

By courtesy of the British Museum.

this one is on a similar basis to that of a great number of others, and we must judge of its authenticity chiefly by the internal evidence of its content, and not allow ourselves to be prejudiced by the recentness of its reception.

Relating the story of the birth of Jesus Christ in a cave, the Gospel of the Holy Twelve says :

" And there were in the same cave an ox and a horse and an ass, and a sheep, and beneath the manger was a cat with her little ones, and there were doves also, overhead, and each had its mate after its kind, the male with the female. Thus it came to pass that he was born in the midst of the animals which, through the redemption of man from ignorance and selfishness, he came to redeem from their sufferings, by the manifestation of the sons and the daughters of God."

The love of the Master for the animals who had shared His birth-chamber is beautifully portrayed in the following legend :

" As Jesus passed through a certain village He saw a crowd of idlers of the baser sort, and they were tormenting a cat which they had found, and shamefully treating it. And Jesus commanded them to desist and began to reason with them, but they would have none of His words, and reviled Him. Then He made a whip of knotted cords and drove them away, saying, This earth, which my Father-Mother made for joy and gladness, ye have made into the lowest hell with your deeds of violence and cruelty. And they fled before His face. But one more vile than the rest returned and defied Him. And Jesus put forth His hand, and the young man's arm withered, and great fear came upon all ; and one said, He is a sorcerer. And the next day the mother of the young man came unto Jesus, praying that He would restore the withered arm. And Jesus spake unto them of the law of love, and the unity of all life in the one family of God. And He also said, As ye do in this life to your fellow-creatures, so will it be done to you in the life to come. And the young man believed and confessed his sins, and Jesus stretched forth His hand, and his withered arm became whole even as the other. And the people glorified God who had given such power to man " (xxiv. 1–5).

Reading on, we again find Christ protecting an unhappy cat, comforting her loneliness, and providing lovingly for her future.

" As Jesus entered a certain village He saw a young cat which had none to care for her, and she was hungry and cried unto Him ; and He took her up, and put her inside His garment, and she lay in His bosom. And when He came into the village He set food and drink before the cat, and she ate and drank, and showed thanks unto Him. And He gave her unto one of His disciples who was a widow, whose name was Lorenza, and she took care of her. And some of the people said, This man careth for all creatures . . . are they His brothers and sisters that He should love them? And He said unto them, Verily these are your fellow-creatures, of the great Household of God; yea, they are your brethren and sisters, having the same breath of life in the Eternal. And whosoever careth for one of the least of these, and giveth it to eat and drink in its need, the same doeth it unto Me; and whoso willingly suffereth one of these to be in want, and defendeth it not when evilly entreated, suffereth the evil as done unto me; for as ye have done in this life, so shall it be done unto you in the life to come" (xxxiv. 7–10).

For the second time in connection with the Cat, the solemn warning is uttered by the Master that all creatures are so closely knitted to Him that our every action towards them is counted as if done unto Himself.

The legends are not unduly overlaid with miracle, but describe events we need feel no great difficulty in crediting, and in the simple narration seem to bear the stamp of truth. Christ, having spent a part of his childhood in Egypt, may easily be supposed to have felt a special sympathy for the sacred symbol of his own prototype, Osiris-Horus, and to have been shocked at the spectacle of his countrymen illtreating the animal he was accustomed to see regarded with so much reverence.

BIBLIOGRAPHY.

"The Gospel of the Holy Twelve." Written down and pub. by the late Rev. G. J. Ouseley. New edition pub. by Edson, Ltd., London, 1923.

CHAPTER IX

THE VIRGIN AND THE CAT

IT has been plausibly suggested that our English word "Puss" is derived from the name of the goddess "Pasht," a form of the Egyptian Isis, and that we therefore pronounce the sacred name whenever we call our feline friend by this title. As we have seen in these pages Pasht has been known by many names. The Greeks invoked her as Artemis, the Romans appealed to Diana, the Buddhists worshipped her as Maya, the Saxons called on Frigga, and the Christian pays homage to the Virgin Mary. But whatever the name she is known under her attributes remain unchanged, for everywhere and always she is the Divine Mother, the feminine Principle of the Deity, the Virgin-goddess, who is yet maternal and fruitful, and bestows fertility even whilst she protects and honours chastity.

The mediæval artist, Baroccio, had perhaps been contemplating this paradoxical parable when he was inspired to paint his conception of the Madonna, entitled "Our Lady of the Cat," and by its means to point a finger that should direct the student's gaze to the essential unity of past and present faiths, however greatly they may differ in outward form. We may learn from his direction how the ancient symbolism of the lunar Virgin Mother, and her solar Son, whom she cradles in the crescent of her arms, or lays to rest in the night sky, was freely adopted and adapted by the Christian Church so that to-day the chief emblems of the Virgin Mary are the Sun, Moon, and Stars (Rev. ii. 1 : Cant. vi, 10). In pictures of the Assumption a crescent moon is placed under her feet ; whilst in representations of the crucifixion, the eclipsed moon appears on one side of the cross, and the sun on the other. As Maury remarked, "the Virgin took possession of all the Sanctuaries of Ceres and Venus." And therefore she is appropriately symbolised by the Cat that represented the attributes of her predecessors.

An interesting example of the connection of the dual symbols of cat and crescent with the Virgin-goddess was discovered when the site of ancient Tarsus was explored by Barker, in 1845. He made a collection of over a thousand terracotta figures which he found in the midst of an old mound or rubbish heap; among these were a number of Sigillaria, one of which he describes as being in the form of "a small cat, having a cord tied round its neck, from which is pendant an inverted crescent, showing that the animal had been sacred to the moon, recalling the collar placed around the neck of the stag of Mount Cercynitis."

It seems probable that this cat was a symbolic representation of the Virgin-goddess Pallas Athena, who was worshipped in Tarsus before that city's conversion to Christianity caused the sacred images of its former faith to be broken and consigned to the rubbish heap. In this case the inverted crescent hung from the cat's neck would refer to the control Athena, like other virgin-goddesses, was said to exercise over the watery element: a doctrine which procured for her a considerable amount of homage from all who went down to the sea in ships.

CARVING FROM A TOMB OF THE GALLO-ROMAN PERIOD
Bordeaux Museum.

As the Moon-goddess of the Athenians, Pallas is sometimes represented as riding on a lion, the head of the feline tribe, and holding her infant son in her arms, and she was invoked on her festivals as the "One Mother of God." We may compare this with the titles accorded by the Christian Churches to Mary, and the identification of Jesus with "the lion of the tribe of Judah," and the "Sun of Righteousness."

It has been suggested that the world-wide game known as

Cat's Cradle took its rise from the Christian Mysteries, and that the name is a corruption of "cratch cradle," meaning manger, or rock cradle, and referring to the manger wherein the Holy Child was laid; but it is certain that the game is far older than Christianity, and it seems probable that it originated in an ancient solar rite. Everywhere the underlying purpose appears to have been to control the Divine Cat of the Sun by means of sympathetic magic. In hot climates the cradle of string invited him to rest from his activities, whilst in Arctic regions its meshes were a trap to entangle his feet, and so postpone his dreaded departure. Professor Starr collected over sixty different designs in Cats' Cradles from among the Congo tribes, and Professor Fraser has described how the Esquimaux of Iglulik play the game when the sun is going southward in the autumn, and sinks lower and lower in the Arctic sky, with the object of preventing his disappearance. Missionaries to certain parts find a knowledge of it essential, since the natives are not only experts in the game, but regard it as a test of intelligence.

The parable of the Virgin and the Cat may be also recognised in the old folk-tale of Cinderella, which, in some of its variants, is entitled "The Hearth Cat."

The heroine represents the Roman modification of Diana known as Vesta, the goddess who guarded hearth and home, or the priestess, who impersonated her. We find her robing herself in a mantle made from cat-skins—just as the witches of later times arrayed themselves for the performance of their mystic rites—and thus being enabled to attend the ball, i.e. the Sabbat gathering.*

The story of Cinderella's early fate shows her darkened by smoke and ashes, and seems to point to an aspect of the Virgin which has not received the consideration it deserves. The text from Canticles, "I am black, but comely," has been held by certain devout writers to describe the Virgin Mary, who, as the womb of Nature, is black, like the Night sky that gives birth to the moon and stars. The imagery helps us to understand why the cat that accompanies the Daughters of Diana (or Cinderella) is of that hue, and the following paragraph from Jennings still further elucidates the matter:

"Black is the Saturnian colour—also that of the Egyptian Isis. Under the strange head of the embodiment of Deity under darkness, the following remarkable facts may be considered: the Virgin and Child are depicted *black* at the Cathedral at Moulins, at the famous Chapel of the Virgin at Loretto, in the

* In many cults the totemic or symbolic animal of the deity is flayed, and its skin used to robe the priest, who by means of it impersonates the god.

THE MADONNA DEL GATTO

The original picture by Baroccio is in the National Gallery.

Church of the Annunciation at Rome, at the Church of St. Lazaro and the Church of St. Stephen at Genoa, at that of St. Francisco at Pisa, at the Church of Brixen in the Tyrol, at a church in (and at the Cathedral of) Augsburgh, where the black figures are as large as life, at the Borghese Chapel in Rome, at the Church of Santa Maria Maggiore in the Pantheon, and in a small chapel at St. Peter's, on the right-hand side, on entering near the door."

The darkness of the Virgin, and the black cat representing her, is not the darkness of evil, but of the Uncreate, of the Great Deep, and the Unknown God. It is the Limitless, Formless and Inexpressible, that, by antithesis, is the One True Light.

BIBLIOGRAPHY

"Lares and Penates," pp. 190–8. By Wm. Burckhardt Barker, M.R.A.S. Pub. by Ingram, Cooke & Co., London, 1853.

"The Rosicrucians," pp. 154 and 259. By Hargrave Jennings. Pub. by Chatto & Windus, London, 1879.

'The Egyptian Religion," p. 61. By E. A. Wallis Budge. Pub. by Kegan Paul & Co., London, 1899.

"The Golden Bough," Vol. I, p. 316. By J. G. Fraser. Pub. by Macmillan & Co., London, 1907.

"Among the Primitive Bakongo." By John H. Weekes. Pub. by Seeley, Service & Co., London, 1914.

CHAPTER X

THE MAY KITTEN

" He seemed fader of all unthryftnesse,
Jagged and garded full ungay,
With a face filled with falsenesse
Berded lyke kitling of May."
(*Barclay*.)

THE above lines are expressive of the deeply rooted distrust with which our forefathers regarded the kitten that was born in the month of May. Indeed, the belief is still strongly prevalent in Celtic districts that May kittens ought never to be reared because they bring snakes into the house, whilst a generally distributed modification of this idea is that May kittens make troublesome, ill-behaved cats.

" May chets
bad luck begets
and sure to make dirty cats,"

is the dictum of an old Huntingdonshire proverb that even to-day makes its influence widely felt at least in country places, and is responsible for the slaughter of many wee innocents.

To trace the origin of so strange a belief we must turn to Celtic mythology: from it we learn that the first of May was the day called Beltaine, sacred to Bile, the god of death. Writing of the mythology of Britain, Squire says:

" If anything uncanny took place, it was sure to be on May-day. It was ' on the night of the first of May ' that Rhiannon lost, and Tiernyon Twryf Vliant found, the infant Pryderi, as told in the first of the Mabinogion. It was ' on every May-eve ' that the two dragons fought and shrieked in the reign of 'King' Lludd. It is on 'every first of May' till the day of doom that Gwyn, son of Nudd, fights with Gwyrthur, son of Greidawl, for Lludd's fair daughter, Creudylad. And it was when she was 'a-maying' in the woods and fields near Westminster that the same Gwyn, or Melwas, under his romance name of Sir Meliagraunce, captured Arthur's queen Guinevere."

May is then an ominous month for people of the Celtic race, and it is easy to understand why they should regard the birth of a creature so closely in contact with the unseen worlds as the Cat was held to be, with superstitious fear, when it took place in this ill-omened season.

But they forgot that May, like the Cat herself, symbolised the ALL. It was not only the month of the god of Death. The first of May was held as a festival by the Druids, who on it kindled the May fires, and offered sacrifices on the mountains to celebrate the revival of earth from her death-like slumber, and the renewal of warmth and rebirth of vegetation. The Druids passed away, but their May Day observances were continued by the witches; in many European countries, and in Finland, long after the introduction of Christianity, the peasants believed demons and sorcerers thronged every hill-top at midnight on Roodmas or Walpurgis-Night—as May Eve was variously named—that they might greet the rising sun on the morn when his power returned.

It is hardly necessary to remind my readers that the demons and sorcerers of the Christianised Finns were the gods and priests of the older religion which was so cruelly misrepresented and persecuted by Christian intolerance.

The witches are said to have arrived on the mountain-tops by magical flight on cats or brooms, as we have described in the chapter on the Cat and the Sabbat. So we may take it that the Cat was with them when they greeted the Sun-god's uprising.

Indeed it is to be feared that often the Cat was there as the victim of the sacrifice, and was burnt alive in the fires that honoured the sun, and celebrated the death of death. A relic of such cruel ritual survived in France until forbidden by law in the reign of Louis the Fourteenth. There, upon St. John's Day, baskets caging living cats, wolves, and foxes were burnt on hill-top fires in the presence of the sheriffs or the mayor of the town. St. John's, or Midsummer Day, was the second of the four great days of the year marking the rise, power, and decline of the sun, but Druidical ritual required sacrificial offerings at each of these festivals, and certainly they were not omitted on May Day, which was the most important of all the celebrations.

We cannot recall May Day observances without being reminded of the Maypole, a survival of the ancient Phallic worship in which the pole and ring (*linga* and *yoni*) symbolise the dual generative principle of Nature. Is it a mere coincidence that the Cat, which is a phallic symbol, is regarded as unlucky if born in May, and that May is " forbidden for marriages," as Hargrave Jennings points out, " although it is the ' woman's month,' or month in which ' May Day ' occurs, and in which ' Maypoles ' used to be set up everywhere ? "

Superstition, or " that which remains " (as its literal meaning is) of the ancient faiths dies hard. " APRIL, THE MONTH OF WEDDINGS. RUSH TO ALTAR BEFORE MAY COMES IN," says the *Daily News*, of April 3rd, 1929, adding that " the traditional superstition that May is an unlucky month in which to be married still prevails in 1929, with the result that April is to see an almost unprecedented rush to the altar."

We have noted that the Cat is not only a phallic symbol, but presents an apparent paradox by also typifying Virgin Motherhood. May and maiden are cognate words. Perhaps the prohibition of May marriages could be traced to a desire to show Virginity reverence :

> " Joy of our hearts, O let us pay to thee
> thine own sweet month of May,"

says a children's hymn addressed to Mary the Mother which is well known in the Catholic Church. Mary was the inheritor of all the Virgin-mother goddesses, and Scott informs us that the ancients had a maxim to the effect that only bad women married in the month of May : " *Malâe nubent Maia.*" It would seem that the Cat, when born as a May kitten, is the accepted symbol of sacred Virgin-motherhood, but, that born on any other date, it is a phallic emblem like the Maypole.

With the idea of a taboo, the idea of a penalty following any breach of it is intimately connected. In course of time the reason for a taboo may be forgotten, but the conception of misfortune attached to its violation is not only remembered, but is often transferred to the subject of the taboo, or even to its symbol, by the popular imagination. Hence yet another reason for the still lingering distrust and dislike of the May kitten.

BIBLIOGRAPHY

" Description of Heaviness." By Alexander Barclay. Printed 1506.

" The Rosicrucians, Their Rites and Mysteries," 2nd edition, pp. 282–5. By Hargrave Jennings. Pub. by Chatto & Windus, London, 1879.

" Celtic Myth and Legend, Poetry and Romance." By Charles Squire. Pub. by The Gresham Publishing Company, London.

" Letters on Demonology and Witchcraft," p. 112. By Sir Walter Scott, Bart. Pub. by Kegan Paul, Trench & Trübner, London, 1926.

" The History of Witchcraft," p. 112. By Montagu Summers. Pub. by Kegan Paul, Trench & Trübner, London, 1926.

" The Occult Review," Vol. XXVI, p. 56. Pub. by Rider & Son, London.

CHAPTER XI

THE CORN CAT

UNTIL quite recent times European legends persisted of a spirit, or minor deity, who made the welfare of the all-important corn his or her special care; and fertilised and guarded the growing crops until the time of its maturity. When harvest arrived, and the corn was cut and bound, this protecting genius took refuge in a sheaf specially dedicated for its use, and there remained until the period for sowing returned, when it followed the seed to the open fields to watch over its welfare once more.

The Corn Spirit usually assumed the form of an animal, and the species chosen by it varied in different districts. But perhaps the most interesting and appropriate of its many guises was the Cat, since in occult lore the Cat is the symbol of both sun and moon; and from a very early age human thought had connected both these luminaries with the growth of vegetation. So closely was the solar orb identified with the corn that to man was the "staff of life," that the Sun-god was worshipped as "the Corn" in Babylon, and in Egypt was known as "the Seed." Thus the Sun-god Osiris, identified with Ra (whose symbol was the Cat), in one of his aspects was a deity of vegetation. His character in this respect, Sir James Fraser tells us, "is brought out by the legend that he was the first to teach men the use of corn; and by the custom of beginning his annual festival with the tillage of the ground." In one of the chambers dedicated "to Osiris in the great temple of Isis, at Philæ, the dead body of Osiris is represented with stalks of corn springing from it, and a priest is depicted watering the stalks from a pitcher which he holds in his hand. The accompanying legend sets forth that 'this is the form of him whom one may not name, Osiris of the mysteries, who springs from the returning waters.' It would seem impossible to devise a more graphic way of depicting Osiris as a personification of the corn; while the inscription attached to the picture proves that this personification was the kernel of the mysteries of the god, the innermost secret that was only revealed to the initiated. In estimating the mythical character of Osiris, very great weight must be given to this monument. The story that his mangled remains were scattered up and down the land may be a mythical way of expressing either the sowing or the winnowing of the grain. The latter interpretation is supported by the tale that Isis placed the severed limbs of Osiris on a corn-sieve. Or the legend may be a reminiscence of the custom of slaying a human victim as a representative of the corn-spirit, and distributing his flesh or scattering his ashes over the fields to fertilise them."

The legend of the murder of the Egyptian god is preserved and re-enacted in the ritual of the harvest fields with the Corn Cat in the rôle of Osiris. Sometimes the celebrants are contented by an imaginary slaying of an invisible corn-spirit, and, as in Franche-Comte, designate the close of harvest as "killing the Cat." Or they may think even this imaginary bloodshed to be superfluous, and, as in the Vosges Mountains, describe the finish of their harvesting or haymaking by the metaphor of "catching the Cat." They describe the "Cat" as lean or fat, in accordance with the poorness or abundance of their crop. The man who cuts the last handful of hay is the hero of the occasion, for it is he who is regarded by his companions as the "Catcher of the Corn Cat." He is accordingly congratulated, and is presented with a nosegay to carry, or in some cases with a small fir tree that has been decorated with coloured ribbons. There are many variations of this custom and formula, and it will be interesting to glance at some of them *en passant*.

In Scotland a handful of reaped grain or straw that has been laid on the ground without being bound into a sheaf is known as a "cat"; but, though the name is so suggestive, it does not seem to be now connected with any ritual custom. However, we may gain light on the original significance of the title by comparing it with the Scotch word "tat," which has the same meaning, and the old English "tath," or "that which is scattered." Tat, Tait, or Taith, was reverenced by the ancient Hibernian Scots as the god who presided over agriculture, and bestowed his name on the first day of the harvest month of August. This god is said to be identical with the Egyptian Thoth, Tauut, or Tat, the chief lunar deity of Egypt, who, as the Reckoner of Time, occasionally displays solar aspects. The meaning of "tath" forcibly recalls the legend of Osiris to our minds, and it seems clear that the Scotch Corn Cat is the result of contact with the Egyptian teaching that can still be traced in so many ancient European customs.

We may instance the harvesters around Vesoul, who, as they cut the last corn, cry triumphantly, "We have the Cat by the tail." Or the ritual at Briançon, in Dauphine, where, when reaping begins, a cat is decorated with ribbons, flowers, and ears of corn, and is designated "The Cat of the ball-skin." Should a reaper be wounded whilst at work, the Cat must be induced to lick the wound. When reaping is over it is again decked out with ribbons and corn-ears, and the workers dance and make merry. When dancing is done, the girls solemnly strip the Corn Cat of its decorations.

Another interesting example is to be seen in the harvest fields of Grüneberg, in Silesia. There the reaper who cuts the last corn is called the Tom-cat. His companions envelop him in ryestalks and green withes, and provide him with a long plaited tail. Sometimes a second man is similarly arrayed, and is known as the She-cat. Their office is to chase and beat everyone in sight. Perhaps some such custom accounts for the warning given to children in the neighbourhood of Kiel against entering a corn-field. "The Cat sits there," they are told, whilst in the Eisenach Oberland they are further threatened that "The Corn Cat will come and fetch them." But in other localities the ritual takes a more literal and less happy form. An actual cat is sacrificed to ensure the welfare of the harvest next year. Sir James Fraser, from whom we have culled most of the above examples, tells us that near Amiens, the phrase indicating that harvest is about to be completed is "They are going to kill the Cat," and when the last corn is cut, the reapers repair to the farmyard and there actually slay a cat. In some parts of France the ritual is more complicated, and throws further light on its origin and meaning. A living cat is placed beneath the last bundle of corn to be thrashed, and is there struck dead by the flails. Its body is reserved until the following Sunday, when it is roasted and eaten as a holiday (holy day) dish. It is clear that this was originally a sacrament. The murdered Sun-god Osiris, now represented by the sacred Cat, is sacramentally partaken of by his faithful servants on the day that is holy to him, when their labours in the cornfield he has so long blessed and guarded are over. For we must remember that the symbolism of Egypt had almost always a double significance, an inner as well as an outer interpretation, and when the Sun-god Osiris became incarnate, the purpose was not merely that he should give his life as a sacrifice for men, but that he might also be the nourishment and mystical food of their souls.

We have seen Isis with the corn-sieve in her hands, and noted that it was in her temple that the mysteries of Osiris as corn-god were celebrated. Like Osiris, one of her best known symbols is the Cat, that personification of motherhood. Diodorus Siculus says, and it is generally admitted, that Isis was the original of the Greek and Roman Ceres, who was worshipped as being the " Mother of Corn." The child she brought into the world was known as *He-Siri*, " The Seed," or in Assyria as *Bar*, a name of double meaning which might be read either as " son " or " corn." To the unlettered multitude Ceres was the Mother of Bar, the corn which fed their material bodies, but to the initiated few, she was revealed as the Virgin-Mother of Bar, the Divine Son, who was the Bread of Life, and the Sun-god incarnate.

Something of the same conception seems to have been embodied in the goddess Ken, who is represented on Egyptian tablets holding in both hands corn, and standing on a lion, the head of the feline family. Her name occurs as early as the period of the XVIIIth and XIXth Dynasties, but she is clearly of foreign origin, and it has been suggested that her worship was introduced by the Shepherds.

We may gain another viewpoint of the Corn Cat by turning to astronomical symbology. The brightest star in the Constellation of Virgo is called " an ear of corn " (Gk. ΣΤΑΧΥΣ (*stachys*) ; Lat. *Spica*). *Stachys* has an extended meaning, and is used also for " offspring " in a general sense. Here also the reference is to the Seed of the Woman, and we never find Virgo pictorially represented without the ear of corn in her hand. Indeed, the importance assumed by it has sometimes been so great as to completely overshadow the bearer. Virgo has sunk into such insignificance as to become known as Ki,* or the Constellation of the Spike. This Heavenly Corn, the *Spica Virginus*, the offspring of the Virgin, has, like its earthly shadow, a Guardian Cat. The White Cat Moon, the Cleanser of the Night, or *mârgâras* who disperses the shadows by her silvery beams, is the Protector of the Celestial Corn that the grey mice of night seek to devour and destroy.

* Ki was the Euphratean name for Virgo.

Or, in a variation of the allegory, the gorgeous tints of the morning and evening skies are compared to granaries of gold that have been laid in store by the Sun, and entrusted to the care of the watchful White Cat.

Another ancient parable figures Night as a cruel stepmother or witch who forces the maiden Aurora to separate the luminous wheat of evening from the tares of darkness. The wronged and virtuous maiden weeps over her impossible task, until the Cat Moon appears as the Madonna or Good Fairy, and cleans the corn of the darkening sky. But when the night is moonless, a demoniacal black cat often represents its gloom, and like the witch, threatens ill to the hapless maiden Aurora.

A third variant of this fruitful theme may be found in a Finnish myth recorded by Frederick Kreuzwald. The old witch of this tale dies, to reappear in the form of a cat, which is seized by its tail and flung into the fire. The witch is said by Gubernatis to typify night which is burned in the flames of the aurora of the morning.

BIBLIOGRAPHY

" Lares and Penates," p. 176. By Wm. Burckhardt Barker, M.R.A.S. Pub. by Ingram Cooke & Co., London, 1853.

" Ehsthnische Märchen." By von Fried. Kreuzwald. Pub. at Halle, 1869.

" Zoological Mythology," Vol. II, p. 42 *et seq.* By Angelo de Gubernatis. Pub. by Trübner & Co., London, 1872.

" The Golden Bough," Vol. VII. By J. G. Fraser. Pub. by Macmillan & Co., London, 1907.

" Myths of Ancient Egypt." By Lewis Spence. Pub. by George G. Harrap & Co., London, 1922.

" The Two Babylons," 8th edition, pp. 160–2. By the Rev. Alexander Hislop. Pub. by S. W. Partridge & Co., London.

" Encyclopædic Dictionary " ; Article : " Cat in Scotch." Pub. by Cassell & Co., Ltd., London.

CHAPTER XII

THE CAT AND THE SABBAT

WHEREVER the ancient cult of Diana was extant, its votaries met four times a year to celebrate the mysteries of their faith, and these gatherings, which were known as Sabbats or Sabbaths, were the very heart of their existence as a corporate society.

Various derivations of the word Sabbath have been suggested, but perhaps none is quite convincing. In Hebrew the grammatical inflexions show that it is a feminine form, properly *shabbat-t* for *shabbăt-t*. The root carries no implication of resting in the sense of enjoying repose, but in transitive forms means to "sever," to "terminate," and intransitively means to "desist," to "come to an end." It cannot be translated "the day of rest," but the grammatical form of *shabbath* suggests a transitive sense —"the divider," and would seem to denote that the Sabbath divides the month, or, in the case of the witches' quarterly festival, the year. The new moon and the Sabbath are almost invariably mentioned in connection with each other in the older portion of the Hebrew Scriptures, and so great was the joy occasioned by the reappearance of the crescent, that it became to the Jews the type of religious festivity in general. But the full moon also occupied a prominent position of religious significance, so that when the great agricultural festivals (which appear to have been originally sabbats) were fixed to take place on set days, the full moon was chosen for their celebration. For similar reasons the ancient Hindus appointed the times of the new and full moon to be days of sacrifice; and called the eve of the offering *upavasatha*.

Thus the Daughters of Diana had precedent for connecting their Sabbats with the phases of Luna, and the sexual rites which figured so prominently in their quarternary social and religious gatherings were held in honour of the moon's supposed activities in fostering the fruitfulness of men, animals, and vegetation.

To them the moon was represented by her age-old Egyptian symbol of the Cat, so this animal was introduced into the Sabbat mysteries. The celebrants of these rites often costumed themselves in skins and masks that they might impersonate the Cat, or some other animal, effectively (as described in the chapter on Witches in Cat Form), the President being arrayed to represent the animal symbolising the deity whose benevolence it was specially desired to invoke.

In later years, when the Church had enthroned Satan as the god of this world, and identified witches as his servants, the President was formally entitled the "Devil," and the twelve officials attending him received the same complimentary designation; a nomenclature which has created much confusion. The group thus formed was known as a Coven (i.e. conventicle), and the rule which governed the number composing it had evident reference to the thirteen lunar months of the year, and was common to the organisation everywhere. But it apparently suggested to the Christians the fatal number formed by Christ and His chosen Twelve, one of whom was the traitor responsible for the Master's death. Thus it was a cause of offence.

The witches generally selected remote fastnesses such as would naturally appeal to the Daughters of Diana for their Sabbat gatherings. Christian Stridtheckh describes their meetings as being "usually convened in woody places, or on mountains, of in caves, or anywhere far away from the habitations of men." He adds that *Mela,* in Book III, Chapter XLIV, speaks of Mount Atlas as their rendezvous, and that in his native land "The Mountain of the Bructeri, by some called Meliboeus, in the duchy of Brunswick, is known as notorious as the haunt or witches." In Germany the witches were said to congregate on the Blocksburg, or the Brocken, which is the highest peak of the Hart Mountains, and to travel from far away Lapland and Norway to these giddy precipices. It was evident that no mortal means could enable the witches to accomplish such superhuman feats, and they were popularly credited with riding thither on flying cats, or sometimes on broomsticks.

But though cats and brooms seem to have been the favourite means of transport, they were not the only mounts available to the witches. Like the goddess they served, these sorceresses were said to possess the power of transforming human beings into animals, and a sculptured stone panel at the entrance of Lyons Cathedral pictures a witch riding a man she has changed into a goat. She is whirling a cat around her unfortunate victim's head, so that it may tear his face with its claws, and is apparently on her way to a Sabbat meeting.

First-hand evidence from the witches and their unhappy mounts confirmed the story on the stone. We may instance the case of

Ann Armstrong, a member of a Northumbrian coven, who in 1673 "saith, that since she gave information against severall persons who ridd her to severall places where they had conversation with the divell, she hath been severall times lately ridden. . . . On Monday last at night, she, being in her father's house, see one Jane Baites, of Corbridge, come in the forme of a gray cat with a bridle hanging on her foote, and breath'd upon her & struck her dead [i.e. unconscious], & bridled her, & rid upon her in the name of the devill southward, but the name of the place she does not now remember. And the said Jane allighted & pulld the bridle of her head." From the context of this account it appears

WITCH, WITH CAT, RIDING TO SABBAT
From panel in Lyons Cathedral.

that Ann was changed into a horse, for Jane to ride in feline form to the Sabbat meeting.

The Sabbat of Dianic cult is referred to by many contemporary writers, who describe its phenomena indignantly, yet somewhat doubtfully, as the result of delusion by the devil, rather than an actual occurrence. We may take, as an example of these outpourings, the diatribe of the famous Benedictine Abbot, Regino of Prum (A.D. 906), who writes: "This, too, must by no means be passed over that certain utterly abandoned women, turning aside to follow Satan, being seduced by the illusions and phantasmical shows of demons firmly believe and openly profess that in the dead of night they ride upon certain beasts along with the pagan goddess Diana and a countless horde of women, and that in those silent hours they fly over vast tracts of country and obey her as their mistress, whilst on certain other nights they are summoned to do her homage and pay her service."

Regino was not isolated in his opinion of the illusions of witchcraft. In similar language Bartholomew Iscanus, Bishop of Exeter (1161–86), condemns " whosoever, ensnared by the Devil's wiles, may believe and profess that they ride with countless multitudes of others in the train of her whom the foolishly vulgar call Herodias or Diana, and that they obey her behests." And among the resolutions of the Council of Ancyra, which was held about the middle of the fifteenth century, is one concerning women who profess to ride abroad with Diana and Herodias. The scepticism expressed by these writers ill accorded with the relentless cruelty that often accompanied it. And we may here note that the feat of levitation which the witches and sorcerers claimed to perform in order to attend their Sabbats is recognised as possible in a large number of religious systems. " Stories of levitation," says Clodd, " specially gather round St. Philip Neri, St. Dunstan, St. Ignatius Loyola, St. Theresa, and many others whose names are written in the *Acta Sanctorum.*

Almost equally famous, and nearer to our own times are the levitational feats of St. Francis Xavier, who was born in the early part of the sixteenth century, and in 1541 visited the East. Eye-witnesses declare that on several occasions they beheld him elevated in the air.

Another Christian example is the levitation of the Franciscan monk, St. Joseph of Copertino, who lived in the seventeenth century. He was often raised in the air, remaining there till called to earth by the general of his Order. Although aged, he is said to have taken a short flight the day before he died. The same power was possessed by the magicians of Mexico ; and Father Acosta, in the sixteenth century, said they were able to fly through the air, and assume any form they chose.

Similar legends come from the East, adding to the list Gautama the Buddha and his disciples, and also Brahmins, who levitated so as to perform more completely the solar rites."

In connection with Buddhism, we may read how the sister of the Raja Kalasoka, who was a devout Buddhist, possessed " the usual Buddhist accomplishment of flying through the air," and used this means of transport to go to the aid of her brother when he was in a tight corner (Speir). Likewise the Buddhist Prince Mahendra, when, accompanied by other devotees, he went on his mission to Ceylon, about 246 B.C., made the journey " rising aloft into the air—and instantaneously alighting on the superb Missa Mountain," where the remains of Buddhist temples may still be seen (*Mahawanso,* Ch. XIII).

To the modern student of spiritualism levitation is a well-attested fact, so that those who record the flights of witches have no need to apologise or endeavour to explain them away.

It is probable that on those occasions when the masked dances of the Dianic cult were performed in caves rather than upon mountain tops the idea was to invoke the goddess in her aspect as Hecate ; and that the use of an underground sanctuary had originally been suggested by the practice of cave burial. The ritual seems to have been, at least in part, for the purpose of enabling the living to commune with the shades. Therefore Hallow-e'en, when, according to Celtic belief, the souls of the departed hover over the earth, was a day of tremendous activity among the Daughters of Diana. On this annual day of festival, the dead, released from the dark temple sepulchres, joined their faithful priestesses, whose bodily bonds were also loosened for its meet celebration. Hecate herself would appear among them, and head a procession of witches and sorceresses, " good neighbours " and ghosts. The company, mounted on tabby-cats, which had been transformed for the occasion into coal-black steeds, would gallop along the roads, or, bestriding flying besoms, would sweep through the air. A spirited account of such a proceeding has been bequeathed to us by the " Rhymer of Scotland," Dunbar, in his " Flyting of Dunbar and Kennedy," a poem which attained great popularity among the poet's contemporaries. The goddess honoured by these Sabbat rides is said to have been appealed to under the name of Andraste, for " victory, salvation, and liberty," by Boadicea, who before engaging in combat with the Roman invaders, exclaimed : " I thank thee, O Andraste, and I will call upon thy name, O kind lady."

This Celtic Hecate became known as Nicneven when a system blending the faiths of the Celts and the Goths on the subject was accepted, and her cult is said to have survived with considerable vigour in Scotland until the eighteenth century. But in England the Dianic cult was dying even before the commencement of the mediæval persecution which so cruelly destroyed its votaries, and left us only distorted fragments of its tenets.

Perhaps just because the Church had adopted so much of the ritual and creed of solar and lunar theogonies, it was furiously energetic against those customs it failed to absorb, and all through the Middle Ages, not only witches, but cats, were persecuted and tortured by the Christian organisations. The older religions had held these animals sacred, and the churches dreaded a revival of their faiths, and did not want the populace to see the connection between the Virgin Mary and the Virgin Diana, and to realise that the new religion was the same in essentials as the old.

BIBLIOGRAPHY

"Superstitions condemned in the Penitential of Bartholomew Iscanus, Bishop of Exeter, 1161–86." See "A Mediæval Garner." By G. G. Coulton. Pub. by Constable, London.

"Flyting of Dunbar and Kennedy." By William Dunbar. Printed by Chepman & Myllar, 1508.

"Letters on Demonology and Witchcraft," p. 126. By Sir Walter Scott. Pub. by John Murray, London, 1833.

"Life in Ancient India." By Mrs. Speir. Pub. by Smith, Elder & Co., London, 1856.

"Life and Letters of St. Francis Xavier." By Henry James Coleridge, S.J. Pub. 1872.

"The Golden Bough," Vol. I, Part VII, p. 226. By J. G. Frazer. Pub. by Macmillan & Co., London, 1907.

"The Pagan Tribes of Borneo," Vol. II, p. 29. By Charles Hose, D.Sc., and Wm. McDougall, M.B., F.R.S. Pub. 1912.

"The Question," p. 92. By E. Clodd. Pub. London, 1917.

"The Philosophy of Witchcraft," pp. 118–20. By Ian Ferguson. Pub. by George G. Harrap & Co., London, 1924.

CHAPTER XIII

WITCHES IN CAT FORM

IN all ages, and among all peoples, the belief has prevailed with varying intensity that Nature was the custodian of secret forces, which might be seized and used by the initiate, either to benefit others, or to destroy them, or for such personal purposes as love, and the acquirement of riches and power. No nation is, or ever has been, without its soothsayers, sorcerers, and magicians; whilst above and beyond the half-hidden creed of which they are the representatives, each nation boasts a religious faith, with terrors and aspirations confirmed by signs and miracles; or tenets disclosed by supernatural messengers and means.

Whatever the stage of development a country may have attained, whether infancy, or decrepit age, or manhood's prime, barbarous or civilised, conqueror or enslaved, in all stages of knowledge or ignorance, a most remarkable similarity in both religious and magical phenomena is forced upon the observer's notice.

In ancient Egypt religion and magic were closely interwoven, and the triform goddess Hecate (Egyptian *Hek,* a sorcerer, with feminine termination), Isis or Bast, is said to have presided over enchantment, and to have appeared at the sacrifices if called seven times. At the completion of the ritual, apparitions were wont to take shape, and these were named Hecatæa in honour of their patroness. Hecate was Diana on earth, and this fact gives us the key to much that is obscure and difficult to understand in witchcraft. For as soon as we turn to the terrestrial deities we recognise immediately in these goddesses and their insignia and attendant priestesses the originals of the later witches. Many of these goddesses were merely specialised or localised variations of Diana, though this fact was only revealed to the few. For example, Juno Lucina, whose office it was to assist women in travail, is thus described by Tooke: "One Hand was empty, and ready, as it were, to receive the new-born Babe; the other Hand held a lighted Torch, by which that Light of Life was signify'd, which all enjoy as soon as they are born. Timæus speaks very handsomely, when he relates that Diana's Temple was burnt the same Night in which Alexander was born: 'It is no wonder she was absent from her House,' says he, 'when her Assistance was necessary at the Labour of Olympias, Alexander's Mother.'"

"Intercidona," the same authority informs us, "was the Goddess who first taught the Art of cutting Wood with an Hatchet to make Fires." These friendly terrestrial goddesses were recognised by the implements of labour that they carried to assist their human sisters in the daily struggle; and the same implements distinguished the witches so maligned by the Christian churches.

Thus Deverra is described in quaint old Tooke's mythology as being "worshipp'd as a Goddess because she invented Brooms, by which all Things are brush'd clean, and those Distempers prevented that proceeded from Nastiness. The Sylvan Gods, who were always hurtful to big-belly'd Women, were driven away by those Deities, and the Mischief they invented was prevented. For, as neither the Trees, says St. Augustin, are cut down without an Ax nor Bread made without a Pestle, nor Things preserved clean without a Brush; so, since those Instruments are thought signs of good Housewifry, it was supposed that these wild, unclean Gods would never dare to enter into the Chamber of a breeding Woman." Certainly it is interesting to find St. Augustin so well informed when we remember the attitude adopted towards witchcraft by his successors. But whenever the Deity is conceived of as an arbitrary Tyrant instead of as an All-loving Parent, religion becomes the potent and terrible instrument of evil. Such was the case when from the sixteenth to the eighteenth century the entire Christian world became obsessed by the terror of witchcraft. Every natural occurrence was regarded as being the work of witches; lightning or hail, milk that turned sour, and every sort of misfortune and disease that attacked human beings or domestic animals was among the supposed effects of these malign sorcerers.

Between "the fierceness of the wrath of God" (Rev. xiv. 19) and the "great wrath" of the devil (Rev. xii. 12), Christians lived in a state of abject and continuous fear. No wonder they were cruel. Their deity was to the full as unmoral as their devil; but they believed that ultimately he was destined to prove the victor, and after his triumph would burn his foes alive in the lake of fire and brimstone, whence "the smoke of their torment" would ascend "for ever and ever" to his throne (Rev. xiv. 11).

So they sought to please him by anticipating the vengeance that he jealously claimed as his own prerogative (Rom. xii. 19), and even expected to gain a high place in Heaven for themselves by hastening the perdition of their brothers and sisters. Oh, God ! what a culmination to man's painful search for Light !

During the reign of the famous British demonologist King James I, who, in the Act relating to the Gunpowder Plot, is described as " the most great, learned, and religious king " that ever reigned in England, the Christian Church made a determined onslaught on the fragmentary and degraded survivals of the once noble, profoundly occult religion of Diana Triformis.

This led to a popular revival of interest in the darker aspect of occultism, for it was as Hecate alone that the uninitiated, irreverent bigots glimpsed the threefold goddess when they sought to tear aside the veil that covered her. " Witchcraft celebrates pale Hecate's offerings," said Shakespeare, voicing the belief of his own times, and it soon became a fashionable study among courtiers and place-seekers. The angle from which the new students approached it, automatically negatived the possibility of any revelation of its higher esoteric significance, whilst the bitter persecution instigated by the Christian churches, brought forth further distortion and concealment of its true tenets.

All this must be continually borne in mind when reading contemporary accounts of witch trials in European courts of justice, and we must also remember that without exception the accounts are recorded by avowed and bitter enemies. We have not a single sympathetic narration to help us in arriving at a just estimation.

That extraordinary product of the Roman Catholic Church known as the *Malleus Maleficarum*, or " Hammer for Witches," which was written by Innocent VIII, in 1489, was held to prove beyond question that the children of Satan were wont to transform themselves into all manner of animals, even as their father the devil had assumed the shape of a serpent for the purpose of tempting Eve (Gen. iii.)

In this chapter we will review some of the weird stories of human beings in feline form which were accepted as evidence by contemporary ecclesiastical courts. A notable instance occurred in 1596, when the witches of Aberdeen were accused of having assumed the likeness of cats that they might celebrate their orgies undisturbed around the Fish Cross. It seems probable from the name of the Cross, that it was erected in a fish-market, and that the supposed witches were actual cats drawn thither by the odour of their favourite food ; but another explanation is possible. If we turn to the chapter on Witch Cats and Repercussion, we shall see that masks and cloaks of fur were used by witches in their ritual dances to suggest their identity with the animal they represented, and popular belief credited them with actually achieving the desired transformation. The dittay against Bessie Thom, who was one of the Aberdeen coven, states that " there, accompanied with thy devilish companions and faction, transformed in other likeness, some in hares, some in cats, and some in other similitudes, ye all danced about the Fish Cross." Support is given to the theory that the Aberdeen witches were costumed to represent the animals sacred to their cult by the stern dictum of Theodore, seventh Archbishop of Canterbury, regarding a similar practice. He says, " If anyone at the Kalends of January goes about as a stag or a bull ; that is, making himself into a wild animal and dressing in the skin of a herd animal, and putting on the heads of beasts ; those who in such wise transform themselves into the appearance of a wild animal, penance for three years because this is devilish." Margaret Murray says that " The witches themselves admitted that they were masked and veiled, and the evidence of other witnesses goes to prove the same. Boguet suggests that the disguise was used to hide their identity, which was possibly the case at times, but it seems more probable, judging by the evidence, that the masking and veiling were for ritual purposes."

But though it would seem that the ecclesiastical authorities must have been aware of the ancient ritual of masked dances, they appear to have upheld and confirmed the popular belief that the witches through powers conferred on them by the devil, effected an actual change of form. Their object probably was to arouse the fears and hatred of the people against the revival of the older religion.

From such doctrine it naturally followed that unoffending animals were often the objects of superstitious fear. This is clearly reflected in contemporary literature. For example, George Gifford in his Dialogue writes : " In good sooth, I may tell it to you as to my friend, when I go but into my closes I am afraid, for I see now and then a hare, which by my conscience giveth me is a witch or some witch's spirit, she stareth so upon me. And—There is a foule great cat sometimes in my barne which I have no liking unto." It must have been somewhat trying even to the strongest nerves to have to face such ever-present threatening perils, but fortunately it was possible to combat them in various ways.

Mrs. Browning has told us that " Whiskered cats arointed flee," and her words have been interpreted as meaning that these animals, so intimately associated and even identified with witches, flee if a branch of the sacred rowan (or roan) tree be shaken against them, since according to an old belief witches are powerless in the neighbourhood of roan-tree wood. It will be realised that "aroint" is here considered to be a corruption of the words "a ronan-tree." But many other derivations have been suggested. Shakespeare is said to have been responsible for the introduction of this doubtful word, and when he makes Macbeth exclaim, "Aroint thee, witch!" some critics think that we should understand it as the equivalent of "avaunt," whilst others suggest that the word is really "anoint," and see in it an adjuration to the witch to annul the evil within her by a sacred rite. Naturally, witch-possessed cats would fly if "arointed," just as the poetess asserts that they do. It may even be that very ordinary cats, whether "whiskered" and witch-possessed or no, would shun the experience in either form, and might not be discerning in the case of the roan-tree, but flee with equal precipitation from a branch of any other wood angrily shaken to scare them!

But let us consider a recorded case of a witch transformed into a cat, where the presence of mind of the victim in repeating a potent incantation saved him from serious harm. We cull the instance from Cotton Mather's celebrated "Wonders of the Invisible World." It formed part of the evidence given during the trial for witchcraft of Susanna Martin at the court of Oyer and Terminer, on June the 29th, 1692. The prisoner pleaded not guilty, but many witnesses appeared against her. Among them was one Robert Downer, who testified as follows: "That this Prisoner being some Years ago prosecuted at Court for a Witch, he then said unto her, *He believed she was a Witch.* Whereat she being dissatisfied, said, *That some She-Devil would shortly fetch him away!* Which words were heard by others, as well as himself. The Night following, as he lay in his Bed, there came in at the Window, the likeness of a *Cat,* which flew upon him, took fast hold of his Throat, lay on him a considerable while, and almost killed him. At length he remembered what Susanna Martin had threat'ned the Day before; and with much striving he cried out, *Avoid, thou She-Devil! In the Name of God the Father, the Son, and the Holy Ghost, Avoid!* Whereupon it left him, leap'd on the Floor, and flew out at the Window. And there also came in several testimonies, that before ever *Downer* spoke a word of this Accident, *Susanna Martin* and her Family had related, *How this* Downer *had been* handled!"

Nor was this a solitary instance of rough handling by a witch in cat form.

In 1607, Isobel Grierson was convicted of witchcraft, and burnt, her ashes being scattered to the winds. The charge against her was that she went into the house of Adam Clark and his wife in Preston Pans, one night, in the likeness of his own cat, accompanied by a mighty rabble of cats, which, by the noise they made nearly frightened to death Adam, his wife, and the maidservant. The cats were accompanied by the devil, who, in the form of a black man, seized the poor maid, and dragged her up and down by the hair of her head.

Isobel was further accused of paying frequent visits to Mr. Brown of the same town in the shape of a cat, and rudely bespringling Brown's wife, and various parts of their domicile, but once being called upon by name, vanished away. Brown died of a disease inflicted by her ; if we may trust the evidence.

An interesting question arises from the testimony, given at the trial of Jonet Irving in 1616, to the effect that the devil, whilst in the form of a woman, on hearing the name of Christ pronounced, made a *second* metamorphosis, and ran " out at the holl of the door lyk a black catt." Why the feline form appeared as a surer refuge to Satan than the one he had adopted is a matter for conjecture. Was it that the Cat, as symbol of both good and evil, Christ and devil, was a recognised flag of truce, sure of respect from both belligerents ?

Another Isobel, the spouse of George Smith, a " portioner " in East Barnes, was tried for witchcraft in 1629, and among other articles of the indictment she was accused of having " resett Christian Grinton, a witch, in her house, whom the pannel's husband saw one night to come out at ane hole in the roof, in the likeness of a cat, and theirafter transform herself in her own likeness ; whereupon the pannel told her husband, that it should not faire weill with him, which fell out accordingly ; for next day he fell down dead at the pleuch."

The City Records of Edinburgh contain an account of a gift of escheat, which was granted by the council to the baron bailie of Canongate, of all heritable and movable goods belonging to the witches thereof (July 17th, 1661). After this there follows a Report made by William Johnstone, baron bailie of Canongate, relating that " wmquhill Jonet Allan, who is condemned and brunt for witchcraft, did delate Barbara Mylne, as one whom the said Jonet did once sie come in at the Watter-gate in lykness of a catt, and did change her garment under her awin staire, and went into her house."

This evidence, weighted, no doubt by the remembrance of the promised gift of escheat, caused the bailey to detain Barbara in prison until he had acquainted the council with the case. But he was instructed by them to liberate her until some course was taken for further examination.

The case of Isobel Gowdie, known as the Queen of Scottish

witches, who made her confession in the April of 1662, is a specially interesting one as casting a light upon the ceremonial ritual of the Scottish witches which we look for in vain elsewhere. Her confession, too, appears to have been freely made, without any compulsion from her examiners, though she seems to have been fully conscious of the peril in which her disclosures placed her. " I do not deserve," said she, " to be seated here at ease and unharmed, but rather to be stretched on an iron rack ; nor can my crimes be atoned for, were I to be drawn assunder by wild horses."

According to Isobel's evidence, the witches of Auldearn were so numerous that they were divided into companies known as *covines*, or *covens*, each of which was commanded by two officers, one of whom was called The Maiden of the Coven, and was usually an attractive girl. Isobel told the court, how on one occasion, at Lammas, 1659, she and her coven disguised in the form of cats, crows, and hares, rambled through the country, eating, drinking, and wasting their neighbour's goods, and how, amongst other exploits, they entered a dye-works in Auldearn, and played such pranks over the vat that ever after it would only dye black, " according to the colour of the Devil."

Isobel has handed down for our edification, the magic formula by which she transformed herself into a cat and back again. The spells had to be thrice repeated, and were as follows :

" I shall goe intill ane catt,
With sorrow, and sych, and a blak shott ;
And I sall goe in the Divellis nam,
Ay quhill I com hom againe."

To effect the return to human form she said :

" Catt, catt, God send thee a blak shott.
I am in a cattis liknes just now,
Bot I sal be in a womanis liknes ewin now.
Catt, catt, God send thee a blak shott."

Another witch who favoured the feline form was Marie Lamont, " a young Woman of the adge of Eighteen Yeares, dwelling in the parish of Innerkip (Inverkip, near Greenock), who willinglie offered herself to Tryell on the 4th of March, 1662." She told the court that " God had moved her heart to confess, because she had lived long in the devil's service." The eighth article of her confession described a witch's meeting in the Bridylinne " where the devill was with them in the likeness of a brown dog. The end of their meitting was to raise stormie weather to hinder boats from the killing fishing ; and she confessed that shee, Kettie

Scot, and Margaret Holm, cam to Allan Orr's house in the likeness of kats, and followed his wif into the chalmer, where they took a herring owt of a barrell, and having taken a byt off it, they left it behind them. The elk herring the said Allan his wif did eat, and yairefter taking heavy disease, died."

On another occasion when Marie, and the coven to which she belonged, assembled together in the night, at the back gate of Ardgowan, to work their evil spells, they appear to have met in their own proper forms. But, " The devill was with them," this time " in the likeness of a black man, with cloven featt, and directed some of them to fetch wyt sand from the shore, and cast it about the gates of Ardgowand . . . ; but shee sayes, when they war about that business, the devil turned them in likeness of kats, by shaking his hands above their heads."

A classical example of this ancient idea is afforded by the fable of Galinthias, or Galanthis, the faithful servant maid of Alcmena, whose sagacity shortened the pains of her mistress in giving birth to Hercules. She was changed by the jealous Juno into a cat, and condemned thereafter to bring forth her young, with the most agonising pains, by her mouth. Probably the cat's habit of carrying her kittens from place to place was the immediate source of this fable. In some versions the cat is replaced by a weasel.

Even to-day in many European countries similar legends find ready credence. For instance, in the Monferrato it is believed that all the cats which wander upon the roofs during the month of February are not really cats but witches, and that it is a duty to shoot them.

In Hungary it is believed that a cat usually becomes a witch from the age of seven years to that of twelve, and that witches ride upon tom-cats, especially black ones. To deliver the cat from the witch it is said to be necessary to make a cut upon its skin in the form of a cross.

It would be easily possible to fill many volumes with attested accounts of these weird transformations. It is not so very long ago since the Church gave the full weight of her authority to the belief in their actuality. The doctrines they exemplified are not dead to-day; though alleged examples of shape-changing no longer inspire us with panic fear, but arouse the desire to discover the laws which we know must underlie all unexplained phenomena.

BIBLIOGRAPHY

"A Dialogue of Witches and Witchcraft." By George Gifford. Printed 1608.

"The Pantheon," pp. 214, 286–7. By Andrew Tooke, A.M. Printed in London.

"Letters on Demonology and Witchcraft," 2nd edition, pp. 156–8 and 277–82. By Sir Walter Scott, Bart. Pub. by John Murray, London, 1831.

"Criminal Trials in Scotland," Vol. III, p. 613. By Robert Pitcairn. Pub. at Edinburgh, 1833.

"Monumenta Ecclesiastica," Vol. II, pp. 32–4. By Benjamin Thorpe. Pub. London, 1840.

"Spalding Club Miscellany," p. 167. Pub. at Aberdeen, 1841.

"Zoological Mythology," Vol. II, p. 63. By Angelo de Gubernatis. Pub. by Trübner & Co., London, 1862.

"The Wonders of the Invisible World," pp. 142–3. By Cotton Mather, D.D. Pub. by J. Russell Smith, London, 1862.

"A Historical Account of the Belief in Witchcraft in Scotland," pp. 98–128, 133–4. By Charles Kirkpatrick Sharpe, Esq. Pub. by Hamilton, Adams & Co., London, 1884.

"Tree Lore." By Francis George Heath. Pub. by C. H. Kelly, London.

"The Witch Cult in Western Europe." By Margaret Murray. Pub. by the Clarendon Press, Oxford, 1921.

"The Occult Review." Pub. by Rider & Co., London, Aug. 1924.

CHAPTER XIV

WITCH CATS AND REPERCUSSION

THE religious origin of Witchcraft is now generally admitted, and the cult recognised as the degenerate offspring or survival of a fallen and dying faith. If we keep this before our mental vision we shall not find it difficult to see the most probable explanation of the animal shapes said to have been assumed by witches. It was an expression of longing for union with their deity that caused devout worshippers to adopt the form that symbolised the divine attributes. The transformation was induced by the same means as in those earlier religions of which the sorcery practised in the Middle Ages was a ghastly relic. It was an article of faith that the worshipper might become the sacred animal that was the god's representative by being robed in its skin—or by wearing a mask of its head, and making sounds and gestures characteristic of its peculiarities, or even by the mere pronunciation of mystical formulæ.

As in the more ancient cults, the witches were often masked and veiled at their ritual dances and other ceremonies, and though it is obvious that their transformation into cats, goats, hares, etc., was not actual, yet the performers called themselves by the names of the animals, and, in their own estimation, and that of their fellow-ritualists, the change took place.

The belief that it was possible was very widely diffused. Indeed, the same thought may be found in modified forms in practically all religions, for, in its first intention the transforming rite was a communion service, which in its degenerate days was misunderstood and profaned.

As Eliphas Levi pointed out, " superstition is derived from a Latin word which signifies survival," and " is the dead body of a Religious Rite." Witchcraft was a survival of the worship of the feminine Principle of God—of the Eternal Virgin-Motherhood of the Creator ; and inseparably connected with it was the Cat, the symbol of this aspect of the Divine. Hence the feline form is represented on the apex of the Sistrum that Isis carries in her hand, and the Cat was the chosen transformation of the great Diana (or Hecate) herself in her hour of peril, when the terrible Typhon forced the gods to hide their divinity in animal shapes, and flee into Egypt. (This legend probably means that owing to the degeneration of humanity Religion had to be veiled in symbolism from profane eyes.) Having assumed feline form, Diana took refuge in the moon, and all lunar goddesses in different countries and ages were inseparately connected with the Cat. Witches, once their priestesses, adored the moon with undiminished reverence, so that the Cat was bound to retain its importance in the cult of Dianism, even after the terrible degradation of Mother-worship.

To explain the downfall of this ancient and beautiful faith, we must remember that the Cat, either by her own multiple nature, or, more obviously, when coiled in a circle, like the changing moon she represented, showed forth the Mother of Nature as All. She was Venus the Beautiful, and Venus the Terrible, the Goddess of Life and Death, whose Eastern name Al-Husa, or Huza, stands for the Egyptian " Divine Woman," or Isis. Al-Husa means the hyacinth or lily, hence the Light, which, being the soul of Matter or Maya is the shadow of God, the very opposite of God's Actuality.

So long as Religion honoured the Real through its manifestation or shadow, and accepted, or even propitiated, the evil and finite, because they were the necessary instruments of the Creator, all was well. But when homage became diverted from the Unknown Darkness that was Spiritual Light, to the visible material Light of Nature, which in Reality is Darkness and Delusion, the falsified conception speedily resulted in Black Magic and Devil Worship, with all its accompanying horrors.

That which is Real is Immutable. The unreal is distinguishable by its lack of stability. The moon is always changing form, and shape-shifting is one of the powers attributed to the daughters of Diana. Hargrave Jennings claims " the calderon of the witches as, in the original, the vase or urn of the fiery transmigration, in which all the things of the world change."

When we come down to practical affairs the belief in shape-shifting involves the corollary that wounds received by a person when masquerading in the form of an animal, will remain on the body after it has returned to human shape, and this alleged phenomenon is known as repercussion. There are an almost endless number of stories illustrating this particular form of zoanthropy, which are even now current in Scotland, France, Italy, and Germany, but in England such tales are rare, the witches' cat being considered rather as an attendant familiar spirit than as the witch herself in this country.

The classic Scotch story of repercussion is as follows, and is woven around the witches of Thurso. In December of 1718, an honest merchant known as William Montgomerie, who lived in the Burnside of Scrabster, handed a petition to the sheriff, representing that his house " was severall times infested with cats to that degree, that he nor his family were in safety to reside there any longer." His maid reported that the cats spoke among themselves ; his wife threatened to leave him and go to Thurso, and one of his servants fled in fear before his term of service had expired.

At last one night Montgomerie lost patience, and, arming himself with broadsword, dirk and axe, he killed two of the cats and struck off a leg from a third, wounding several others as they fled. Shortly afterwards a suspected witch, named Helen Andrew, died suddenly, whilst another, M'Huistan, threw herself off some rocks into the sea, where she drowned. Then an old woman, Margaret Nin-Gilbert, who lived about a mile and a half from Montgomerie, was seen by some of her neighbours " to drop at her own door, one of her leggs from the midle." Of course there was no hesitation in identifying these three women with the slain and wounded cats. Margaret's black and putrefied leg was taken to the Sheriff-Depute, and he immediately ordered her to be imprisoned. A few days later she was examined, and confessed that she had been bodily present in Montgomerie's house, and that he had " broke her legg either by the durk or ax, which legg since has fallen off . . . ; and that she was in the likeness of a feltered cat."

Two or three weeks after this forced confession the poor old woman died in prison ; probably as a result of the gangrene or leprosy (?) from which she seems to have suffered, though popular gossip suggested that she had been murdered by some of her fellow-prisoners, whom she had named as her confederates. There are variations of this story.

According to one account, when Montgomerie cut off the cat's leg, he found it to be the leg of a woman, and next morning Margaret was minus the corresponding limb. After Margaret's death an attempt was made to force confessions from "other three defamed by her who continues incarcerated," but finally the Lord Advocate stopped all further procedure.

Another Scotch story is related by a Captain Burt, who, writing in 1730, tells us he had it from a clergyman. A certain laird, noticing that his wine was mysteriously diminishing, suspected witchcraft to be the cause of his loss. Accordingly he went armed to his cellar one night, expecting to find the unhallowed gang at their orgies.

But when he entered, he was surrounded by cats, and laying about him with his broad sword, soon rid his premises of their presence. Examining the floor, he saw by the blood drops on it, that his attack had wounded one of the cats ere it had departed, and next day, when the house of an old woman, reputed locally to be a witch, was entered, she was found in bed with one of her legs off.

Tales of repercussion in England are rare, but that celebrated divine and philosopher of the seventeenth century, Joseph Glanvil, one of the most active members of the Royal Society, and a firm believer in witchcraft, has recorded an interesting case for us. He tells of "an old woman in Cambridgeshire, whose astral spirit, coming into a man's house (as he was sitting alone at the fire) in the shape of an huge cat, and setting herself before the fire, not far from him, he stole a stroke at the back of it with a fire-fork, and seemed to break the back of it, but it scrambled from him, and vanisht, he knew not how. But such an old woman, a reputed witch, was found dead in her bed that very night, with her back broken, as I have heard some years ago credibly reported."

It is recorded by Bodin, the French lawyer and political writer of the sixteenth century, that the witches of Vernon who were tried in 1566, used to assemble in an old ruined castle in the shape of cats. Four men of valour arranged to spend a night in the haunted precincts, but they paid dearly for their temerity. The witch-cats assailed them by myriads, and one of the bold intruders was killed, whilst the others were severely injured. However, they managed to leave their mark on the cats, and next day a number of old women in the neighbourhood were found to be suffering from ghastly wounds.

Boguet relates several stories of repercussion. According to one of these a labourer of Strasburg was attacked by three huge cats, and in self-defence wounded them seriously. Within an hour he was arrested on a charge of maltreating three well-known ladies of the town. He professed himself amazed at the accusation and vigorously denied it, telling how he had been assaulted by the cats. He produced what were considered to be proofs of his statement, and the three ladies when medically examined were found to be suffering from the wounds he had inflicted on them in their cat shape.

Meier relates a Swabian story of a young woman and her soldier lover. He used to visit her when off duty, but one day the girl told him not to come Friday nights as it was not convenient to her to see him then. This aroused suspicions in him, and the very next Friday he set out to go to her house. As he went a white cat ran up to him in the street and followed him closely, refusing to be driven off. This so annoyed him that he drew his sword and slashed off one of her paws, whereupon she bolted. The soldier walked on, but when he arrived at his sweetheart's house he found her in bed, and when he asked the cause her reply was confused. Seeing bloodstains he drew down the coverlet and found the girl had one of her feet chopped off, and was weltering in her gore. "So that's what ails you, you witch!" said he. He left her, and in three days she was dead.

Repercussion was still believed in among the Basques in recent years, as was proved by an experience of the Rev. Wentworth Webster when he was collecting material for his Basque Legends (1877). He tells us that "Witches still appear in the shape of cats, but generally black ones. About two years ago," he adds, "we were told of a man, who at midnight, chopped off the ear of a black cat who was bewitching his cattle, and lo! in the morning it was a woman's ear, with an ear-ring still in it. He deposited it in the Mairie, and we might see it there, but we did not go to look as it was some distance off."

Nor are these beliefs confined to the countries of Europe. One of the primitive tribes of Bengal, the Oraons, or Uraons, firmly holds that "some women have the power to change their soul into a black cat, who then goes about in the houses where there are sick people. Such a cat has a peculiar way of mewing quite different from its brethren, and is easily recognised. . . . Any wound inflicted on the cat will be inflicted on her [the witch], and if they cut its ears or break its legs or put out its eyes, the woman will suffer the same mutilation."

The following account of a modification of the same superstition in modern Egypt, related about three-quarters of a century ago by Lady Duff-Gordon, is certainly of interest in this connection.

"Do you remember the German story of the lad who travelled 'um das gruseln zu lernen' (to learn how to shudder?) Well, I who never 'gruselte' (shuddered) before, had a touch of it a few mornings ago. I was sitting here quietly drinking tea, and four or five men were present, when a cat came to the door. I called, and offered milk, but puss, after looking at us, ran away.

"'Well dost thou, Lady,' said a quiet sensible man, a merchant here, 'to be kind to the Cat, for I daresay he gets little enough at home: *his* father, poor man, cannot cook for his children every day.' Then, in an explanatory tone to the company: 'That's Ali Nasseree's boy, Yussuf, it must be Yussuf, because his twin, Ismain, is with his uncle at Negadeh.'

"'Mir Gruselte' (I shuddered) I confess: not but what I have heard things almost as absurd from gentlemen and ladies in Europe, but an 'extravagance' in a Kaftan has a different effect from one in a tail-coat.

"'What! My butcher boy who brings the meat—a Cat?' I gasped.

"'To be sure, and he knows well where to look for a bit of good cookery, you see. All twins go out as Cats at night, if they go to sleep hungry, and their own bodies lie at home like dead, meanwhile, but no one must touch them or they would die. Why, your own boy, Achmet, does it. Ho, Achmet!' Achmet appears.

"'Boy, don't you go out as a Cat at night?'

"'Non,' said Achmet tranquilly, 'I am not a twin. My sister's sons do'

"I enquired if people were not afraid of such cats.

"'No, there is no fear: they only eat a little of the cookery, but if you beat them, they tell their parents next day. So-and-so beat me in his house last night,' and show their bruises. No, they are not afreets: they are beni-Adam. Only twins do it, and if you give them a sort of onion broth and some milk, the first thing when they are born, they do not do it at all.'

"Omar professed never to have heard it, but I am sure he had, only he dreads being laughed at. One of the American missionaries told me something like it, as belonging to the Copts; but it is entirely Egyptian, and common to both religions. I asked several Copts, who assured me it was true, and told it just the same. Is it a remnant of the doctrine of transmigration? However, the notion fully accounts for the horror the people feel at the idea of killing a cat."

The Copts are followers of the Eutychian "heresy," or Jacobite sect of Christianity, but are supposed by some writers to be descended from the ancient Egyptians, as certain of their ceremonies resemble the customs of those people. It is noteworthy that chivalrous feelings of protection are aroused in their breasts by the thought that a fellow-human may be abroad as a helpless cat, and stands forth in striking contrast from the murderous instinct of European Christians in like circumstances. I leave the former cases to speak for themselves of the achievement of centuries of Christianity in conjunction with the then highest known form of civilisation. Was the Master quite forgotten? It would seem so. The Churches had slain Him, and the animal that was the age-old symbol of the Christ was persecuted and slain, too.

BIBLIOGRAPHY

"Six Lives de la République." By Jean Bodin. Printed 1576.

"Discours des Sorciers." By Henri Boguet. 3rd edition. Pub. at Lyons, 1590.

"Saducimus Triumphatus, or Full and Plain Evidence Concerning Witches and Apparitions." By Joseph Glanvil, London, 1681.

"Miscellanies." By John Aubrey. Pub. 1696.

"Ovid's Metamorphoses, Translated by the most Eminent Hands," 4th edition, Vol. I, Book V, p. 180. Printed for T. Davies and others. London, 1773.

"Letters on Demonology and Witchcraft," 2nd edition, p. 326–7. By Sir Walter Scott, Bart. Pub. by John Murray, London, 1833.

"Witch Stories." By Mrs. E. Lynn Lynton. Pub. 1861–2.

"Primitive Culture," Vol. I, p. 314. By Sir Edward B. Tylor. Pub. London, 1873.

"Basque Legends." By the Rev. Wentworth Webster. Pub. 1877.

"A Historical Account of the Belief in Witchcraft in Scotland." By Charles Kirkpatrick Sharpe, Esq. Pub. by Hamilton, Adams & Co., London, 1884.

"Witchcraft and Second Sight in the Highlands and Islands of Scotland." By the Rev. Gregorson Campbell.

"Transcendental Magic: Its Doctrine and Ritual." By Eliphas Levi. Trans. by Arthur Edwarde Waite. Pub. by Wm. Rider & Son, London, 1923.

"Cat Gossip." Edited by H. C. Brooke. Pub. at Taunton, Feb. 9th, 1927.

"Religion and Customs of the Uraons." By the Rev. P. Dehons, S.J.

CHAPTER XV

SECRET SECTS AND CAT WORSHIP

PERHAPS the most renowned of the three great military Orders founded in the twelfth century* for the protection of Jerusalem, is that of the Knights Templars. The story of their phenomenal growth in numbers, wealth, and power, which made them for more than a hundred years one of the most influential forces in the moulding of European politics, is dramatically followed by their even more sudden downfall and annihilation during the reign of Phillip the Fair of France.

This king, to gratify a private grudge against certain eminent Templars, instituted a bitter persecution of the whole Order, accusing them of heresy and incredible crimes. On October 13th, 1307, he had all the French members arrested, and, in order to extract confessions of guilt from them, tortured and racked.

A very short time previously Phillip had spoken of his special love for the Order that now he had determined to destroy, but strange rumours about the secret rites practised by its members at their midnight meetings afforded him a measure of justification for his change of front.

Two principal classes of accusation were brought against the Order. First, the denial of God and of Christ, embodied in the Articles I to XIII, and second, the worship of the devil and the practise of sorcery. It was affirmed that Satan himself presided over the Templars' secret midnight assemblies, and made appearance among the celebrants in the form of a black Tom-cat, or some other hideous four-footed monster, and that on these occasions sacrifices of infants and young girls were offered to propitiate the fiend.

Without any proof of the truth of such terrible charges the Templars were there and then denounced as the enemies of God. Their profession of Christianity was said to be a mere cloak to conceal their blasphemous rites and obscene orgies. The king's

* Suppressed by Pope Clement in 1312. Abolished by Council of Vienne, 1313.

suspicions were confirmed by confessions extracted under torture. Out of the Templars examined by the Inquisitors in Paris, between October 19th and November 24th, 1307, hardly one refused to admit that the crucifix had been dishonoured at his reception ceremony, whilst many confessed to other terrible charges, even the most loathsome, such as the *osculum infame* said to be demanded of the juniors by their superiors.

Although modern investigation confirms the idea that the monstrous accusations brought against the Templars were untrue, and the confessions that were extracted by torture valueless as evidence, yet it seems fairly clear that the Templars were members of a secret religion which combined the heretical doctrines of the Bogomilians, and the closely connected Luciferans or Satanists. The name of the former signifies in Slavonic tongue "The Friends of God," and the sect believed in a Supreme Deity whose eldest son, Satanael, worshipped by the Jews as Jehovah, created the world after revolting against his father; and whose younger son, Jesus, became man to counteract the wicked work of his brother. The Bogomilians did not venerate the Cross, because they saw it as the instrument of Christ's sufferings. But the Luciferans worshipped God's eldest son, who had power over wealth and worldly happiness. They are said to have adored a black cat as the symbol of Satan, when celebrating their mysteries, and to have sacrificed children at their nocturnal orgies, and used the victim's blood in making the Eucharistic bread of their Order.

M. Loiseleur considers that the Templars borrowed from the Bogomilians their belief in the Supreme Deity, and from the Satanists their worship of the god of this world. In support of his theory he points out many remarkable coincidences, verbal and otherwise, between the creed of these sects and that of the Templars. Eliphas Levi also accuses the Templars of following the occult practices of the Luciferans, and further asserts that they were "initiated into the mysterious doctrine of the Kabala."

Certainly the intercourse of this Order with the East brought them into contact with many religious conjectures and opinions which at that period were totally unknown to European thought, though the loss of Constantinople and the immigration of numerous Eastern refugees afterwards introduced these ideas to Western minds. It has been claimed that the revival of learning, the study of Greek, and the rise of free thought all date from this event, which led to the introduction of Oriental learning and mysticism into Europe. The Templars possibly anticipated some of these results, because of the long sojourn of their Order in Palestine, and by displaying the wider knowledge thus gained, shocked the limited home-staying clergy.

Antiquarians have identified many of the curious symbols carved in the churches of the Templars with the signs in use among ancient Gnostic sects, and drawn the conclusion that their opinions and practices were probably similar. This is confirmed by the fact that although the persecution of the Templars was carried out so ruthlessly by their religious antagonists, it failed to exterminate their doctrines, rites, and ceremonies. Dormant for a period, the fourteenth century saw their revival, and their recovery was further aided in the fifteenth by the development of the Rosicrucian Society in Germany.

Like the Templars, the Gnostic sect of the Manicheans were accused by their persecutors of many terrible and incredible crimes, and were said to worship the devil in the form of a black cat. They were the disciples of Mani, or Manes, a Persian who was born in Babylonia about A.D. 216, and who is said to have been learned in all the wisdom of the Magians, and to have been physician, astronomer, artist, philosopher, and poet. His teachings, however, are supposed to have been partly derived from books he inherited, written by a Saracen disciple of Empedocles named Scythianus, and treating of the wisdom of Egypt. His gospel, which he first proclaimed about 242, combined this doctrine with ideas borrowed from Buddhism, Zoroastrianism, Judaism, and Christianity, and certain of his own originating. His fundamental tenet was Dualism. He believed Jehovah to be a subordinate Demiurgic minister of Ahriman, the eternal principle of evil. The human race was therefore of Satanic origin, and the powers of darkness, being co-equal with the powers of light, must be placated. Christ or Mithras, the Spirit of Life, resided in the sun by his power, and in the moon by his wisdom, and those who confessed him must renounce Jehovah. The heavenly orbs were the visible symbols of the deity Ormuzd, or the good Principle, and, allowing for the fact that Manichean doctrines have only reached us in the distorted form their enemies bestowed on them, it seems probable that the Cat was honoured by this sect because of its association with the sun and moon, and was representative of Christ or Mithras. Even so, it must be admitted that the Dualism of this creed gives cause for suspicion that the accusations brought against its votaries may not have been wholly unfounded. Like the Templars, the Manicheans were accused of unspeakable abominations in connection with their secret ritual. They were said to meet on certain days in an appointed house, each carrying a lantern, and there to sing the names of various demons, as if chanting a litany, until the devil suddenly appeared in their midst in the form of a cat, or other animal. This was the signal for the lights to be extinguished, and a sexual orgy to commence. We are further told that when a child was born to a member of the sect, they called an assembly on the eighth day, and lighted a large fire through which the babe was ceremonially passed. Afterwards the child was burnt, and its ashes preserved for use in their communion service. The ceremonial violation of a maiden of tender years in the presence of the "perfect" (i.e. the fully initiated) is said to have been also part of their ritual. More sympathetic accounts describe the hymns of the votaries as being addressed to beings whose names recall the functions and attributes of angels.

Still, we can hardly wonder that the sect was relentlessly persecuted by the Roman Church, and that, following her usual

CAT REPRESENTED ON A CAPITAL IN THE FRENCH CHURCH AT CANTERBURY
From "Archæologia."

policy of casting out Satan by Satan, she burnt many of its members alive. Mani himself is said to have been crucified in 276–7, or according to another account flayed alive, and his carcase cast to the dogs. But in spite of this bitter opposition, aiming at nothing less than extermination, the creed spread to a surprising extent and gave birth to many sub-sects. It was held and preached by the great Augustine for a period, and preserved a vigorous life in Europe during a thousand years, and still, it is alleged, survives in Asia.

According to Montagu Summers, early in the eleventh century Manichee and warlock were recognised by the Roman Church as synonymous. He recalls how in 1022 a number of Manicheans were burnt alive by order of Robert I, after trial by a synod at Orleans, and adds, "A contemporary document clearly identifies them with witches, worshippers of the Demon, who appeared to them under the form of an animal."

Similar accusations were brought against the Waldensians or Vaudois, a Manichean sect which originated in the eleventh century at Lyons. According to some authorities their name was derived from that of their founder, Peter Waldo, but others consider that Vaudois was a corruption of the Provençal word *Vaudes*, which meant a sorcerer. The sect was accredited with all kinds of dark practices, and a very rare tract of the fourteenth century charges them with the following: " Item: *in aliquibus aliis partibus apparet eis dæmon sub specie et figura cati, quem sub cauda sigillatim osculantur.*" (The devil appears to them in the form of a cat, and they kiss him *sub cauda.*)

The kindred sect known as the Albigenses arose about the same time as the Waldensians and took their name from the city of Albi. The Roman Church found herself seriously embarrassed by the spread of these heretical doctrines, and the murder of a papal delegate afforded her an excuse for drastic measures of revenge. Pope Innocent III* proclaimed a crusade against both the sects, which resulted in the brutal massacre of tens of thousands of men, women, and children. The few Waldensian survivors of the holocaust fled to the more inaccessible valleys of Piedmont, and in spite of the devastating persecution which pursued them even there, succeeded in maintaining their Church until the Reformation; but the Albigenses were slowly and secretly exterminated by the strong hand of the Inquisition. The awful narrative of Leger describing the Piedmontese Massacres makes the blood run cold. Infants snatched from their mothers' arms were torn asunder, or their heads were dashed against the rocks. The sick and old were burned alive in their homes. Some were flayed alive, some were roasted alive, some disembowelled; or fastened to the trees of their own orchards whilst their hearts were torn out. Some were atrociously mutilated and their mangled remains flung on the highways to be devoured by beasts, whilst of others the brains were boiled and eaten by these devils in human shape. Some were fastened into the furrows of their own fields and ploughed into them. Others were buried alive. Fathers were marched to death with the heads of their children suspended from their necks. Deeds too terrible to mention were committed against them. " My hand trembles," says Leger, " so that I can scarce hold the pen, and my tears mingle in torrents with my ink, while I write the deeds of these children of darkness—blacker even than the Prince of Darkness himself."

Wordsworth sympathetically refers to these heroic victims of Christian intolerance as

* 1198–1208.

> " . . . the Waldensian bands whom Hate
> In vain endeavours to exterminate,
> Whom Obloquy pursues with hideous bark :
> But they desist not ;—and the sacred fire,
> Rekindled thus, from dens and savage woods
> Moves, handed on with never-ceasing care,
> Through courts, through camps, o'er limitary floods ;
> Nor lacks this sea-girt Isle a timely share
> Of the new Flame, not suffered to expire."
>
> (" Ecclesiastical Sonnets," Part II, 12.)

And in a note he explains how their persecutors " even consolidated their miseries into one reproachful term, calling them Patarenians, or Paturini, from *pati* to suffer.

> " Dwellers with wolves she named them, for the pine
> And green oak are their covert ; as the gloom
> Of night oft foils their enemy's design.
> She calls them Riders on the flying broom ;
> Sorcerers, whose frame and aspect have become
> One and the same through practices malign."

Whether Wordsworth was correct or not in thus identifying the Waldenses with the Patarenians or Paturini (who originated at Milan, and flourished in our eleventh century), similar charges to those made against the Templars were proffered in condemnation of both these sects. The Paturini were accused of celebrating midnight rites resembling those of the witches' sabbath, in which cats and goats played important rôles. According to a description given of one of these meetings, the celebrants sang hymns in their den of infamy until the first watch of the night. Then a black cat was lowered into their midst. Its appearance gave the signal for the lights to be extinguished, and license succeeded devotion just as was said to be the case in the Manichean ritual, and in that of their successors the Waldensians.

Mr. Churchward has pointed out that the study of the mysteries of the past reveals the fact that " the Druids, the Gymnosophists of India, the Magi of Persia, and the Chaldeans of Assyria had all the same religious rites and ceremonies as practised by their priests who were initiated to their Order, and that these were solemnly sworn to keep the doctrines a profound secret from the rest of mankind. All these flowed from one source—Egypt." " It is admitted that the secret system of free Masonry was originally founded on the mysteries of the Egyptian Isis," says Hislop. We may remember that the goddess Bast sits as a Cat upon the Sistrum of Isis, and thereby gain a new light on Cat worship as practised by secret sects. I have reviewed this aspect more fully when dealing with The Virgin and the Cat, and The Taigheirm, so I will not enlarge on it here, except to remark the degeneration brought about by the doctrine of Dualism in originally lofty and beautiful symbolic conceptions. Isis (or Bast) is degraded, and seen and worshipped only in her shadow form as Hecate or Proserpine wherever Dualism has entered and corrupted the Mysteries.

The strange religious rituals, at some of which we have been glancing because of the importance given by them to the symbol of the Cat, have for us a more than passing interest, for we are told by modern writers (as e.g. Nesta Webster and Montagu Summers), who have made a study of secret sects and societies, that " these amazing cults, these strange perverted rites which we associate with the Dark Ages, are going on around us to-day. Illuminism, Cabalism, and even Satanism are still realities," says the first-named writer, and the evidence she presents to us seems incontrovertible.

BIBLIOGRAPHY

" Histoire Générale des Eglises Evangéliques des Vallées de Piemont ou Vaudoises," Part II, p. 111. Par Jean Leger, Pasteur et Moderateur des Eglises des Vallées, et depuis la violence de la Persecution, appelé à l'Eglise Wallonne de Leyde. A. Leyde, 1669.

" Recherches Historiques sur les Templiers." By Fabré Palaprat. Pub. Paris, 1835.

" Histoire et doctrine des Cathares ou Albigeois," Vol. I, p. 31. By Schmidt. Pub. Paris, 1849.

" La doctrine secrète des Templiers," p. 66. By Jules Loiseleur. Pub. Paris, 1852.

" The History of Magic," Vol. II, p. 150. By Joseph Ennemoser. Trans. by Wm. Howitt. Pub. by Henry G. Bohn, London, 1854.

" The Military Religious Orders of the Middle Ages." By F. C. Woodhouse, M.A. Pub. by S.P.C.K., London, 1879.

" Faiths of Man." By J. G. R. Forlong. Pub. by Bernard Quaritch, London, 1906.

" Signs and Symbols of Primordial Man," p. 185. By Albert Churchward. Pub. 1910.

" Secret Societies and Subversive Movements," p. 323. By Nesta H. Webster. Pub. by Boswell Printing and Publishing Company, London, 1924.

" The History of Witchcraft and Demonology," p. 24. By Montagu Summers. Pub. by Kegan Paul, Trench, Trübner & Co., London, 1926.

" The Liberation of Mankind," p. 108. By Hendrik Willem Van Loon. Pub. by George G. Harrap & Co., Ltd., London, 1926.

CHAPTER XVI

THE CAT AS SACRIFICE

THE usual conception of sacrifice as a banquet which gods and men share in common is completely placed out of court when we come to consider the Cat as a sacrificial victim. It is clear that here we are dealing with that higher idea which visioned the sacred animal as sharing the nature of the god it symbolised, so that the deity in a mystical sense died for his people when it was immolated. This was especially the case in ancient Egypt where, as Sextus Empericus has recorded, the Cat (the symbol of the Sun-god) was sacrificed to Horus, the rising sun.

Not being a " food animal," no thought that it had been slain to appease the hunger of an anthropomorphic deity could stain the thoughts of the worshippers. It was either identified with the bright god it represented, who daily died for the world's inhabitants, and rose again in the morning sky, or it was connected with the Great Mother Isis in one of her many aspects and personifications. Sacrifice, when thus viewed, is but the circulation of the one Divine Essence through the being of God, Nature and Man. The Rig Veda speaks of the sacrificial plant in this sense, stating that it contains all the worlds and is father of the gods (ix. 86, 10 ; 109, 4), and of the sacrificial horse which assumes the names and nature of the gods (i. 163, 3).

So long as this purity and sublimity of conception was the basis of sacrifice, whatever form it took, only good to all concerned could be the result. But like the symbol of the Encircled Serpent, the Cat represented God as All, and as life became more complicated, Evil took stronger and more definite form, and could no longer be left out of man's reckoning. Dualism quickly brought about the downfall of spiritual religion. The Unity of the Trinity was no longer recognised. Luna, Diana, and Hecate were torn asunder, and no more seen as the triple aspects of the one Great Mother. There was war in Heaven.

Religion has sometimes been regarded as the sublimation of magic, but, generally speaking, it would be more correct to see in magic a retrogressive form of religion. Sorcery originated as a sacred art, and the possession of magical knowledge was an attribute of the very gods. The sorcerer ranked with prophet and priest, and the highest honour was attached to his calling. The character and position of magic in the earlier pre-Christian period, was entirely different from that it assumed in late Egyptian thought, and in the Judaic-Christian creed of Mediæval Europe. Long before the introduction of Christianity, however, the originally high ideals of the ancient religion had begun to disintegrate, and had been misinterpreted and cruelly degraded. The votaries of corrupt practices in the cult of Dianism saw in the Great Mother only Hecate, or Proserpine, the dread ruler of Hell, who presided over demons and unhappy ghosts, and evil enchantments. Her head was said to be covered with frightful snakes instead of hair, and her feet to be formed like serpents. She would come to the sacrifices when called upon seven times, and when they were concluded, apparitions, called after her Hecatea, were wont to appear. The object of evoking such definitely evil and hostile powers at first sight is obscure, but the sorcerer hoped by magical devices to render the demons subservient to his will. As Malinowski commented, we must see in magic " the embodiment of the supreme folly of hope."

Nor were the forces of evil approached solely from the standpoint of Dualism. As ancient religion fell into decay, a pernicious idea took root and grew. The Kingdom of Heaven might be taken by violence ; where prayer and entreaty had failed to move the gods the strong and courageous man would force from reluctant Heaven the coveted blessing. Sacrificial ritual gradually gave place to the dark practices of Black Magic. The gods were no longer reverenced or even feared. Invocations so presented and worded as to be commands were addressed to them, and their resentment of the impertinence frustrated by the protective charms with which the operator encircled himself.

> " The face of earth hath maddened me, and I
> Take refuge in her mysteries, and pierce
> To the abodes of those who govern her,"

said Byron ; and this resolution was but an echo of the grim purpose pursued by the votaries of the Left Hand Path all through the ages.

" Our philosophy is mysticism," says a modern Spanish author, " . . . eternal combat with God to wrench from Him His secret, the secret of our destiny. . . . This our furious passion not to die, this madness of immortality, takes us far away from the æsthetic calm demanded by science." Those who peruse this chapter will certainly agree that it does so, when allowed to overrule all considerations of abstract right and wrong in order to glorify or perpetuate the personal concrete ego.

Perhaps because of its nocturnal habits, the Cat from ancient times had been considered the most acceptable offering to the gods of darkness, and the subterranean deities. To sacrifice a cat was a sure means of contacting these deities, and persuading them to confer the gift of second sight, which the Cat, as their representative, was believed to possess.

But, as the idea of forcing the gods gained ground, the Cat sacrifice was newly interpreted. The gods loved the Cat as their chosen and sacred symbol. To torture it mercilessly would be to oblige them to grant any request that its persecutor made the condition of its release. Here was an invincible weapon that the strong and unscrupulous might wield.

In this dark period Christianity was launched upon the world, and quickly completed the destruction of the older religions, by teaching its proselytes to regard their former deities as devils.

The effect of the new creed was to strengthen and even justify the idea we have outlined. The devil had usurped the powers and position of the ancient gods, and he retained their symbol, the Cat, as his chosen representative. Who could object to see the archfiend forced to obey a human being, or the animal sacred to him, tortured? Yet in justice to the Church, we must note that this black magic which she recognised as real and potent, was strictly forbidden by her. She did not distinguish the would-be masters of Satan from his servants, but sought by means no less desperate and terrible than their own to exterminate them. Bitter as was her hostility on other occasions to any rival interpretation of Divine mystery, it was long before the Christian Church entirely lost touch with the older Egyptian tradition. Efforts at amalgamation and reconciliation were continually being made by those who realised the basic unity of the two creeds. As late as 1757 a symbolic appeal was directed to the imagination of the Christian populace, by introducing the figure of the Cat, as the symbol of Horus, into the Christian mysteries.* Until this date a weird ritual was annually celebrated at Aix, in Provence, in which a cat was the central figure. On these occasions the finest Tom-cat in the country was swathed in swaddling clothes like an infant, and exhibited to the adoration of the devout in a magnificent shrine. Flowers were strewn along the route ere he passed, and every knee was bent as his litter approached. The Cat was now identified with Horus who daily died for his people, and a terrible culmination followed.

* Christ was to be regarded as a new manifestation or incarnation of the the Egyptian Sun-god.

When the sun crossed the meridian on June 24th, the cat was placed in a wicker basket, and thrown alive into an enormous bonfire which was kindled in the city square. Apparently this ritual had the full support of the Christian Church. Bishops and priests sang anthems in honour of the sacrifice during its performance, and after its conclusion held a solemn procession.

The following account of cat sacrifice under Christian auspices is taken from "Notre Ami le Chat."

"M. Edelestand du Meril, dans un brochure sur les usages populaires, écrit 'qu'on croyait encourager les bonnes mœurs en jetant quelques chats dans les feux de la Saint-Jean.' En effet, l'abbé Lebœuf cite une quittance de cent sols parisis signée par un certain Lucas Pommereux en 1573, 'pour avoir fourni durant trois années tous les chats qu'il fallait aux feux de la Saint-Jean, comme de coutume.' . . . Cette déplorable coutume de jeter des chats dans les feux de la Saint-Jean s'est conservée très longtemps, témoin ce quatrain accompagnant un dessin grossier daté de la fin du XVII siècle :

> Un chat qui, d'une course brève
> Monta au feu saint Jean en Grève,
> Mais le feu ne l'epargnant pas
> Le fit sauter de haut en bas.

Cet usage persistait encore en 1750 à Metz : ce n'est que vers cette époque que la maréchale d'Armentieres obtint de son mari la suppression de ces inutiles hécatombes felines.

"Dans sa 'Lettre sur les Chats,' Moncriff raconte cette scene : 'Il se passe à Metz tous les ans une fête qui est à la honte de l'esprit : les magistrats viennent gravement sur la place publique exposer des chats dans une cage, placée audessus d'un bûcher auquel on met le feu avec un grand appareil ; et le peuple, aux cris affreux que font les bêtes, croit faire souffrir encore une veille sorcière qu'on prétend s'être autrefois métamorphosée en chat lorsq'on allait la brûler.'

"Il n'y a pas bien longtemps—en plein dix-neuvième siècle—ces cruels divertissements étaient encore pratiqués en Picardie dans le canton d'Hirson. Le premier dimanche de carême on célébrait le *Bihourdi ;* dès que le signal était donné, tous les habitants apportaient leur part à un bûcher dressé au milieu du village ; la ronde alors commençait, les garçons tiraient des coups de fusil, les ménétriers jouaient du violon : à la perche du *bihourdi* était attaché un chat qui finissait par tomber dans le feu. Il fallait a ces barbares un feu de joie avec un chat rôti ! L'animal sauvé du feu est la marque du pas qu'a fait la civilisation dans les campagnes."

In England a custom was observed until quite recent times of whipping a cat to death at Shrovetide. It would seem to have been specially popular in the Midland village of Albrighton, in Shropshire, where an inn sign formerly commemorated it with the rhyming couplet : *

> "The finest pastime that is under the sun
> Is whipping the cat at Albrighton."

Apparently this barbarous rite was a relic of the worship of Apollo. In some places the solar symbol of a cock (or hen) was substituted for that of the cat.

> "All which we on this stage shall act or say
> Doth solemnize Apollo's shroving day ;
> Whilst thus we greet you by our words and pens,
> Our shroving bodeth death to none but hens."†
>
> (*W. Hawkins.*)

The birds were beaten to death, like the cat, and afterwards eaten.

The building of Westminster Abbey was the occasion of a feline sacrifice in a Christian church. One of the exhibits in the once famous collection‡ of curiosities, formerly on view in Don Saltero's Coffee House, in Cheyne Walk, Chelsea, was a starved and shrivelled corpse of a cat, which had been found between the walls of the Abbey when the east end was being rebuilt. Apparently the cat had been walled in alive, and doubtless was a sacrifice to the Sun-god, an identification of Horus with Christ.

But such sporadic efforts to incorporate the dying faith with the newly born creed were fated to fail. The forces of disintegration were too strongly at work in the old to admit of its rebirth in the new. We have already noted the degradation of the gods, and a period of dense spiritual gloom now followed. According to the doctors of Christian teaching, "the whole of the British Islands, yea, and also the Highlands of Scotland [were] overrun by demons who were like the legions of base spirits whom Solomon enclosed in a kettle, and sunk at Babylon, but which, on the kettle being opened in quest of treasure, streamed up into the air, and spread themselves over the whole heavens, and thence over all Asia." It will probably surprise some of my readers to find Britain mentioned as the headquarters of evil spirits, but we must remember that from prehistoric times the Highlands and Islands of Scotland were the home of the supernatural. It would seem as if the inhabitants of these wild regions

* Sidmouth "Observer," 16-4-30.
† "Appollo Shroving" (1626), p. 6. Nares.
‡ The collection was opened in 1690, and sold by auction in 1799.

had succeeded in establishing a sympathetic and strong rapport with the unseen worlds of magic and miracle which elsewhere is unparalleled. Our ancestors, not unnaturally, believed that condemned spirits were banished to those Western Islands, where wailing winds and eternal fog seemed to suggest the presence of unhappy shades. Even Plutarch was impressed by the weirdness of these islands, which, amid savage and incessant storms, rose utterly barren and desolate in dizzy precipices from the seething sea. We are told that ghostly apparitions were familiar sights to the few unfortunate human beings condemned to spend their sombre lives in the continual terror these surroundings inspired.

FELINE DEMON ON ST. JOHN'S CHURCH AT WESTON-SUPER-MARE
(ABOUT 1268.)

Many centuries later, such descriptions were confirmed by an ecclesiastical writer, the Venerable Bede. In his "History of the English Church," he tells us how until the eighth century the Island of Lewis (which is one of the largest of the Western Isles), was not only almost destitute of men, fruits, trees, and herbs, but was the favourite rendezvous of wicked and malicious spirits, who there practised their devilish ceremonies until the pious Cudbrecht forced them to depart.

The efforts of that worthy man were not crowned by the complete success that doubtless they deserved, for the atrocious Cat sacrifice under the name of the Taigheirm* persisted, and as recently as 1750 was extant in the Hebrides. Its actual origin

* Gaelic, *Taish*, unreal or shadowy appearance, *Taishitaraugh*, second sight, *Taishatrin*, visionaries, seers.

is lost in the mists of antiquity, though we have indicated the way in which it probably arose. But whence its infernal rites were introduced to the Western Isles is not known. The most probable conjecture is that the first settlers in these islands, who came from Iceland, Greenland, Norway, and the Faroe Islands, brought it with them. We know that until the Middle Ages, Scotland was thought to be peopled by fairy folk and nature deities from northern lands, who mingled with her native sprites, and remarkably affected the everyday life of her people. The subterranean deities or demons were known in the Highlands and Islands as the Black Cat Spirits, and were the powers invoked in the celebration of the Taigheirm.

The Scottish title of the sacrifice has a double meaning, and according to the way its syllables are pronounced, implies an armoury or the cry of cats. The pun seems to be intentional, for the shrieks of the tortured cats are the weapons with which the celebrant overcomes the resistance of the spirits to his demands. Though white was the distinguishing colour of the priestly garments of all nations from India to Gaul, yet black was worn when they sacrificed to the subterranean gods, probably in allusion to the darkness in which these deities dwelt.* Hence the reason why the cat offered to them must be black, and why midnight was the proper hour for the commencement of the rite. The time officially prescribed was 12 midnight between Friday and Saturday, and the duration of the ceremony was four whole days and nights, during which the operator must take no nourishment. "After the cats were dedicated to all the devils," says Horst, "and put into a magico-sympathetic condition by the shameful things done to them, and the agony occasioned them, one of them was put at once upon the spit, and, amid terrific howlings, roasted before a slow fire. The moment that the howls of one tortured cat ceased in death, another was put upon the spit, for a minute of interval must not take place if they would control hell; and this continued for the four entire days and nights. If the exorcist could hold it out still longer, and even till his physical powers were absolutely exhausted, he must do so."

When the sacrifice had continued a certain time, infernal spirits appeared in the form of cats. These came in continually increasing numbers, and mingled their unearthly cries with the howlings of the tortured victim on the spit. Finally a cat of monstrous size appeared with dreadful menaces. When the Taigheirm was complete, the sacrificer demanded the reward of his offering from the spirits. This took various forms, such as

* Osiris, the Egyptian god of the Underworld, was black.

riches, children, etc. But the gift of second sight was the usual recompense, and, when granted, was retained until the celebrant's death.

According to Horst, one of the last Taigheirms was held in the middle of the seventeenth century on the island of Mull. Ennemoser says that " the inhabitants still show the place where Allan Maclean, at that time the incantational and sacrificial priest, stood with his assistant, Lachlain Maclean, both men of a determined and unbending character, of a powerful build of body, and both unmarried—Allan Maclean continued his sacrifice to the fourth day, when he was exhausted both in body and mind, and sank into a swoon ; but from this day he received the second-sight to the time of his death, like his assistant. In the people the belief was unshaken that the second-sight was the natural consequence of celebrating the Taigheirm.

" The infernal spirits appeared, some in the early progress of the sacrifice in the shape of black cats. The first who appeared during the sacrifice, after they had cast a furious glance at the sacrificer, said : 'Lachlain Oer,' that is, 'Injurer of Cats'. Allan, the chief operator, warned Lachlain, whatever he might see or hear, not to waver, but to keep the spit incessantly turning. At length the cat of monstrous size appeared ; and after it had set up a horrible howl, said to Lachlain Oer, that if he did not cease before their largest brother came, he would never see the face of God. Lachlain answered that he would not cease if all the devils in hell came. 'At the end of the fourth day, there sat on the end of the beam in the roof of the barn a black cat with fire-flaming eyes, and there was heard a terrific howl quite across the straits of Mull into Morven' (Horst). Allan was wholly exhausted on the fourth day, from the horrible apparitions, and could only utter the word 'Prosperity.' But Lachlain, though the younger, was stronger of spirit, and perfectly self-possessed. He demanded posterity and wealth. And each of them received that which he had asked for. When Allan lay on his death-bed, and his Christian friends pressed around him, and bade him beware of the stratagems of the devil, he replied with great courage that if Lachlain Oer, who was already dead, and he, had been able a little longer to have carried their weapons, they would have driven Satan himself from his throne, and at all events, would have caught the best birds in his kingdom.

" When the funeral of Allan reached the churchyard, the persons endowed with the second-sight saw at some distance Lachlain Oer, standing fully armed at the head of a host of black cats, and everyone could perceive the smell of the brimstone which streamed from those cats. Allan's effigy in complete armour is carved on his tomb, and his name is yet linked with the memory of the Taigheirm."

Shortly before the events just related, another Scotchman, Cameron of Lochiel, performed a Taigheirm, and received from the infernal spirits a small silver shoe which they directed him to put on the left foot of every new-born son of his family, saying it would bring to each, who was thus made its wearer, fortitude and courage in the presence of his foes. The shoe was applied as directed to each new son until 1746, when Cameron's house was burnt to the ground. The only boy of the family that the shoe did not fit inherited a larger foot from his mother, who was of a different clan, and he fled before the enemy at Sheriff Muir. So was the prediction justified.

In many of these ancient myths and legends, the original divinity of the devil is still traceable, so that Harsnet's remark, " The prince of darkness is a gentleman," is not unjustified. He is acknowledged as true—to his friends or foes and to himself.

We have marked how the faithfulness of the devil to his favourite animal was exploited by the unscrupulous in the terrible Taigheirm. In the legend related below we may see how Satan honoured his word, even at that creature's expense, when he found himself outwitted by human cunning. He accepts defeat with gallantry, nor uses his power in unfair or unsportsmanlike manner. The ancient legends certainly do not justify the Biblical description of the devil as " the father of lies." It is almost always the Christian who stoops to lying in bargaining with the prince of darkness: and the chroniclers invariably praise his deceit, holding that the end justifies the means. Such a legend is woven around the prehistoric bridge known as the Tarr or Torr Steps, which crosses the River Barle, near Dulverton, in Somersetshire. It is said to have been built in a single night by the devil, who intended to reserve it for his own private use, and allow no mortal to traverse it. The bridge is 180 feet long and 5 feet wide, and is formed from slabs of stone, the longest of which measures 8 feet 6 inches. To deter mortals from trespassing, the devil condemned to destruction the first creature that should cross by its means, and hid to see if any would be bold enough to do so. The local inhabitants cunningly decided that the devil's own favourite animal, a cat, should be the victim, and sent one across. The devil's threat was fulfilled, for the cat was torn to pieces, when it reached the further bank, and thus the spell was broken. The parson was the next to go over, and had some words with the devil, who called him a black crow, but mindful of his promise did not molest him, and ever since the bridge has been open.

The following interesting legend from the " Revue Féline Belge," translated by H. C. Brooke, and published in "Cat Gossip," is a romantic example of the Cat sacrifice:

"In 1787, when the Revolution was beginning to threaten in Paris, Brittany was still steeped in superstition. Anne Marie de Trégor, daughter of an old family of the lesser Breton nobility, shared her love between her two cats and her lover, Jean Louis, a handsome young fisherman whom she met in secret. But she was also beloved by the son of a neighbouring seigneur, Count Alain de Kerguelen, an equally handsome youth, but of an arrogant and cruel nature, who, unable to bear the thought that a poor fisherman should be preferred to him, vowed hatred and revenge to his humble rival. The great Pardon* of Roscoff was to take place on Sunday, and Anne had arranged a rendezvous with Jean Louis. But the Count of Kerguelen had been watching, and he had Jean Louis seized by his men and immured in the dungeons of Kerguelen. Although this was well known in the district, the power of the Count imposed silence, except in the evening, when groups of old Bretons would meet and work diabolical spells. Anne Marie was on the point of yielding to the Count to save Jean Louis when a number of old Bretons told her that they had learnt that if she agreed to wall up her cats alive Jean Louis would be saved. Agonised at the thought of sacrificing her pets, Anne bethought herself that a year before she had saved a young girl from drowning, Yvonne le Goff, the pride of her father, who was a gaoler at Kerguelen. Hard and severe though he was known to be, could she not work upon him through his love for his rescued daughter? The Count frequently visited Jean, and finding him obdurately persisting in his love for Anne, ordered Yvonne's father to throw him into the oubliette. All seemed lost, and Anne was in despair. Must she sacrifice her innocent pets curled at her feet? Kneeling, Anne Marie murmured prayers, placing these innocent creatures amongst the host of the martyrs. A convent was being built in the shadow of the Creisker.† It was in the ceiling of the prayer-room here that Anne Marie caused her poor pets to be immured.

"On the same day Yvonne was wandering sadly near the Castle of Kerguelen, when her father's dog suddenly disappeared in a heap of brushwood which concealed a deep hole. Endeavouring to recall the dog, she discovered an old stairway almost entirely covered up, a long-abandoned entrance to an old cellar of the Castle, and passing close to the oubliettes. Yvonne informed Anne Marie, and together, returning at night, they succeeded in piercing the wall and rescuing Jean Louis, still living, but in an

* Pardon, a Brittany religious festival.

† Criesker, tower or belfry.

emaciated condition. Thus saved, but dead in the eyes of the world, he reappeared at St. Pol in the rags of a beggar, only known to the two who had saved him.

"Not long after he was fishing at high tide when he perceived theCount trapped in a quicksand. His efforts to save his enemy nearly resulted in his being himself engulfed, and he was forced to watch the Count slowly disappear in the quicksands. Thus freed from his bitter foe, Jean Louis appeared in his proper person and soon was married to Anne Marie, who did not forget the poor little creatures to whom she felt she owed her happiness. She had embroidered upon the arms of the House of Trégor the two cats in the agonised posture she imagined for them, with the device:

> " 'By virtue of my sufferings
> I bring happiness.' "

Occasionally when witches sacrificed to the devil the chosen victim was a cat. Danæus, writing of the newly initiated witch, says: "Then this ungracious and new servant of satan, euery day afterward offreth something of his goods to his patrone, some his dogge, some his hen, and some his cat." And Scot states that after the Sabbath the witches depart "not forgetting euery daie afterwards to offer to him dogs, cats, hens, or bloud of their owne." The record of an unpublished trial in the Justiciary Court at Edinburgh, which took place in 1630, relates that when Alexander Hamilton consulted the devil, "afoir the devill his away passing the said Alexr was in use to cast to him ather ane kat, or ane laif [loaf ?], or ane dog, or any uther sic beast he come be."

So much for the legendary past.

The sensational witchcraft murder trial of John Blymer and his assistants, Wilbert Hess and John Curry, which took place at York, Pennsylvania, in January, 1929, revealed the astounding fact that three-fourths of the population of York County, numbering 150,000 souls, retain the mediæval belief in witchcraft that their Moravian ancestors brought from Germany two hundred years ago. The records of York County register a lengthy catalogue of sorceries, malpractices, and mysterious murders that were brought to light by the Kinzel-Metzer case in 1922. "To-day," says the correspondent of the "Sunday Express" (January 13th, 1929), "the farm lands and the cities of York County are in the grip of a witches terror, the villages fear-ridden at the thought of 'hexes' and evil spirits. The country barns, and the cowsheds and the cattle shelters bear strange crosses and painted hieroglyphs against the 'hex.' Black cats have practically disappeared from the countryside, for it is known that a sure way of making one's peace with Satan is to plunge one alive into boiling water, keeping the last bone for an amulet."

The intention of this sacrifice is somewhat obscure; perhaps it is not blackmail, but the gratification of Satan by the offering of the gift he so highly values, just as Jehovah was placated by the savoury odours of burnt cattle or sheep*. Extremes meet, and the evidence does not justify a conclusion.

The extraordinary complications of motive and doctrine inspiring the cat sacrifice, together with the biased nature of much of the evidence on the subject, make it often difficult, or even impossible, to be certain if we are reviewing White Magic or Black. Sacrifice of the animal sacred to the god is righteous or impious according to the determining motive of the celebrant; that alone is the test. In either case, the Cat, from the special love the gods bore to it, was an oft-chosen victim.

Mediæval witchcraft provides many problem cases. One of the articles in the indictment of Isobel Young, who was tried for witchcraft in 1629, stated that "for thir forty years, for curing of hir bestiall, she has been in use to take a quick ox, with a cat, and a great quantity of salt, and to burie the ox and cat quick with the salt in a deep hole as a sacrifice to the devil." This is probably one of the cases in which an ancient god, possessed of healing power, was identified with Satan, and his priestess, far from seeing any cruelty in the horrid ritual, thought she honoured and favoured the victims by sending them "quick" to his presence.

The doubt ever present in the heart of man when making such offerings is illustrated by an old custom of the Laplanders, who sacrificed "dogs, cats, hens, and chickens to their gods"; but evaded responsibility by first enacting the following ceremony to discover whether or not the slaughter would be acceptable. Hurd says: "After they have tied up the victim behind their hut, they strip off some of the hair from under the neck of the animal, which they fasten to one of the rings of a drum appropriated for that particular service, and which one of their priests beats, while the whole assembly of the people sing a short prayer. If the bunch of rings to which they fastened the hair of the victim, and which before was immovable, should turn about in an instant, and point to their god Thor, they look upon it that the sacrifice is acceptable to that god. But on the contrary, if the bunch of rings remains fixed and immovable, notwithstanding the motion of the drum, they present the victim to another god while the drum is beating, and the people singing a second prayer or hymn."

* According to some writers the bull was the symbol of Jehovah, so that the god was sacrificed to himself.

BIBLIOGRAPHY

"Dialogue of Witches," Chapter IV. By Lambert Danæus. Printed 1575.

"Discoverie of Witchcraft," Book III, p. 44. By Reginald Scot. Printed London, 1584.

"Masque of Queens." By Benjamin Jonson. Pub. about 1600.

"Declaration of Egregious Popish Impostures." By Samuel Harsnett. Pub. 1603.

"Archæologia: or Miscellaneous Tracts relating to Antiquity," Vol. VIII, pp. 174, 176. Pub. by the Society of Antiquaries of London, 1787.

"The Talmud." Treatise Berakhoth. Folio 6.

"The Magus or Celestial Intelligencer." By Francis Barret, F.R.C. Printed for Lackington, Allen & Co., London, 1801.

"The History of Magic," Vol. II, pp. 102–7. By Joseph Ennemoser Trans. from the German by William Howitt. Pub. by Henry Bohn, London, 1854.

"A Historical Account of the Belief in Witchcraft in Scotland," p. 99. By Charles Kirkpatrick Sharpe, Esq. Pub. by Hamilton, Adams & Co., London, 1884.

"The Religious Rites, Ceremonies and Customs of the Whole World," p. 360. By William Hurd, D.D. Printed for Alexander Hogg, London.

"The Natives of the Northern Territories of the Gold Coast," pp. 30, 93. By A. W. Cardinall. Pub. by George Routledge & Sons, London.

"Notre Ami le Chat," p. 45. Par Paul Mégnin. Pub. by J. Rothschild, Paris, 1899.

"Cat Gossip," April 10, 1929.

CHAPTER XVII

THE CAT AND TRANSMIGRATION

"If dying mortals' dooms they sing aright,
No ghosts descend to dwell in dreadful night:
No parting souls to grisly Pluto go,
Nor seek the dreary silent shades below:
But forth they fly immortal in their kind,
And other bodies in new worlds they find."
(*Rowe's* "Lucan.")

THERE is nothing inconsistent in the doctrine of the materialist who claims that the "soul" is simply a function of the brain, and that in man and animal alike it is dissolved by the death of the body. But when the teacher of theology, who lays it down that the soul of man is immortal, simultaneously tells us in the very words of the materialist that the animal soul dissolves into nothing when the body dies, being too imperfectly organised to survive its loss, we recognise that he is in an untenable position. The latter half of his doctrine is dangerously antagonistic to the belief in human continuance, for we see him compelled to admit that a mere difference of degree in evolution is sufficient to decide eternal destiny. The one is immortal without any merit, the other doomed without any fault. Another difficulty arises when we consider prehistoric man and his relationship with the anthropoid apes. The low mentality and total lack of morality which even to-day are displayed by certain primitive races make one ask, "At what degree of elevation does the soul become strong enough to resist the crisis of separation from its body? Where may we draw a certain dividing line? Ought we to assert that our barbarous primitive ancestors, scarcely distinguishable from the anthropoid apes, merited the gift of immortality, whilst a noble, generous, loving cat, or horse, or dog, that would willingly give its life to save its master or its young, is only worthy of extinction?"

We turn with relief from such absurdities to the only doctrine capable of explaining spiritual evolution, that of Reincarnation, and as we do so we note with satisfaction that it is the solution arrived at by the intuition of by far the greater number of the world's inhabitants, and has been handed to us from a remote antiquity, having survived through innumerable vicissitudes in vastly varying races, and climes, and religions.

About seven hundred and fifty million of our fellow-men hold that the soul must progress by taking in turn every earthly form, from gas to mineral, and on through plant, and animal to man, till all the lessons of mortal life have been learned. According to Herodotus, the Egyptians were the first who taught this doctrine, and the cycle of experience undergone by every soul was fulfilled in three thousand years.

The Egyptian belief in metempsychosis is curiously reflected in the paintings on some of the monuments. These show the ignominious return to earth, in animal form, of souls which when weighed in the scales before Osiris were found wanting. The practice of representing men under the character of animals having thus been introduced was soon more widely applied, and animals were often figured as following the various occupations

FROM AN EGYPTIAN PAPYRUS
Now in the British Museum.

of mankind. Several examples of this have been salvaged from the wreckage of time. The drawing here given is from a picture on papyrus now in the British Museum, and represents a cat in charge of a flock of geese.

Pythagoras is said to have visited Egypt in his youth, and to have been instructed by the priests in its mysterious religion, afterwards travelling to the East, where he was received by the Persian and Chaldean Magi, and the Indian Brahmans. He taught the Egyptian doctrine of metempsychosis, warning his disciples that souls never die, but now inhabit one body, now another, passing from the form of an animal into a human shape, and back again. As wax may be stamped with various figures, melt and be stamped anew, yet always remain the same substance, so may the same soul appear in fresh likenesses. "Therefore," appealed the philosopher, "if you yet bear love to your kindred, refrain, I entreat you, to violate the lives of those who may perchance be your own relations" (Ovid).

The teachings of Virgil respecting metempsychosis were in conformity with the doctrines of the Pythagoreans: and the Roman poet puts into the mouth of Anchises a description of how souls too corrupted to be entrusted with human bodies are imprisoned in brute animals, cats, lions, dogs, tigers, monkeys, etc.

Perhaps it was because of his residence in Egypt that the Phrygian Æsop conceived his wonderful fables. My readers will recall the tale which tells of the Cat who was so madly beloved by her master that

> ". . . his tears and praying,
> By wizard charms and much soothsaying,
> Wrought things so well, that Destiny,
> One fine day, changed the Cat into a Woman."
>
> . . . . . .
>
> "Mad friends became mad lovers then;
> And not the fairest dame e'er known
> Had ever such affection shown
> To him she'd chosen from all men."

At first all went well, and it seemed that

> ". . . not a trace of Cat was left at all,
> No scratch or caterwaul."

But alas! when mice appeared, the lady's feline instincts reasserted themselves, and made her run on all fours in vain attempt to catch them as of yore.

> "This aberration on her part
> Was grief perpetual to his heart.
> It never ceased to be the way
> Whenever mice were out at play."

It seems at least possible that many otherwise unaccountable attractions and repulsions are explained by subconscious recollections of life in other than human form. Two children, well known to the writer, had distinct recollections of having been horses, and were never so happy as when, imagining themselves to be once more in equine form, they imitated the prancings and curvetings of the steed, or, when as they grew older and opportunity offered, they rode or drove, or caressed and groomed and trained their horses.

It is claimed by many writers of to-day that Transmigration was among the accepted doctrines of the early Christian Church. The adjoined drawing of a carving on a choir stall in Beverley Minster shows a cat playing a viol, and teaching her kittens to dance. Egyptian influence persisted in the new religion long after it ceased to be acknowledged, and was probably the source that

FROM A CHOIR STALL IN BEVERLEY MINSTER: SOUTH SIDE, LOWER ROW

inspired the Christian sculptor, even though he may not have been aware of it. The thought underlying the Cat and Geese and the Cat playing the viol is so obviously one that it is difficult to realise that centuries divide the two conceptions. It would be easier to think that the same artist had drawn both designs. Well! Perhaps he did! The student may also compare the design drawn on p. 226.

Modern Spiritualism has provided a certain amount of confirmation of the ancient Egyptian doctrine. Certain cases of phantom animals do not seem to be accounted for by the supposition that they are elemental spirits, or ghosts of earthly animals. The suggested explanation in such instances is that the apparitions represent spirits of human beings, who in their earthly existence have been guilty of sins corresponding to vices associated with certain species of brutes, as cruelty with the tiger, or filth with the hog. Dr. Kerner has illustrated this in his work, " La Voyante de Prevorst." He there describes how on one occasion the somnambulist asked a spirit whether he could manifest under a different form to that in which he had spent his life, and received the reply: " If I have lived as a beast, I must appear to you as such. We cannot, however, take the forms that we would, and we must appear to you such as we were in life." On another occasion the spirit is quoted as saying: " The debauchee can appear under the form of an animal which he resembled in the manner of his life."

Because evolution works in parallel lines on spiritual and physical planes, the spiritual is ever able to use the material as a ladder. Once we grasp this conception we see clearly that however prodigally wasteful of life and effort Nature may appear to be, actually nothing is lost.

In India the doctrine of transmigration is firmly held. The Indian natives scruple to take the life of any living creature, lest it be one of their own relatives in a different bodily form. A startling instance of the practical working of this belief in modern India is provided by the following strange story which General Sir Thomas Edward Gordon related of a cat that was said to enshrine the soul of a dead man.

" For twenty-five years an oral addition to the written standing orders of the native guard at Government House near Poona had been communicated regularly from one guard to another on relief, to the effect that any cat passing out of the front door after dark was to be regarded as His Excellency the Governor, and to be saluted accordingly. The meaning of this was that Sir Robert Grant, Governor of Bombay, had died there in 1838, and on the evening of the day of his death a cat was seen to leave the house by the front door and walk up and down a particular path, as had been the Governor's habit to do after sunset. A Hindu sentry had observed this, and he mentioned it to others of his faith, who made it a subject of superstitious conjecture, the result being that one of the priestly caste explained the mystery of the dogma of the transmigration of the soul from one body to another, and interpreted the circumstance to mean that the spirit of the deceased Governor had entered into one of the house pets. It was difficult to fix on a particular one and it was therefore decided that every cat passing out of the main entrance after dark was to be regarded as the tabernacle of Governor Grant's soul, and to be treated with due respect and the proper honours.

This decision was accepted without question by all the native attendants and others belonging to Government House. The whole guard, from sepoy to sibadar, fully acquiesced in it, and an oral addition was made to the standing orders that the sentry at the front door would 'present arms' to any cat passing out there after dark."

The faithful and chivalrous nature of the Hindu people is touchingly exemplified by this story. Their general was their general still, though now without authority, and inhabiting the humble form of a cat.

We may fittingly conclude this chapter with the following quotation from "The Light of Asia":

> "For while the wheel of birth and death turns round,
> Past things and thoughts, and buried lives come back.
> I now remember, myriad rains ago,
> What time I roamed Himâla's hanging woods,
> A tiger, with my striped and hungry kind;
> I, who am Buddh, couched in the kusa grass
> Gazing with green blinked eyes upon the herds
> Which pastured near and nearer to their death
> Round my day-lair; or underneath the stars
> I roamed for prey, savage, insatiable,
> Sniffing the paths for track of man and deer.
>
> . . . . . .
>
> The wheel of birth and death turns low and high."
>
> (*Sir Edwin Arnold.*)

BIBLIOGRAPHY

"A Varied Life," pp. 56–7. By General Sir Thomas Edward Gordon. Pub. 1906.

"The Fables of La Fontaine." Trans. into English Verse, by Walter Thornbury. Pub. by Cassell, Petter & Galpin, London.

"La Voyante de Prevorst," pp. 120, 190. By Dr. Kerner.

"The Light of Asia," p. 26. By Sir Edwin Arnold, M.A. Pub. by Kegan Paul, Trench, Trübner & Co., London, 1906.

CHAPTER XVIII

THE TEMPLE CAT

WHEN we remember the long sojourn of the Israelites in the Land of Egypt, and the veneration in which the Cat was held by the Egyptian priests, it is certainly somewhat strange to discover that the animal is only once mentioned in the Bible, and that this solitary instance occurs in the Apocryphal Book of Baruch. Even here the reference is not to the Sacred Cats of Egypt, but is part of an argument intended to demonstrate the vanity of the Babylonish "gods of silver, and of gold, and of wood . . . which cause the nations to fear" (vi. 4). We are told how "Upon their bodies and heads sit bats, swallows, and birds, and the cats also." The writer adds triumphantly: "By this you may know that they are no gods: therefore fear them not" (vi. 22, 23).

It will be interesting to examine the fact Baruch adduces as proof of the non-divinity of the Babylonish deities, where it refers to the subject of our book. Obviously the cats which sat upon the statues of the gods were sacred animals belonging to the Temple. It is clear, even from the text just quoted, that they were well-fed felines, not hungry strays; or the "bats, swallows, and birds" would not have shared their perches. They were in fact, highly venerated, and had their part to play in the aspect of religion accepted by this ancient people. It was believed that each cat had an important mission to fulfil, for when a human being who had attained a certain degree of holiness died, the cat acted as the host of his soul for the rest of its natural life. Only by this means could the departed soul gain Paradise, and as none was privileged to attain this coveted reincarnation as a

THE SACRED BURMESE CAT
From "Cat Gossip," Oct. 3rd, 1928.

sacred cat within the holy temple without the express sanction of the presiding goddess, Baruch's arguments cannot be maintained. Even to-day the Burmese and Siamese believe that their beautiful sacred cats enshrine the spirits of the dead, and with this in mind they introduce them into their religious ritual. Years ago, when a member of the royal house of Siam was buried, one of his favourite cats used to be entombed alive with him. The roof of his burying-place was designed with small holes piercing it, and if the cat succeeded in escaping through one of these, the priests knew that the soul of the prince had passed into its body, and they conducted it to the Temple with appropriate honours.

Ancestor worship is still an impelling force in Oriental countries. It was probably in order to show reverence to the departed monarch that when the young King of Siam was crowned in 1926, a white cat was carried by the Court chamberlains in the procession to the Throne Room. The old king would of course wish to occupy a recognised position in the coronation of his successor, and his former courtiers were not unfaithful. Along with the

SIAMESE CAT

Photo. Mrs. Veley. Block by "Cat Gossip."

sacred Cat were borne a grindstone, symbolising firmness, a gherkin for happiness, and grain for prosperity.

The Temple Cats of Siam, especially the golden-eyed, black-coated variety, have a part to play in religious ceremony. They are often enclosed in gilded cages before which incense is burnt, and offerings of food are made to them.

Mrs. Cran, an authority on Siamese cats, writing in "Cat Gossip," has described what is known as The Temple Mark, though she says her information is but scanty. Two distinct markings may be found on the backs of some highly bred Siamese which are said to be the distinguishing feature of the True Temple cats. The priests consider such cats to be especially sacred, but Mrs. Cran does not know the full story, or the name of the god who "once picked one up and left the shadow of his hands for ever on its descendants." The shadowy marks do not form a saddle, but suggest that someone "with sooty hands had lifted a pale-coated cat, gripping his neck rather low down. They are not often seen." But, she adds: "They are certainly a distinctive mark, and not an accidental marking."

We may compare the "Legend of the Tortie and White" given in another chapter.

Another characteristic of the Siamese cat is the kink in its tail which is said to have been there for two hundred years. It also is the subject of a Siamese fable which no one seems able to relate in full, but the gist of it is that the Siamese cat had a knot tied in its tail to remind it of something which it hasn't remembered yet, though who the tier was we are not told; presumably some divinity.

For two hundred years Siamese cats were only to be found in that portion of the Royal City of Bangkok where the monarch and his court resided. But though we can trace the variety for so long a period, its origin remains obscure. The Hon. Russell Gorjon, (Gordon ?) who made a study of the subject, considers it is derived from a cross between the Sacred Cat of Burmah, and the Annamite Cats that were introduced into the religiously sealed and guarded Burmese and Cambodian Empire of Khmer, when this succumbed to the attacks of the Siamese and Annamites in the seventeenth century.

About 1885, the wife of a British Consul brought two of the species to Europe, and an immediate demand for them arose in England.

The Sacred Cat of Burmah is yet more veiled in obscurity than its supposed descendant the Siamese, and we are indebted to Russell Gordon for the only authentic account of this species that has reached our shores. He gained his information during the Burmese War of 1885 whilst serving as an officer in the English Army occupying Burmah. His position enabled him to protect certain *kittahs*, or priests, whose lives were in danger, and in return they bestowed on him unprecedented privileges of entry into their secret and sacred places.

From his account we learn that the Indian Brahmins were the bitter enemies of the people of Khmer and their beloved kittahs. From the commencement of the eighteenth century they had mercilessly pursued and massacred these priests, who, to escape from their persecuting zeal, fled to North Burmah, where the mountains afforded security from pursuit. There, amid chaotic labyrinths and dizzy precipices, the indomitable kittahs founded the marvellous subterranean Temple of Lao-Tsun (the Abode of the Gods), and practised the secret rites that were closed to all but the higher castes among their own people.

Gordon describes the Temple of Lao-Tsun, as "one of the greatest marvels of the East—situated to the East of Lake Incaougji, between Magaoung and Sembo, in an almost desert region of immense peaks and chaotic labyrinths, it offers a barrier of insurmountable walls. Here there still existed in 1898 the last kittahs (priests), and as a most extraordinary favour I was permitted to see and observe them and their sacred animals. Following the rebellion and the English occupation, at the base of Bhamo (a base very isolated and distant from Mandalay), we had to protect the kittahs against a Brahmin invasion, and we saved them from certain massacre and pillage. Their Lama-kittah received me, and presented me with a plaque representing the Sacred Cat at the feet of a bizarre deity, whose eyes are made of two long sapphires (specimen No. 4108 in my collection at Mildenhall), and after having shown me the sacred cats, in number about a hundred, explained their origin to me." This he did by relating the following beautiful legend :

"When, with the malevolent moon, the barbarian Siamese Thais came to the mountains of the Sun, Mun-Ha was living in the Temple of Lao-Tsun. Mun-Ha, the most precious among the most precious, for whom the god Song-Hio had woven the beard of gold. This venerable priest had ever lived in rapt contemplation of Tsun-Kyanksé, the goddess with eyes of sapphire who presided over the transmutation of souls about to receive their dues, whose searching gaze none could evade. Mun-Ha had an oracle who dictated his decisions, and this was his cat Sinh, whom the kittahs fervently revered.

"Seated close to his dread master, Sinh lived in the contemplation of the goddess. The beautiful animal! His eyes were yellow like gold from the reflection of the metallic beard of Mun-Ha, yellow like the amber body of the goddess with the sapphire eyes.

"One night, at the rising of the moon, the Thais menacingly approached the sacred Temple. Then, invoking destiny, Mun-Ha died, weighed down by years and anguish. He died in the presence of his goddess ; close beside him was his divine cat, and the kittahs lamented their cruel loss. But suddenly, the miracle of immediate transmutation took place. Sinh bounded on to the holy Throne. Supported on the head of his stricken master he faced the goddess. And the hair along his spine blanched to a golden hue. His eyes, golden of the gold of the beard woven by the god Song-Hio—his eyes changed to blue—immense, abysmal, sapphire—like to the eyes of the goddess. His four feet, brown as the earth, his four feet which contacted the venerable skull, whitened to the claws, to the toe-tips, thus purified by the touch of the puissant dead.

"Sinh turned towards the South Door, his imperious gaze, in which could be read an imperative order, possessed of an invincible force the kittahs obeyed. Then they closed on the ancestral enemy the bronze doors of the holy Temple, and passing by their subterranean tunnel they routed the profane invaders.

"Sinh refused all nourishment, and would not quit his Throne. He continued standing erect and facing the goddess—mysterious priest—fixing his steadfast gaze on her eyes of sapphire, partaking of their fire and sweetness.

"Seven days after the death of Mun-Ha, erect on his purified feet of white, without lowering an eyelash, he died. Thus was borne away towards Tsun-Kyanksé the soul of Mun-Ha, which was too perfect for earth. But, for the last time, his look turned slowly towards the South Door

"Seven days after the death of Sinh the kittahs assembled before Tsun-Kyanksé to choose the successor of Mun-Ha. Then —Oh wonder!—There came in slow procession the hundred cats of the Temple. Their feet were gloved in white; their snowy hair emitted the reflection of gold, and the topazes of their eyes had changed to sapphires.

"The kittahs fell prostrate in an attitude of devout fear, and waited. Did they not know that the souls of their masters inhabited the harmonious forms of the sacred animals? And these, solemn and grave, surrounded Legoa—the most youthful of the priests—and so revealed the will of Heaven. When a sacred cat dies in the temple of Lao-Tsun, the soul of a kittah re-enters—to quit no more—the mysterious paradise of Song-Hio, the god of gold. Unhappy are those who even involuntarily hasten the end of these formidable and venerable cats: the most dreadful torments are reserved for them, that the soul in pain may be appeased." (From the French of Marcelle Adam.)

Gordon, who does not relate this legend, in the remarks from which I have quoted, says of it, that "The legend is pretty but explains nothing scientifically. . . . One may feel assured that the Burmese Cat is a very ancient race, but it will, I think, be impossible ever to obtain documentary evidence about a race so rare that no breeder or author in the two continents with whom I have corresponded within the last thirty years, has anything more than a sketch of them, and only knows them by the writings of Auguste Pavie and of myself."

Gordon describes the Burmese cats as being much like the Siamese in colouring, but says they had white toes on all four feet, long hair, and magnificent bushy tails which they usually carried over their backs in squirrel fashion. Their eyes were intensely blue, deep and melancholy—gentle when at rest, but wild and fiery if angered.

An interesting glimpse of sacred cats in religious ritual may be gained from Lane's detailed account of the Muslim religious procession of the Kis'weh, or covering of the Ka'abeh, as he witnessed it on February 15th, 1834. In this pageant " came several tall camels, slightly stained with the red dye of the *hhen'na* and having high ornamented saddles—upon each of these were one or two boys and girls ; and upon some were cats. These were followed by a company of Baltagee'yeh (or Pioneers), a very good military band,

A JAPANESE "KIMONO" CAT
Photo. Mrs. Veley. Block by "Cat Gossip."

and the Basha's guard," etc. What was the significance of the cats in this procession ? Without actual knowledge it is hazardous to guess, but evidently the cats were sacred animals.

Dr. Lilian Veley, writing in " Cat Gossip," describes the sacred Japanese cat, and Mr. Brooke has kindly lent me the blocks of the photographs illustrating her article. She says :

" As far as I know, no other ' sacred ' cat than this one, which I photographed in 1910, has ever been brought out of Japan. I am told that every cat in Japan which is born with a certain marking is considered as sacred—at least by some sects or some portion of the public—it is held to contain the soul of an ancestor, and is sent to a temple. No such cat would ever be parted with ; this one, I was informed, was stolen by a Chinese servant, and carried on board a ship. Here it became the property of an

English officer, who would have wished to return it to its temple, but dared not do so on acount of the feeling aroused by the theft. It was brought home, and eventually came into the possession of an English family in Putney, who respected its traditions, and with whom it enjoyed a happy home and lived to an honoured old age. It died about 1911, soon after I had photographed it. The cat was black and white in colour, the black patch on the back being the 'sacred' mark—which is supposed to resemble a woman in a kimono. Its tail was short, black, very broad, and almost triangular in shape. It was almost uncannily human in its ways, and lived entirely on raw meat, refusing all other foods. I was

A JAPANESE "KIMONO" CAT
Photo. Mrs. Veley. Block by "Cat Gossip."

grateful for the opportunity afforded me of photographing it, and never even showed the photos to anyone, though I gave a copy to its owners, who wrote and informed me when its death took place. I understand that the cat, which was a female, refused all mates, and never had any kittens."

Mr. Brooke, commenting on the above, reminds us that "An analogous instance of certain markings, occurring in an ordinary species, being held, at least by some sects, to confer sanctity—though very probably in the first place due purely to priestcraft—may be found in that of the sacred bull Apis, in ancient Egypt. Here also black and white were the colours; but white on a black ground. . . . At Memphis he was worshipped as being the re-incarnated god Phtha; he was kept in great pomp by the priests in the Temple, and the whole land mourned his death."

The wondrous changeful luminous eye of the Cat is the reason for much of the adoration it has received. The ancient Greek historian, Horapollon, who saw an analogy between the eye of the cat and the sun tells us " that the cat was adored in the Temple of the Sun at Heliopolis, because the pupil of this animal follows in its proportions the height of the sun above the horizon, and in this respect resembles the marvellous planet."

But we have in other chapters dilated at some length on the position of the Cat as Solar Symbol, so will not follow up this aspect here, although it is perhaps an even stronger factor in the reverence felt for the Temple Cat than that we have been examining.

BIBLIOGRAPHY

" Manner and Customs of the Modern Egyptians," Vol. II, p. 245. By E. W. Lane. Pub. by Nattali & Bond, London, 1835.

" Cat Gossip," Vol. I, No. 6, p. 5 ; Vol. II, pp. 158, 159. Pub. by the Ed tor, H. C. Brooke, Taunton.

" Animals," p. 242. Article by H. C. Brooke. Pub. Jan., 1926.

" The Daily Express." Pub. by " The London Express Newspaper Ltd.," 24th Sept., 1926 and 22nd Sept., 1927.

" The Daily News." Pub. by " News and Westminster Ltd.," London, 27th Sept., 1928.

" Revue Féline Belgé." Article by Marcelle Adam. Pub. by Arthur Goemaere, Anvers, Dec., 1929.

CHAPTER XIX

ANIMATED CAT IMAGES

WHENEVER an Egyptian temple was dedicated to the sun, an image or symbol of a cat was prominently placed within it, and ancient and modern legends agree in attributing strange potentialities to such images, or even pictures, of the sacred animal. These powers are sometimes explained by the idea that a spirit resides within the form, and sometimes by the theory of sympathetic magic. In this chapter I have brought together two or three examples of such stories, leaving it to my reader to place his own interpretation thereon.

ANCIENT EGYPTIAN PAPYRUS PAINTING
Showing a cat of Abyssinian colouring
By courtesy of the Natural History Museum.
Block by "Cat Gossip."

The first of these weird tales was related by the Cairo correspondent of "The Sunday Express" and published on August 24th, 1919, headed "The Temple Cat of Karnak." "The hero of this tale was an Australian soldier named William Nerley, who had been invalided to Egypt from the Dardanelles in 1915, and a pretty

Greek girl, with an unspellable name, was the heroine. The story commences when Netley, an invalid in one of the hospitals of Alexandria received permission to drive out one day. Availing himself of this he hired an *arabiyeh* and went round the city. As he passed along one of its meaner streets he saw a beautiful Greek girl, and fell in love with her on the spot. He called to the driver to stop, but the Arab either did not or would not hear, and drove on. Netley walked back, when his drive ended, to find the girl, but failed to discover a trace of her. After this he was invalided out of the army and returned to his home in Australia. But the spirit of the Greek girl haunted him, and he could not forget her. He returned to Egypt that he might make a systematic search for her, but again his effort to find her was without success. He decided to visit Assouan and Luxor, and then to give up his quest and sail for home. Whilst at Luxor he dutifully paid homage to the Temple of Karnak, and during his visit seems to have become fascinated by the ruins of the mighty past. Instead of returning to Cairo he prolonged his stay and spent the greater part of his time among the broken columns of sacred stone. On the sarcophagus of a mummy was the image of a cat, and, gazing intently on this, it seemed to him the engraved figure was assuming animation. The eyes held him, and the figure became lifelike. Then something touched his leg, and he was astounded to find the cat of the image on the stone was at his feet. It made no sound, but its eerie aspect rather unnerved the hero of the Dardanelles. To cut the story short (and its details might prove too great a strain on my reader's credulity), the cat moved slowly away, and the soldier followed it down the mean street at the back of the temple. The animal stopped outside a little *pension*, then, noting that the Australian was following, darted within. The soldier, whose curiosity was now so thoroughly aroused that he no longer remembered his nervousness, went after it, and there met face to face the Greek girl he had sought so long."

In the above remarkable story the spirit animating the image of the cat was a benevolent one, but as a rule, such spirits manifest hatred and destruction.

An extraordinary instance of the apparent possession of a mummified cat by an active and malevolent spirit is related by Arthur Weigall. His account is such a vivid one that I hesitate to mar it by expressing it more shortly in my own words. So I hope he will forgive the liberty I take in quoting the story intact.

"In the year 1909 Lord Carnarvon, who was then conducting excavations in the Necropolis of the nobles of Thebes, discovered a hollow wooden figure of a large black cat, which we recognised, from other examples in the Cairo Museum, to be the shell in which a real embalmed cat was confined. The figure looked more like a small tiger as it sat in the sunlight at the edge of the pit in which it had been discovered, glaring at us with its yellow painted eyes and bristling its yellow whiskers. Its body was covered all over with a thick coating of smooth, shining pitch, and we could not at first detect the line along which the shell had been closed after it had received the mortal remains of the sacred animal within; but we knew from experience that the joint passed completely round the figure—from the nose, over the top of the head, down the back, and along the breast—so that, when opened, the two sides would fall apart in equal halves.*

"The sombre figure was carried down to the Nile and across the river to my house, where, by a mistake on the part of my Egyptian servant, it was deposited in my *bedroom*. Returning home at dead of night, I here found it seated in the middle of the floor directly in my path from the door to the matches; and for some moments I was constrained to sit beside it, rubbing my shins and my head.

"I rang the bell, but receiving no answer, I walked to the kitchen, where I found the servants grouped distractedly around the butler, who had been stung by a scorpion and was in the throes of that short but intense agony. Soon he passed into a state of delirium, and believed himself to be pursued by a large grey cat, a fancy which did not surprise me since he had so lately assisted in carrying the figure to its ill-chosen resting-place in my bedroom.

"At length I retired to bed, but the moonlight which now entered the room through the open French windows fell full upon the black figure of the cat; and for some time I lay awake watching the peculiarly weird creature as it stared past me at the wall. I estimated its age to be considerably more than three thousand years, and I tried to picture to myself the strange people, who, in those distant times, had fashioned this curious coffin for a cat which had been to them half-pet and half-household god. A branch of a tree was swaying in the night breeze outside, and its shadows danced to and fro over the face of the cat, causing the yellow eyes to open and shut, as it were, and the mouth to grin. Once, as I was dropping off to sleep, I could have sworn that it had turned its head to look at me; and I could see the sullen expression of feline anger gathering upon its black visage as it did so. In the distance I could hear the melancholy wails of the unfortunate butler imploring those around him to keep the cat away from him, and it seemed to me that there came a glitter into the eyes of the figure as the low cries echoed down the passage.

"At last I fell asleep, and for about an hour all was still. Then,

* See illustrations on p. 144.

suddenly, a report like that of a pistol rang through the room. I started up, and as I did so a large grey cat sprang either from or on to the bed, leapt across my knees, dug its claws into my hand, and dashed through the window into the garden. At the same moment I saw by the light of the moon that the two sides of the wooden figure had fallen apart and were rocking themselves to a standstill upon the floor, like two great empty shells. Between them sat the mummified figure of a cat, the bandages which swathed it round being ripped open at the neck, as though they had been burst outward.

"I sprang out of bed and rapidly examined the divided shell; and it seemed to me that the humidity in the air here on the bank of the Nile had expanded the wood which had rested in the dry desert so long, and had caused the two halves to burst apart with the loud noise which I had heard. Then, going to the window, I scanned the moonlit garden; and there in the middle of the pathway I saw, not the grey cat which had scratched me, but my own pet tabby, standing with arched back and bristling fur, glaring into the bushes as though she saw ten feline devils therein.

"I will leave the reader to decide whether the grey cat was the malevolent spirit which, after causing me to break my shins and my butler to be stung by a scorpion, had burst its way through the bandages and woodwork and had fled into the darkness; or whether the torn embalming cloths represented the natural destructive work of Time, and the grey cat was a night wanderer which had strayed into my room and had been frightened by the easily explained bursting apart of the two sides of the ancient Egyptian figure. Coincidence is a factor in life not always sufficiently considered; and the events I have related can be explained in a perfectly natural manner if one be inclined to do so."

With which comforting reflection we will pass on to our next case. T. H. Kerner of Wernsberg, "a literary man of some note in Germany," is responsible for the following weird story which appeared in the Editor's pages of the "Occult Review." Again I must apologise for the liberty I take in quoting the account *in extenso*.

Herr Kerner writes:

"One day Count Alexander of Wurtemburg sent to my father a picture in an ordinary black frame. It was the life-size picture of a wild cat, drawn with black chalk upon a bluish paper, and the same bluish tint was to be seen in the eyes of the cat, the animal being of a dark colour. The most remarkable feature of this picture was that the longer one looked at it the more did the cat seem to be living. The eyes then assumed a malignant, dismal look, making one feel quite uncomfortable. Even now, after years have passed, I cannot forget that look. The picture was accompanied by the following letter :

" 'My Dear Justin,

'I send you this picture, it is so well painted that I do not like to burn it ; nevertheless I cannot keep it any longer, as it would make me crazy. I saw it once hanging on the wall in the room of a forester in my service. The man seemed to be in excellent circumstances and happily married, but two months ago *he shot himself without any apparent cause.* I bought the picture from the widow and hung it up in my room ; but I cannot bear the eyes of that cat any more ; they constantly attract my attention and render me so melancholy that I feel I should finally end in the same way as the forester unless I gave the picture away. I therefore send it to you, as you are known to be a master over the spirits ; to you this evil spell will do no harm.'

" *Soon afterwards Count Alexander died.* The picture now hung in our room and my father had a dislike for it, but as it was the last gift of his friend he would not part with it. One day, however, he gave it to me, desiring me to put it away. He said he could not bear any longer to have it about him.

" For nearly a year the picture hung in my room, and I paid no attention to it. One night in winter, while I was writing a letter, it suddenly seemed to me as if I were *not alone in my room,* as if something strange were sneaking near me. I looked up and saw the eyes of that cat. I then knew instantly that there would be no more peace between us. Those eyes seemed to persecute me. I hated them, and the worst thing was that I felt they were stronger than I. The eyes of that cat seemed to suck the very life out of my nerves and to absorb my thoughts. I did not wish to give it away, but finally I found an excuse for doing so. I knew a gentleman who was a great lover of sport and hunting and just getting ready to furnish his new house. To him I gave the picture. He was very glad to receive it and hung it up in the hall. Six months afterwards *he killed himself,* having become melancholy without any apparent cause.

" A relative of this gentleman took the cat with him. A few months passed away, when he *was found dead in his bed.* Whether he was murdered or committed suicide has not been ascertained. I do not know what afterwards became of the cat."

Dr. Franz Hartman, who sent the above account to Mr. Ralph Shirley, remarked that it seemed clear " that it was not the painting itself which exercised such a deleterious influence upon its possessor, but that some living power, whether we call it an 'elemental' or a 'thought-form' or a 'magic spell' had been attached to it . . . Such things," he added, " will naturally be incomprehensible to our physicists so long as they are unable to realise the fact known to every occultist, that the ' astral and mental planes are worlds of their own, invisible to our physical eyes, but nevertheless real and substantial and having inhabitants of their own with powers to will and think and act, be it instinctively or intelligently '."

It is difficult for those who are not conscious of psychic influences to realise the extent to which they are affected by inhabitants of unseen worlds. Seers assure us that we are never actually alone, and the invisible beings who surround us are not always merely passive witnesses of our actions, but at times play a very definite rôle in our lives.

The extraordinary feature shared in common by the cases recorded in this chapter is that in every instance the spirit of which the tale is told had taken up its domicile in an image of a cat.

CHAPTER XX

THE CAT IN THE NECROPOLIS

IN this chapter we propose to follow the sacred and symbolic Cat in its descent to the tomb. For the Sun-god, whom the Cat represented, was not only The Fount of Life and Light. As Kephera he nightly sank into the mysterious grave below the world, to all appearance slain and buried. In this aspect, personified as Ptah or Osiris, he was god of the dead, and the realm of darkness and night. The cat that walketh in darkness was still his fitting glyph.

The chief picture on one of the Papyri in the British Museum (Salt, 825) is interesting as proving the importance attached to feline symbolism in portraying the life of man beyond the tomb. It is described by Sharpe in the following words: "Osiris is standing with the lion-headed goddess Mout seated behind him. Before him are Pasht, as a lion with ram's horns, Isis, a cat-headed man, four asps, and a sphinx. Nepthys is standing behind. Beyond is the mummy of the deceased seen. . . . Beyond is a cat-headed man in the act of worship."

The cat-headed men may be thought of as having by devotion identified themselves with one of the feline deities, or, at least, as having assumed a cat-shaped mask for carrying out the ritual prescribed for this purpose, and through its means, attaining the presence of the gods.

Among the most beautiful of the many works of art found in Tut-ankh-amen's Tomb, is a gold statuette of the youthful monarch riding on a black feline which bears him into the nether world. The king stands upright on a plinth which rests on the shoulders and hips of the feline steed, and holds in his hand what seems to be a scourge. The animal resembles a leopard in form but there is some doubt as to whether this is the species the artist intended to represent since black leopards are an Asiatic variety, and are not found in Africa. Anyhow, the statuette is another instance of the importance of the feline tribe beyond the tomb in Egyptian religious thought.

One of the most ancient effigies of a cat may be seen in the Necropolis at Thebes which contains the sepulchre of Hana who

CASE FOR HOLDING MUMMIED CAT. FROM MEMPHIS
Now in the British Museum, No. 676.

ANOTHER CASE FOR A MUMMIED CAT
British Museum, No. 35852/24.

is thought to have belonged to the XIth Dynasty. There the monarch is represented standing proudly with his favourite cat, Borehaki, at his feet. The coffin of one of the sacred cats dedicated by Amenophis III, is still preserved at Cairo.

The well-known Egyptologist, Borckhardt, describing a sculptured stone mummy case, says: " The form of this little sarcophagus is a reduced copy of those used for the Dead in the XVIIIth Theban Dynasty. . . . The larger sides show us the little cat sitting upright, its tail drawn between its legs in the usual attitude of a seated cat. Before it on a table are rich offerings, which, constantly renewed by the power of magic, assure to the little gourmand succulent provender through eternity. The sarcophagus bears the seal of a Thotmes prince, and appears to date from the brilliant XVIIIth Dynasty, that of Amenothes and Thotmes, at the zenith of the Theban, 1580 to 1320 B.C."

The pious Egyptians mummified cats in uncountable numbers. Recent research at Bubastis revealed that thousands of feline corpses were interred there. And at Beni Hassan an Egyptian fellah who accidentally discovered a cat cemetery in the grottoes found himself in the midst of hundreds of thousands of mummies ranged in order on shelves.

Once the discovery of the corpses became public property, the inhabitants of neighbouring villages turned up in force, and seized, burnt, or buried large numbers of the mummies, whilst Levantine antique dealers took possession of many more to sell to tourists. But the supply still far exceeded the demand, and seemed well-nigh inexhaustible.

At last a utilitarian Alexandrian speculator saw a way to turn the corpses into money by offering them as manure. He accordingly shipped the tons of corpses yet remaining to England. A cargo, consisting of 180,000 mummied cats was landed in Liverpool in March, 1890, and disposed of by auction. The unimaginative salesman actually used one of the corpses as a hammer, and knocked down the strange lot at the price of £3 13s. 9d. a ton, less than a single specimen of a mummied cat would fetch to-day.

Surely Fate has seldom played a stranger trick than bringing to such an inglorious end the once sacred objects of so much reverent care and skill!

A visit to the British Museum testifies to the importance of the position occupied by the Cat in the days of Egypt's glory. Cat mummies of extraordinary variety may there be found. Some of these are wrapped by linen bandages, so arranged as to form a pattern of two colours, and have painted linen discs sewn on to represent eyes and nostrils, whilst midribs of palm leaves imitate

MUMMIED CAT FROM ABYDOS. ROMAN PERIOD
Now in the British Museum, No. 37345. (Brit. Mus. photo.)

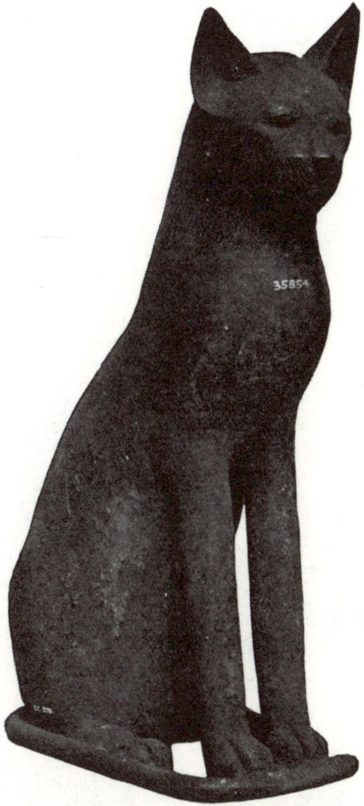

BRONZE CASE FOR HOLDING A MUMMIED CAT
Now in British Museum, No. 35854. (Brit. Mus. photo.)

ears. Others are interred in mummy cases of wood, or bronze, or clay, made to resemble the feline form, or shaped as a jar or coffin. Among these cases are some with eyes formed of crystal inlaid with gold, the pupils being of black obsidian. There are also bronze feline images of various sizes, some engraved with necklace and scarab, others with necklace, and eyes inlaid with gold; figures of cats represented in various stones, in crystal, blue marble, glazed ware and porcelain, exquisite groups of cats and kittens, cat amulets of different sizes which had been suspended around the owner's neck in his lifetime, finger-rings of gold on which are engraved the form of a cat, even a child's wooden toy, representing a cat with a movable jaw, may there be seen. Some of these images were intended for erection in temples, but others were buried in the tombs as funerary offerings.

In those towns and cities of ancient Egypt where the deities to whom special animals were sacred held an important position in the sanctuary, the ceremony of removing the bodies of these animals, after death, to the city peculiarly dedicated to the god they represented was dispensed with. This is why the remains of cats were embalmed and buried at Thebes, Speos, Artemidos, and other towns where the rites of Bast were duly observed

Herodotus says that those cats that died in the vicinity of Bubastis were sent to repose within the precincts of that place specially dedicated to them. But others were deposited in consecrated spots set apart for the purpose near the town where they had lived. And though some Egyptians so honoured and loved their sacred pets as to send their bodies long distances to the Necropolis of Bubastis, this was done with the same object as made a zealous votary of Osiris ask on his death-bed that his body might be removed from his native town to the city of Abydos.

Plutarch explains this was in order that it might appear to rest in the same tomb with Osiris himself. It was similarly thought Pussy's soul would rest in greater security near the abode of her patroness. To this feeling of loving reverence for the "ka" that still needed its bodily casket may be ascribed the multitude of cat mummies near Sheikh Hassan, where a small rock temple marks the site of the Speos Artemidos.

The veneration bestowed upon the individual animal chosen by the deity to incorporate one of the doubles representing his or her person was in the course of long time extended to all its kind; so that the people of Bubastis no longer limited their worship to the few cats which represented their goddess in the temple dedicated to her honour, but included all cats in their reverential esteem. As Maspero phrases it: "The god of the

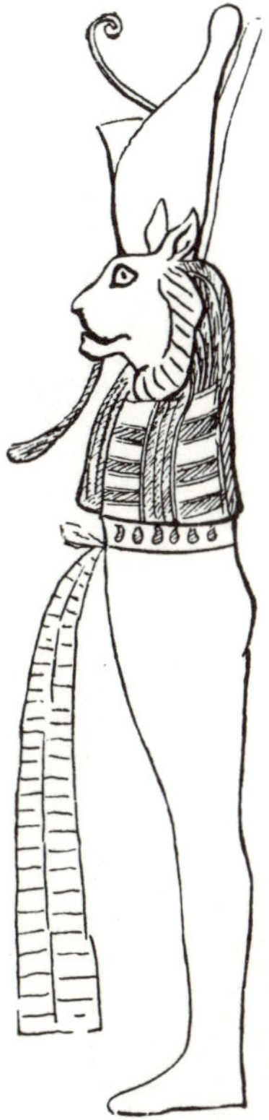

CAT OR LION-HEADED FIGURE, PAINTED ON THE COFFIN OF A PRIEST OF AMEN-RA AT THEBES. (ABOUT 1150 B.C.)

Now in British Museum, No. 24789A.

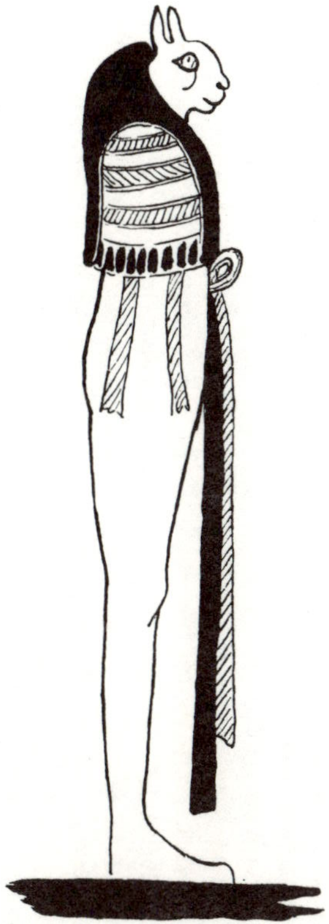

CAT-HEADED FIGURE PAINTED ON THE INNER COFFIN OF THE "DIVINE FATHER" AMEN-EM-APT, A PRIEST OF AMEN-RA AT THEBES. XXTH TO XXIST DYNASTY. (ABOUT 1100 B.C.)

Now in British Museum, No. 22941.

IN A WOODEN COFFIN OF AN OFFICIAL OF THE TEMPLE OF AMEN-RA AT THEBES. (ABOUT 1100 B.C.)

Now in British Museum, No. 6664.

nome ceased to be a special cat and became the cat species in general."

Cemeteries for cats and other animals were introduced at the time when Egypt, realising that contact with Western civilisations was bringing about a gradual degeneration in her ideals, reacted strongly against foreign influences, and emphasised her own peculiarities. Thus she passed from the veneration of certain specially selected animals to that of the whole species, and their mummified remains were properly buried side by side in the cemeteries with as much honour as if they had been men. To provide for their burial was regarded as a meritorious work, and its ritual was performed with some ostentation in a sanctified place. The expenses of such funerals were considerable, but were contributed by the pious, or were dependent on the peculiar honours paid to that goddess of whom cats were the emblem. Like men, Egyptian animals were graded in rank, and it is probable that these cats which during their lifetime were worshipped in the temple as the living symbols of the goddess Bast were treated with additional honours after death and buried more sumptuously, even when the reaction we have noted had made all cats sacred. The distinguished office assigned to the Temple Cats when alive raised them from the rank of mere emblems to the proud dignity of being actual representatives of the goddess. Viewed thus, it is easy to understand why, when a cat died, pious Egyptians would shave their eyebrows in token of their grief, and with the idea of preventing the loss or misfortune they would anticipate as likely to follow the severing of the link that had secured for them divine favour and protection.

BIBLIOGRAPHY

"Egyptian Antiquities in the British Museum," p. 146. Described by Samuel Sharpe. Pub. by John Russell Smith, London, 1862.

"The Ancient Egyptians." By Sir J. Gardner Wilkinson, D.C.L., F.R.S., F.R.G.S. Pub. by John Murray, London, 1878.

"A Handbook of Egyptian Religion." By Adolf Erman. Trans. by R. Griffith. Pub. by Constable & Co., London, 1907.

"New Light on Ancient Egypt," p. 213. By G. Maspero. Pub. by T. Fisher Unwin, London, 1908.

"Myths of Ancient Egypt." By Lewis Spence. Pub. by George G. Harrap & Co., London, 1922.

"The Bazaar and Exchange Mart." Article by H. C. Brooke. Pub. May 3rd, 1924.

CHAPTER XXI

THE CAT IN PARADISE

THE wonderful religion of the ancient Egyptians, like other creeds, was evolved from crude commencements. Originally this people had no conception of a soul. Life was a breath, a fluidic motive power which vanished suddenly when its possessor fell into that state which we call death, characterised by the absence of breath and movement, the cessation of consciousness, the corruption of the flesh, and final destruction of the body. The three first-mentioned phenomena constantly occurred without bringing about the state of death, as in sleep, hypnotism, catalepsy, swooning, etc., in which, after a varying lapse of time the individual returned to life.

The only apparent difference between deep unconsciousness and death is that when the latter takes place decomposition follows. It was therefore an obvious inference from observed facts that if it was possible to prevent decomposition, life would return to the body, as it did when the sleeper awoke from his dreams.

Thus the Egyptians reasoned that death ought to be considered as a merely temporary suspension of life which might be remedied by the resources of magic, if these were applied before decomposition commenced. Hence their practice of mummifying and embalming the corpse, and employing magic ritual or Mysteries. The devotion and faithfulness which inspired these services to the departed extended them to the sacred cats. By such rites and practices the little body of the cat (or, perhaps, its astral counterpart) retained the possibility of motion and the use of its organs. Not only might it reawaken, but, if accident was avoided, it might attain to an eternal and exhaustless life. To guard against disaster, loving care provided a second vehicle for the soul in the form of a statuette made in the likeness of the departed, which automatically took the place of the mummy if that perished.

At first the revival of life in the tomb was conceived of as wholly material in its nature. The cat continued its existence in conditions analogous to those it had known on earth, but these were fixed at what had been the happiest period of its past. For example, if it had at one time had a good and powerful master who had made its life joyful, this state was re-entered under the earth.

But the idea of Paradise was not yet born. The survivor passed to the tomb, where its mummy, reanimated by magic, found a little nest, cool in summer, warm in winter, surrounded by offerings and provisions that were continually renewed by virtue of the incantations recited by the priests during the course of the funeral ceremony.

Little by little this crude conception ceased to satisfy. Something more than a material life under the earth was desired and imagined. The corpse became thought of as animated by a spirit who could choose whether he would remain in the tomb, or leave it for a happier place. The Osirian Mysteries celebrated during the funeral rites assimilated the being of the dead to Osiris, god

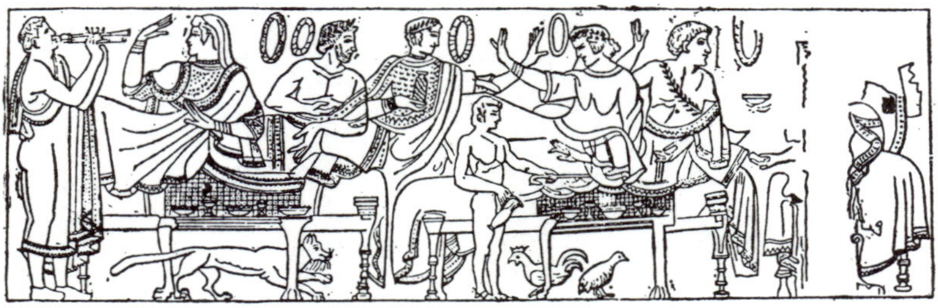

CAT AND FOWLS AT A FESTIVAL

From an ancient tomb-painting. Block by "Les Tablettes."

of the dead, who in his own person had died and lived again. The soul of the dead cat was "osirified," and ascended to the heavens to live with the gods. But it was by paths bristling with perils that the little feline soul arrived in the country of the West on the margin of those fields where the followers of Osiris were assembled.

The beautiful Amenti, goddess of the West, showed them the route, and thither they marched like the Chat Botté of the legend. A god grasped the delicate paws to guide them along the wonderful Pathway of the soul, or *ka*, and the offerings that had been deposited in the tombs magically attended them to sustain them on the journey. At the confines of the sky they found a ladder erected, but the gods held it firm, and they scaled it without mishap. If on the last rung, the feline pilgrims, still timid as when on earth, hesitated, the gods Horus and Set held them each by one of their paws, and hoisted them all fluttered into

Paradise. Once there they were quickly reassured by the bliss which awaited them. Before them was an idealised Egypt, with her Nile, her fishponds, her luxuriant vegetation, and her houses. There they might pass an easy life of hunting and play more happily than on earth. Yet there also they must work, though but lightly, and still they must wrestle for life. But if the struggle again proved too hard for them, a more distant and lovelier Paradise was disclosed. This was known as the Field of Offerings. There, thanks to the terrestrial offerings that had been so piously deposited in pussy's Tombs, the *kas* of which had been released by breaking or burning, the table was spread, and no effort needed. But a third, and infinitely more brilliant destiny was beyond. This was life with the Sun-god Amon-Ra, who navigated the

TEACHING A CAT TO DANCE TO THE LYRE

From a basso-relievo in the Museum of the Capitol.

Block by " Les Tablettes."

heavens in the sun-ship. The divinised soul who attained this glorious consummation became a sparkling spirit of light, lost in the radiant disc of the king of gods. So supreme a joy was not given to all the world. It was the Paradise of the great and glorious Pharaohs, sons of Amon ; yet, without doubt the cats of those princes followed them to this glory. Thus the soul of the Egyptian cat journeyed through the centuries from the humble grave dug in the darkness of the desert to the starry fields of the sky, where for ever it might hunt and roam in the glorious life life of Eternity. (*Steens*).

Few, if any, are the creeds that can equal the Egyptian depiction of a future life for our feline friends. Moreover, as we have seen, the certainty of its reality was so firmly established in the Egyptian mind that no effort imagination could suggest as likely to help the little pilgrims on the farther side of death was spared by their faithful human friends.

In the earlier ages of Etruria, the art and religion of that country were strongly influenced by Egypt, and we find the cat introduced into wall paintings representing happy souls in the other world. In the Etruscan *Tomba Golini* at Orvieto the bliss of the departed is symbolised by their presence at a banquet presided over by the King and Queen of Hades. On a low stool beneath the couch of the revellers a cat named Krankru is tearing her prey.

In the *Grotta del Triclinio* (also known as the *Grotta Marzi*), which was discovered at Corneto in 1830, a similar scene of joy and festivity is depicted. In front of each couch is a graceful Trapeza or four-legged table laden with dishes of various foods. Beneath the table the cat is seen, this time in company with a cock and a partridge, two sacred birds.

It has been questioned whether such scenes are emblematic of the bliss of the departed, or represent actual feasts held in their honour; but the presence of the gods should be sufficient answer; however, in either case they are doubtless truthful delineations of Etruscan manners, and show that the cat, perhaps because of its symbolic significance, was present at the sacred repasts that honoured the dead.

Our next glimpse of the Cat in Paradise is afforded by an Indian legend translated by H. C. Brooke from the French of Fréret—who discovered it, and it relates the story of how an earthly cat visited Heaven.

"An Indian King, named Salangham, had at his court a Brahmin and a Penitent, both celebrated for their virtue, which caused a rivalry between them leading to constant disputes. In the course of one of these arguments before the King the Brahmin declared one day that his virtue was pleasing to the god Parabaravaraston, a deity of the first class, by whose aid he could at will transport himself into one of the seven Heavens. The Penitent accepted the challenge, and the King, appointed arbiter, directed the Brahmin to penetrate the Heaven of Devendiren, and to bring thence a flower of the tree Parisadam, the mere scent of which confers immortality. The Brahmin saluted the King and took his leave, the whole Court expecting him to lose his wager, the Heaven of Devendiren being well known to be inaccessible to mortals. It is the dwelling-place of forty-eight million goddesses, who have for spouses twenty-four million gods, Devendiren being the chief; and the flower, Parisadam, of which he is very jealous, is the chief delight of this Heaven. The Penitent was dilating on these difficulties, and anticipating with joy the failure of his rival, when the Brahmin reappeared with the sacred flower; he was received with homage by King and Court, but the Penitent refused this homage, saying that the

King and Court were too easily pleased, and that he could, if he wished, send his Cat thither, confident that he would be received by Devendiren with distinction. Speaking thus, he summoned his Cat Patripatan, and whispering in his ear, the Cat disappeared in the clouds to the wonder of the beholders, and entering the Heaven of Devendiren was received in the arms of the god with a thousand caresses.

"So far the Penitent had succeeded admirably, but now he received a check, for the favourite goddess of Devendiren, smitten with love for Patripatan, would on no account agree to the departure of the Cat. This latter, having explained the state of things to Devendiren, the god supported him, explaining how the absence of the Cat would reflect upon and affront the Penitent. The goddess refused to listen, and the best Devendiren could do was to obtain her promise to return the Cat to earth after a few centuries.

"King Salangham meanwhile awaited with impatience the return of the Cat; the Penitent alone remained unmoved, and they waited for three centuries without inconvenience beyond that of suspense, for the Penitent, by the power of his goodness prevented old age from attacking the witnesses. At the end of this period the sky suddenly became brilliant, and in the cloud of a thousand colours appeared a throne formed of the flowers of Devendiren.

"The Cat was seated in majesty upon this throne, and on arriving near the King presented the Monarch with an entire branch bearing the flowers of Parisadam. The whole Court shouted 'Victory.' The Penitent was congratulated, but the Brahmin disputed his triumph, representing that the virtue of the Penitent was not to be given credit for this success, it being known how favourable were Devendiren and his favourite goddess to the Cats, so that without doubt half the credit was solely due to the Cat Patripatan. The King, on considering this argument, dared not decide between the Brahmin and the Penitent, but all united in admiration for Patripatan, and ever after this illustrious Cat was one of the chiefest ornaments of the Court, and supped every evening on the shoulder of the Monarch."

Among the more primitive peoples still with us to-day, who venerate the Cat, and believe that its soul attains Paradise, we must number the Jakuns, who are one of the semi-wild Malayan Tribes. They differ from the Egyptians in thinking of the Cat as giving, not as requiring, assistance, on the toilsome road between earth and heaven. For it is their firm conviction that when they die a cat leads the way on the weary journey they must make through Hell to Paradise, and eases their labour by spraying water on the infernal atmosphere, so that they may find it more bearable. No wonder that natives of Malay hold the Cat in high regard and believe that should any among them fall so low as to kill one, he will be severely punished in the future life. For every hair that Puss possessed, he must carry and stack a tree-trunk of the thickness of a cocoa-nut palm. There are few slayers of cats in Malay!

A very restricted conception of Paradise is outlined in the verses by Goethe given below, but one cat at least is there.

THE FAVOURED BEASTS

" Of beasts there have been chosen four
To come to Paradise,
And there with saints for evermore
They dwell in happy wise."

These beasts are the Ass which carried Jesus, the Wolf " to whom Mahomet spake," the Hound of the Seven Sleepers, and lastly

" Abuherrira's Cat, too, here
Purrs round his master blest,
For holy must the beast appear
The Prophet* hath caress'd."

Like the cats of the Pharaohs, this nameless Puss seems to have attained his high position by reflected glory.

But as we have seen in the cases of the Indian Cat, and the Cats of the Jakuns, in some countries the intrinsic merits of Puss were held to be sufficient to secure her admission to Paradise. And certainly this is the view the majority of cat lovers would hold!

BIBLIOGRAPHY

" Immortalité de l'ame." By A. Moret.

" The Poems of Goethe," 2nd edition. Trans. by E. A. Bowring, C.B. Pub. by George Bell & Sons, London, 1874.

" The Cities and Cemeteries of Etruria." By George Dennis, 3rd ed. Pub. by John Murray, London, 1883.

" Cat Gossip," Vol. II, p. 156; quoting " Unzere Katze." Pub. by the Editor, H. C. Brooke, Taunton.

" Cat Gossip," Vol. II, No. 28, p. 8. Legend discovered by Fréret, of l'Académie des Inscriptions et Belles-Lettre. Trans. by H. C. Brooke.

" Revue Féline Belge." Article by Armand Steens on " Les petit chats de l'Egypte." Pub. by Arthur Goemaere, Anvers, 1929.

* Mohammed was a lover of cats, and on one occasion cut off a portion of his robe to avoid disturbing a cat who sat upon it.

CHAPTER XXII

GHOSTLY CATS

" Millions of spiritual creatures walk the earth
Unseen, both when we wake and when we sleep."
(" Paradise Lost," lines 677–8.)

IN this world of matter man finds himself everywhere mocked by Illusion, which stretches a veil between him and Reality, varying in density, but usually impenetrable. Occasionally, however, almost as if by accident, a rent appears, through which he may obtain a tiny hurried glimpse of that which lies behind. The phenomena of ghostly apparitions in one form or another have persisted throughout history in every stage of civilisation. Ancient religious literature abounds with examples, and modern psychical investigation confirms their actuality. Not only do the ghostly entities exist in a mental or astral sphere, but have the power to demonstrate their being on the physical plane. The importance of their doing so lies for us in the fact that we are forced thereby to admit life and mind to be realities, capable of existence independently of what we know as matter, and not to be accounted for by mechanical explanations.

It is interesting to note that the ghosts of animals are manifested in the same manner as are the ghosts of human beings, so that we cannot accept the appearance of the latter as evidence of survival, unless we admit the same applies to the apparitions of the lower creatures and even to those of what we are accustomed to regard as inanimate objects.

According to the accounts of the local peasantry, a striking example of the latter, in conjunction with a ghostly cat, may be found in the Castle of Combourg. A former Count of Comburg, who had a wooden leg when he died, is said to have left behind him the wraith of his artificial limb, and on certain occasions it has been met perambulating the grand staircase of the Tower and accompanied by a spectral black cat.

Elliott O'Donnell remarks that " The most common forms of animal phenomena seen in houses are undoubtedly those of cats," and adds that the number of places reported to him as being haunted by cats is " almost incredible—in one street in Whitechapel there are no less than four." He goes on to tell that "from endless experiments made in haunted houses," he has proved, at least to his own satisfaction, that "the cat acts as a thoroughly reliable psychic barometer. The dog is sometimes unaware of the proximity of the Unknown. . . . I have never yet had a cat with me that has not shown the most obvious signs of terror and uneasiness both before and during a superphysical manifestation."

I have here brought together a few instances of the reappearance of cats after their physical death. It would of course be possible to multiply such almost indefinitely, but space forbids, and I can give but one short chapter to such direct evidence of the survival of our feline friends. Those who have taken the pains to study cats intimately and gained a real understanding of their complex occult personalities, will need little proof. Those who have not done so, have before them a subject that will richly repay patient investigation by the absorbing interest it unfolds, and the sidelights on other problems which it affords.

The Society for Psychical Research in their "Journal" for May, 1912, published an account of the reappearance in her old haunts of a favourite cat which had recently died. The cat was "Smoky," a small blue Persian of a peculiar shade, quite unlike any other feline in the village. The cause of her death had been the attack of a dog which had broken her ribs and left her very lame, so that she was easily identified. The gardener had buried her body and planted a dahlia over her grave, and her mistress, knowing she could not recover, was relieved rather than grieved, to feel her pet's sufferings were ended. About three weeks later Smoky's mistress and her sister were breakfasting together, and the latter was sitting with her back to the window reading a letter aloud, when she suddenly saw her companion "looking absolutely scared," and gazing out of the window which was on her left. "What *is* the matter?" she asked, and her sister replied: "There's *Smoky* walking across the grass!" Both ladies rushed to the window, and saw Smoky, "looking very ill, her coat rough and staring, and walking lamely across the grass in front of the window, three or four yards from it." Her mistress called her, and as she did not respond, ran after her, calling; but to her surprise Smoky took no notice, and disappeared among the shrubs. In about ten minutes, however, the sisters and a friend who lived with them, saw her again, going through a hedge in front of the window. Again her mistress went out after her, but could not find her. The servant was the next to see her, this time in the kitchen passage. She ran to get her some milk, and followed her with it, "but the cat walked away, and from that moment she disappeared completely." The ladies " made every enquiry of the neighbours, but no one had seen her, or any cat like her." They thought a mistake must have been made about her death, although their friend, the gardener, and the boy, had all seen her body, and finally the indignant gardener, outraged by the suggestion that he had not buried the cat, dug it up again.

I would suggest that this apparition was not the actual ghost or soul of Smoky—for that would have responded to the advances of its mistress*—but an astral photograph, which the sufferings of the cat had impressed on the psychic atmosphere. I cannot believe that no one on " the other side " would have helped the poor unhappy newcomer to escape from her troubles in the earth sphere, and realise the freedom from bodily ills to which she had attained. Whilst Justice may bind criminals to the scenes of their crime, it cannot also bind their victims to perpetual re-enactment of a tragedy. Still, I include the story of " Smoky " among ghostly cats, since the astral photo theory has not attained the general recognition it certainly deserves.

A very remarkable instance of a ghost cat is related by Henry Spicer, who says: " Dr. A. has, among his numerous patients, one who is almost constantly attended by a spectral tabby! The fond and playful animal not only sits behind him in his studious hours, but frolics after him about the house, more especially on the stairs, where its amusement is to slip in and out of the rails of the balustrade, working an imaginary *crochet* from the top to the bottom, arriving thither at the same moment as its master. It has been ascertained that no mortal cat of its apparent size could possibly perform this feat. By far the most remarkable part of the story is, that the animal has been, on more than one occasion, visible to other eyes than those of the original seer."

Mr. Spicer makes no comment on the above story, but adds that " A gentleman, now resident in London, enjoys the occasional society of a cat with a human face."

M. Bozzano quotes a case from " Light " (1915, p. 215), where the Rev. Charles L. Tweedale, author of several works on metaphysics, relates how a ghostly cat made itself heard by its former owners, but remained unseen. I translate from Bozzano's French:

" About two years ago (I have recorded the happening in my note-book) my wife and the maid were sitting chatting one evening in a small room of the house. Suddenly they heard the clamorous calling of a cat, beside Mrs. Tweedale. Both located the noise as arising from the same spot, close to my wife's skirt. It continued

* Compare with Henry Spicer's account in this chapter of a ghostly cat.

for some time, then ceased, and they clearly heard in its place the delicate sound produced by the tongue of a cat lapping milk. Puzzled to account for the phenomena, Mrs. Tweedale called her cat; then, aided by the maid, she minutely searched the room, but fruitlessly. They resettled themselves and renewed their conversation. But almost immediately the loud cries of an invisible cat recommenced, and were again succeeded by the sound of a cat's tongue lapping a liquid. They searched the room a second time, but again in vain.

"It should be remarked that some days before, our cat had disappeared. When Mrs. Tweedale and the maid told me what had taken place, I said to them: 'This signifies that we shall not see our cat alive again.' It was even so; the poor beast had met with the end of many cats of this country, which are killed maliciously."

I am also indebted to Bozzano for the following account taken by him from the "Proceedings of the S.P.R." (Vol. X, p. 127). I translate freely from his pages. Mrs. Gordon Jones is the speaker:

"I have always felt a strong aversion to cats—aversion which I inherited from my father, who could not bear their presence. I never allowed a cat in my house until the day when an invasion of mice made it necessary. I then procured a common cat, the coat of which was striped alternately black and grey; but I took no notice of it, and never allowed it to ascend to the upper part of the house.

"One day someone said to me that the cat was mad, and asked me to authorise its being drowned. I had not the moral courage to go and find out if the information was worthy of credit, but accorded the permission without more ado. A little later I was told that the kitchen-boy had drowned the cat in a boiler. As the animal had never been my pet or companion its disappearance left me indifferent.

"The evening of the day that the animal had been destroyed, I was alone in the dining-room immersed in reading (I am sure that I never dreamt of cats or of phantoms), when suddenly I was impelled to raise my eyes, and look beside the door. I saw, or I seemed to see, that the door slowly opened, and permitted the entrance of the cat which had been sacrificed that morning. It was the same without doubt; but it seemed meagre, and was completely drenched, and streaming with water. Only the expression of the gaze was not the same, for it regarded me with human eyes, so sad that I was pained; this look long remained impressed upon my memory as an obsession. I was so sure of what I saw that I did not doubt that the cat had actually escaped from drowning. I rang for the parlour-maid, and as soon as she came, I said to her, 'Here is the cat; carry it away.' It seemed to me impossible that the maid could not see it, for I saw it plain and solid, as the table or the chairs; but she looked at me, frightened, and replied: 'Madame, I was present when William carried the dead cat into the garden to bury it.' 'But it is there,' I interpolated: 'do you not see it near the door?' The maid saw nothing, and soon after the cat began to become transparent and slowly disappeared so completely that finally I saw it no more."

A remarkably convincing case of the reappearance of a cat after death was described by Norah Chesson in the "Occult Review." She says: "Sickness of some kind had kept me to my room for a week, and I had wondered why my cat Minnie had not courted my company as usual, but accounted for her sudden indifference by a possible reflux of motherly devotion to her kitten, now about six weeks old. The first morning of my convalescence the bedroom door, which stood ajar, opened a little further, and Minnie came in. She rubbed her pretty tortoise-shell tabby coat against me in affectionate greeting; she clasped my hand with ecstatic paws in a pretty fondling gesture that was all her own; she licked my fingers, and I felt her white throat throbbing with her loud purring, and then she turned and trotted away. 'Minnie has been in to see me at last,' said I to the maid who brought in my lunch. 'I wonder why she has kept away from me so long.'

"'Minnie's been dead and buried these two days, and her kitten's fretting itself to skin and bone for her,' said Louisa, looking scared. 'Your mamma wouldn't tell you while you weren't well, Miss, for she knew you'd take on, being *that* fond of the little cat.' Minnie was undoubtedly dead and buried, and a stone from our garden rockery was piled upon her place of burial, yet as undoubtedly, Minnie came to welcome my return to health. Is this explicable? I know that it is true.

"I was a child and a girl, normal in mind and body, imaginative but not a visionary, and bred up in a family that heartily disliked and feared any talk of things supernatural."

From the context of this interesting account it would appear that the writer had natural, but untrained psychic powers, and these she used in collaboration with the poet, W. B. Yeats, in psychic experiments. Between 1905 and her death in 1906, she contributed various poems and book reviews to the "Occult Review," and the editor of that paper considered her a promising contributor.

Striking evidence of the survival of her favourite cat is given by Clarice Taylor in a letter published by the "Psychic Gazette" of May, 1918. This animal, a Persian tabby, was known as "Muffy," and had a peculiar little trick of springing over the door-mat when entering any room from the hall. Muffy died, and a few months later her mistress had a white kitten called "Dandy" given to her, and about the same time opened Spiritualist services in Coventry. Mrs. A. E. Cannock, the well-known medium, went to spend a week-end with her, and soon made friends with the new pet. In the morning Mrs. Cannock opened the door after breakfasting, but suddenly jumped back, exclaiming: "Oh, pussy, you *did* startle me!" "Dandy is asleep in her basket," said Kitty's owner. "I don't mean the little white-nosed one," Mrs. Cannock replied, "it's the old one. She jumped over the mat and passed by me."

She then fully described the departed "Muffy." Clarice Taylor adds that her guest had never heard of her previous favourite, and that it was not even in her thoughts, as she had transferred her affection to the new pet. She justly remarks that "if it grieves our spirit-friends to see us and not be seen, how hurt must be our departed pets, who cannot understand the change, at our seeming indifference. Surely a cat, more faithful than many a mortal, deserves our continued affection and consideration after she has 'crossed the border.'"

Mrs. Osborne Leonard's description of the "vagaries" of her wonderful cat "Mickey" on "two planes," which appeared in the "Psychic Gazette" of April, 1918, is of interest alike to cat lovers and to students of the occult. From his earliest days on earth, Mickey, who was a white cat with black markings, manifested extraordinary intelligence, character, and devotion. He was never separated from his people except once for three days when he was twelve months old. Then he refused food and drink, and simply lay moping till they returned, so they determined never to leave him again. After that Mickey went everywhere with his owners, and travelled thousands of miles. They took him to hotels, boarding-houses, and apartments, in Scotland, Ireland, and England, and at each new place he would slip out from his basket when night came, and after smelling round the front door-step to enable him to identify it again, would go forth on a prowl, always returning in the morning. He even accompanied his friends for long walks amidst the busy traffic of London, and never got hurt. In fact, he manifested a preference for towns, and seemed bored by country places. Nine months before Mickey passed over, a friend gave his mistress a Pekinese dog named Ching, and Mickey graciously took the newcomer into his family circle, allowing her to eat off his saucer and even take pieces of food from his mouth. But Ching was unresponsive and rough, and often teased Pussy so that he would jump on to the furniture to escape from her play.

For some weeks after Mickey's death nothing happened, but one night, about eleven o'clock, his mistress was sitting quietly reading, when something made her look up from her book. Then she " saw Mickey, in the astral body, sitting on a kind of shelf under a table." Before she could draw her husband's attention to him, " Ching, who was asleep on the hearth-rug, suddenly began to growl fiercely " ; her hair stood up on end, and her eyes bulged, whilst " her cheeks puffed in and out with excitement." She fixed her eyes on the spot where Mrs. Leonard saw Mickey sitting, and made a rush at him. Mickey leaped out of her way, just as he had been wont to do, and perched on a little side-table in the corner of the room where he looked down contemptuously on Ching, who kept leaping around the table trying to get at him. When Ching returned to the hearth-rug, Mrs. Leonard walked over to Mickey and stroked him. She could distinctly feel him arch his back under her hand as she did so, and noticed what she had forgotten, namely, that he had some coarse white hairs at the end of his tail mingling with the black. In fact, the only difference she could perceive between Mickey's former body and his ghostly one, was that he was now spotlessly clean for the first time in his life ! Whilst she petted him, Ching rushed round barking angrily. After a little while she sat down, and when she looked up again Mickey had vanished. Mr. Leonard was unable to see him. After this Mickey made many appearances, and came almost every night between 11 and 11.30. When the Leonards had friends, Mick walked in at the usual time, made a little grunt of disgust, and went off again.

His mistress went to several séances at Mr. Craddock's, hoping some of her friends on the other side would mention Mickey. One night " Joey " said to her : " Your mother is here, Mrs. Leonard, and she has a cat with her."

Mrs. Leonard was delighted, thinking her Mickey had come ; but she asked what Puss was like, and to her disappointment Joey described him as " a black cat with a little white patch on his chest," and said he belonged to her mother, who always called him " Old Tom." Not till she went home did Mrs. Leonard remember that her mother had had such a cat, which " she simply adored," and believed to possess a soul which eventually would reincarnate in a higher form of life. But on another occasion Mickey did appear at a séance, and even made " the little piping sound " so peculiar to himself through the trumpet there provided. Mrs. Leonard gives yet more stories of her pet, but these will suffice as evidence of Pussy's survival.

The *Weekly Dispatch* of April 3rd, 1921, contained a vivid account of a spectral figure which, at the time of writing, nightly stalked about, accompanied by a large white cat, in Ferryford, a little village near Trenton, New Jersey. "The inhabitants," says the *Weekly Dispatch* cable, "have become so unnerved that most of them are leaving the place, and determined efforts are therefore being made to lay the ghost.

"The spectre is said to be that of John Koch, who once kept a wayside motor repair shop in the village. Six months ago he quarrelled with his mechanic, whom he shot. Believing he had killed him, Koch committed suicide. Koch last Monday, with an enormous white cat, is said to have entered the living-room of the cottage where he had lived, and after spreading panic among the widow and her family, who were gossiping with a number of friends, Koch whistled to the cat and departed. He repeated his performance twice during the week.

"Last night fourteen people, headed by the local policeman, formed a ring round the cottage, determined to solve the mystery. Among them was a man from whom Koch borrowed money the day before his death, and a dog—the latter to investigate the spectral cat.

"Shortly after midnight a loud crash was heard in the cottage. Entering, the watchers found a portrait of the dead man's mother-in-law on the floor. Then a hollow laugh was heard, and Koch appeared at the window surrounded by what was described as 'a faint blue mist.' On a small pear tree behind him was a large white cat with long whiskers. With a loud bark the dog made for the cat as it sprang to the ground. But to the dog's amazement he passed right through the cat, and his jaws snapped in empty air apparently. Feeling unequal to the situation the dog uttered a loud howl and fled.

"Meanwhile, states a representative of the New York 'Evening World,' who accompanied the investigators, the remainder of the party bombarded the 'ghost' with lamps, flat-irons, and other things. But the spectre merely smiled sardonically, called the cat, and faded away.

"The villagers are in such a state of nervous tension that the police have ordered all fire-arms to be confiscated."

It seems strange that none among the watchers thought of approaching the ghost sympathetically as one needing brotherly counsel.

An extraordinary case of the haunting of a house by the apparition of a cat is recorded in the "Journal of the Psychical Research Society" for May, 1926.

"The house is an old one—probably built between 1400 and

1500, but not popularly supposed to be haunted. Fifteen years ago it was an inn, and before that a farm-house. The first percipients of the ghostly cat seem to have been a Mr. and Mrs. S., who lived in the place during 1924 and 1925, and their friend, Miss A., who stayed with them. All saw it several times, and described it as long-haired, and practically black. It never walked towards the seers, but always either by their side, or away from them so that they never saw its eyes, and it carried its tail on end. At nine feet or more, it appeared like an ordinary cat, but when quite close to it, you could see through it, and Miss A. said she knew it was not an ordinary cat as it vanished whilst she looked. Mr. S. had always been sceptical about ghosts until he met the Bogie cat. The first time he saw it he was in the dining-room, when he noticed a cat trying to get into the dresser cupboard, about nine feet away. He walked over and bent down to push the cat off, but found he could see right through it. It went away, and he followed it through the dining-room doorway, across a lobby, through the scullery, and into the pantry, the doors of these apartments being all open. In the middle of the pantry floor it vanished. Mr. S. and his wife both saw Bogie several times before they mentioned it to one another, and had said nothing about it to Miss A. till she remarked: 'I see a cat about your place which vanishes—it cannot belong to you.' Mr. S. thinks that other occupants of the house may have seen Bogie without realising its ghostly nature. No object is apparent in its manifestations, and it seems to be quite happy. Mrs. S. says she is sure its interest is in the house and not in their party."

Such examples of spiritual apparitions as we have here been considering, unsought, confirmed by independent witnesses, certainly go a long way towards proving the continued existence of our dumb friends after they have laid aside the most material of their bodily envelopes. And though in some cases the astral photo theory may be held accountable (as when figures perpetually repeat certain courses of action, without regard to the changes wrought by time and circumstances in their environment), it clearly cannot account for those cases in which the spirit shows a ready recognition of, and adaptation to, new factors in the situation.

For an interesting collection of such cases I would refer the doubter who has not time to peruse heavy tomes to Elliott O'Donnell's "Animal Ghosts." The serious student will find a big literature open before him in any library worthy of the name.

BIBLIOGRAPHY

"Facts and Fantasies," p. 72. By Henry Spicer. Pub. by T. Bosworth, London, 1853.

"The History of Magic," Vol. I, p. 180. By Joseph Ennemoser. Trans. from the German by William Howitt. Pub. by Henry G. Bohn, London, 1854.

"Journal of the Society for Psychical Research," Vol. XV, p. 249; Vol. XXIII, p. 66. Pub. by the Society, London.

"The International Psychic Gazette." Pub. by the "International Psychic Gazette," Ltd., London, April and May, 1918.

"The Occult Review," Vol. II, pp. 9, 10. Pub. by Rider & Co., London.

"La Revue Scientique et Morale du Spiritisme," p. 351. 1920.

"The Weekly Dispatch." Pub. by The Associated Newspapers Ltd, London, April 3rd, 1921.

"Cat Gossip," No. 33, p. 45. Edited and Pub. by H. C. Brooke, Taunton.

"Les Manifestations Métapsychiques et les Animaux," pp. 44, 168. By Ernest Bozzano. Pub. Paris, 1926.

CHAPTER XXIII

DEMON CATS

. . . Those midnight hags,
By force of potent spell, of bloody characters
And conjurations horrible to hear,
Call fiends and spectres from the yawning deep,
And set the ministers of hell to work.

T. E. Hook (?).

THE Celtic tribes, by whom Europe was at an early period peopled, divorced the two-fold aspects of God, and like savages of other races, thought it necessary to propitiate the malignant powers whom they conceived of as guiding and ruling the destructive forces of the material world. The good God might safely be trusted to fulfil His Own Nature, even if His altars were sometimes neglected, but the vengeful jealousy of the Evil One must be constantly propitiated at any cost.

The introduction of Christianity to these peoples confirmed their dualistic creed, and added new terrors hitherto undreamed of. The devil was going about as a roaring lion, seeking whom he might devour. Like the Deity, the Adversary was omnipresent, and if not omnipotent, was at least sufficiently powerful to thwart his Divine Antagonist in most of His good intentions, and seize for his own purposes the creation God had made to glorify and pleasure Himself.

Demoralised by fear, it is little wonder that many of the wretched and credulous people who imbibed such teaching with their mothers' milk, sought to establish sympathetic communication with the Christian devil and his hosts of attendant demons. Abstract right and wrong were undreamt-of conceptions. Whether Jehovah or Satan was the power invoked, fear and selfishness were the motives of the suppliant.

In the ancient Celtic mythology the Cat had been a favourite form of the demons who imperilled the heroes in their wondrous adventures. Together with red-hot swine, and ants as large as calves, stinging cats were among the opponents of the Celtic braves.

The Christian Church, thinking to increase its power thereby, incorporated such monstrous conceptions with its own demonology, so that mediæval superstition recognised a disguised devil in every black tom-cat. The bare fact of an old woman being seen once or twice in the proximity of such a feline, was sufficient reason to brand her as one who held intercourse with Satan. The Cat became known as a familiar because it was said to be the devil's favourite form, and hence witches were believed to harbour demons in their cats.

According to Ennemoser, it was in the thirteenth century that the devil first appeared amongst male heretics in the forms of tom-cats and he-goats ; and amongst the women as toads and geese, and finally as cats.

We may judge of the remarkable spread of witchcraft at this period from the account of Raynald, who says, " that in Germany and Italy especially, such numbers of men were seduced to sorcery that the whole earth was overflowed by it, and would have been laid waste by the devil, had they not in both countries burnt some 30,000 heretics."

Nor was witchcraft eliminated by these desperate means. Cotton Mather, writing four centuries later, quotes Bishop Hall as saying : " Satan's prevalency in this Age, is most clear in the marvellous Number of Witches, abounding in all places. Now Hundreds are discovered in one Shire ; and if Fame Deceives us not, in a Village of Fourteen Houses in the North, are found so many of this Damned Brood. Yea, and those of both Sexes, who have professed much Knowledge, Holiness and Devotion, are drawn into this Damnable Practice."

Mather comments on the above, that he supposes " the Doctor in the first of those passages, may refer to what happened in the Year 1645, when so many Vassals of the Devil were Detected, that there were Thirty try'd at one time, whereas about Fourteen were Hang'd, and an Hundred more detained in the Prisons of Suffolk and Essex." He warns the people of New England that " we must no more be Haughty, because of the Lord's Holy

Mountain among us ; No, it becomes us rather to be Humble, because we have been such an Habitation of Unholy Devils ! "

This widespread and long-continued epidemic of witchcraft had produced a number of professional witch-finders, who made it their special business to seek out, and bring to trial, witches and wizards. The German Sprenger was one of the most assiduous of these, and is said to have been responsible for about five hundred victims a year. A certain judge of Lorraine made boast that he had personally condemned nine hundred, whilst an Archbishop of Treves, who attributed the inclement spring of 1586 to the machinations of witchcraft, burned 118 women at one time. Nor must we omit to mention King James VI of Scotland, who published his famous treatise on demonology in 1597 and condemned so many of " these detestable slaves of the devil, the witches or enchanters," to horrible tortures and death.

Richard Bovet, the seventeenth-century writer on sorcery, has given us an account of how the witches, by means of their demon cats tormented the wife of J. H. Seavington, and her son, aged 18, in the county of Somerset. This lady was a clergyman's widow, who had married for the second time, and had arrived at the age of 57, when a neighbour was suspected of causing her torments. Among her nightmare visions was a large black cat, which together with seven or nine other felines would make a dreadful yelling for about fifteen minutes, and then suddenly disappear. When they had gone Mrs. Seavington would be attacked by fits and internal pains, and flashes and " heaps of light like fire " would appear to her.

The afflicted lady had two favourite cats of her own, and " as soon as the other sort of cats entered the room they would fly as if they were Devil-drove, sometimes into the fire, sometimes the Oven, sometimes up the Chimney, or any way to avoid the room, whilst the rest were there, nor could they ever be brought to enjoy themselves after, but starved and pin'd away after a piteous manner."

Their mistress lived seventeen years, and finally died of pain and grief. Happily, in this instance, no one person appears to have been held to be responsible for the misdoings of the demon cats, but it was somewhat exceptional. A more typical case is related by Roger North, brother of the then Lord Chief Justice, who describes a witch trial which took place at the Exeter Assizes, where, on the testimony of her neighbour, and her own confession, an old woman was condemned to be hanged. The neighbour had seen a cat jump into her cottage window at twilight one evening, and said he believed the cat to be the devil. No further proof of the accused woman's guilt was required.

Not less remarkable was the confession of the celebrated wizard Alexander Hunter, *alias* Hamilton, *alias* Hattaraick, a " Warlok Cairle " accused of having " abused the Countrey " for a long time, who was burned upon Castle Hill, in Edinburgh, in 1631. The devil, it seems, was wont to meet him under a variety of forms. Sometimes Satan would be riding on a black horse, or he would appear in the shape of a cat, a corbie, or a dog. He taught his disciple to summon him in a very disrespectful fashion, by striking the ground with a wand of fir-tree, and crying, " Rise up, foul thief." But, as Thomas Ingoldsby warns us, the devil is " easier at all times to raise than allay," and Alexander declared that he could not rid himself again of his master's presence until he presented to him a quick cat, or dog, or " other some such like thing."

This presentation of the animal " quick " to Satan, and his assumption of the same or similar form as the devoted creature, emphasises the fact that it was not thought of as a food offering, like the cattle sacrificed on Jehovah's altars, whose roasted flesh, by its savoury smell, so often deflected that god's anger from his unhappy " Chosen People." It was usually the services of the living animal that Satan required, and the great majority of ritual sacrifices to the devil make this clear. For even when the death of the victim is involved, the object is generally* to release the creature's soul, and so make it a more efficient servant of the dark spirit to whom it is dedicated. It is not slain, but transferred from a mortal to a demonic existence, in which its powers are enormously magnified.

One of the alleged victims of such demons was Loyse Maillat, a little French girl, eight years old, who lived with her father and mother in the village of Courieres.

On Saturday, June 15th, 1598, this child was attacked by impotence in all her limbs, so that she was obliged to walk on all fours, and at the same time her mouth was curiously drawn and distorted. Weeks passed, but Loyse showed no signs of recovery. Her parents decided she must be possessed, and took her to the Church of the Holy Saviour. There, their fears were confirmed, for no less than five demons were discovered, whose names were said to be *Loup*, *Chat*, *Chien*, *Joly*, and *Griffon*.

In reply to a question by the priest, Loyse pointed out a woman named Françoise Secretain, who had assisted with the rite of exorcism, as being the source of her troubles. At first the devils refused to leave their hostess, but after her parents had spent all night in prayer, they came forth from her mouth in the form of large pellets as big as an orange. *Chat* was black, but the

* For other objects of immolation see chapter on The Cat as Sacrifice.

other demons were a fiery red in hue. Their disappearance was followed by the restoration of Loyse to her usual health. Françoise confessed that she had caused the five demons to take possession of the child, and added that for a considerable time she had served Satan, who appeared to her in various shapes, as a black man, a cat, a dog, and a fowl.

Henri Boguet, the recorder of her case, says that "the glory of God was made manifest in the imprisonment of Françoise."

The same indefatigable investigator tells us that Rolande de Vernois acknowledged "Le Diable se presenta pour lors au Sabbat en forme d'un groz chat noir."

Such beliefs are still prevalent in the remoter parts of Europe.

FELINE DEMON IN IFFLEY CHURCH, OXFORD. (NORMAN)

We may instance the peasants of Southern Slavonia who are firmly persuaded that the devil dwells in a black cat. They try to keep clear of such felines by night, as during the hours of darkness the Fiend has power suddenly to resume his proper form and seize and destroy the unwary traveller.

Modern Spiritualism confirms the testimony of ancient creeds, that the spirit worlds are not only peopled by celestial beings, and ghosts of former earth-dwellers, but by grotesque and monstrous demons of every gradation of wickedness, intelligence, and power. In all these spirit realms, animal forms occupy a well-marked position, but the cat figures with special prominence in ancient and modern accounts of demoniacal apparitions, and adventures of the bold explorers of this dark *terra incognita*. Much evidence has been adduced that this world, although happily invisible to most human beings, has as actual an existence as our own. The literature on the subject is readily available, therefore all I have sought to do in this chapter is to lay before the reader a few illustrations of the appearances and actions of feline demons, or devils in cat form. Since shape would seem to be far less fixed in the spirit worlds than in our own, it is, perhaps, impossible to know whether what appears to the seer as a demon cat (or other creature) is actually such, or merely a temporary mask assumed by an occult intelligence to fulfil a passing purpose. Therefore in appraising the value of the evidence we must constantly bear in mind the power of transfiguration possessed by spiritual beings, and to that limitation we must add the untrustworthiness of man's physical senses in this world of Maya.

To illustrate the survival of the old beliefs in our enlightened land, I append the following testimony from two modern writers ere concluding this chapter.

The well-known ghost-hunter Mr. Elliott O'Donnell assures us that " there are, at the present moment, many houses in England haunted by phantasms in the form of black cats, of so sinister and hostile an appearance, that one can only assume that unless they are the actual spirits of cats, earthbound through cruel and vicious propensities, they must be vice-elementals, i.e. spirits that have never inhabited any material body, and which have either been generated by vicious thoughts, or else have been attracted elsewhere to a spot by some crime or vicious act once perpetrated there. Vice-elemental is merely the modern name for fiend or demon."

Pastor Richard Howton, famous in certain circles as a healer, relates a remarkable case from his own experience of a demon, which, exorcised from a man, entered into a cat and possessed it. The unfortunate man was brought to Mr. Howton " with a fighting demon in him, which made him always want to be boxing." He threatened to box the Pastor, who had to show him that even a minister was not always ignorant of the noble art of self-defence. Mr. Howton says : " When I cast the demon out in the name of the Lord, the unclean spirit entered into a favourite cat, which ran violently out of the house into a pond and tried to drown itself. When rescued and brought into the house, it ran into the fire, and ultimately had to be destroyed. The man was completely healed. To God be the glory ! "

BIBLIOGRAPHY

"Discours des Sorciers," 3rd edition. By Henri Boguet, Lyons, 1590.

"Mystery of Witchcraft." By Thomas Cooper. Printed in London, 1617.

"The Wonders of the Invisible World: Being an account of the Tryals of Several Witches, Lately Executed in New England," pp. 142–3. By Cotton Mather, D.D. To which is added "A Farther Account of the Tryals of the New England Witches." By Increase Mather, D.D. First Printed at Boston, and reprinted at London, 1693. Pub. in "Library of Old Authors." By J. Russell Smith, London, 1862.

"Historical Essay." By Francis Hutchinson. Pub. London, 1718.

"Lives of Francis North, Baron Guildford, and his Brothers." By Roger North. Pub. 1740–2.

"The History of Magic," Vol. II, p. 148. By Joseph Ennemoser. Trans. by William Howitt. Pub. by Henry G. Bohn, London, 1854.

"Divine Healing and Demon Possession," 2nd edition, p. 96. By Pastor Richard Howton. Pub. by Ward, Lock & Co., Ltd., London, 1909.

"Animal Ghosts," pp. 49–50. By Elliott O'Donnell. Pub. by Rider & Co., London, 1913.

"Cat Gossip," Vol. II, p. 156. "Some Catty Superstitions."

CHAPTER XXIV

VAMPIRE CATS

" The witches' circle intact, charms undisturbed
That raised the spirit and succubus."
(*Browning*, " Ring and Book," I. 236.)

THE Cat occupies an important position in the mythology of Vampirism, and, according to the Sephardim, or Spanish Jews, its appearance on our planet in this unlovely character was an early one, actually preceding the creation of Eve. Hebrew folk-lore informs us that the Semitic witch-queen Lilith was Adam's first wife, but that she refused to give him her obedience and flew away, later becoming a vampire. She still lives, and assumes the form of a huge black cat named El Broosha, when she seizes the new-born human babe that is her favourite prey, and sucks its blood.

Lilith is referred to in Isaiah xxxiv. 14, but in the Authorized Version her name has been translated as " Screech-Owl," whilst the Revised Version renders it as " Night-monster," so that it is apt to baffle recognition. The screech-owl, like the cat, is closely associated with all kinds of witchcraft, but especially with vampirism. The explanation of this is that the ghosts of those who, because they had died before their time, were actual or potential vampires, were thought to wail and cry. The *stridores* of the necromancers were an imitation of the ghostly lamentations, and the doctrine of sympathy supposed that this similitude produced power to control the unhappy spirits. Owls, cats, disembodied ghosts, wailing necromancers, who could distinguish the weird sounds? The magic rule is that the part may not only stand for the whole, but is able to draw the whole to itself if aided by magic. He who would evoke the dead, used the strange cries to establish *rapport.*

In the legend of Lilith we recognise the origin of the widespread superstition that cats will suck the breath of a sleeping child, and it is also clear why black cats are banished from children's cradles. In mediæval times witches were thought to assume cat form to play the part of vampire, and seem to have usurped the rôle of Lilith.

Picken, whose "Poems" were published about 1830, has described in verse:

> "How the auld uncanny matrons
> Grew whiles a hare, a dog, or batrons,*
> To get their will o' carles sleepan,
> Wha hae nae staulks o' rountree† keepan,
> Ty'd round them when they ride or sail,
> Or sew't wi' care in their sark-tail."

According to Ennemoser, Zoroasterism, through its doctrine that spirits are sexed, is responsible for the gruesome belief current in the Middle Ages, and accepted by Church and State, that male and female demons, known as incubi and succubi, consort with human beings. An alleged example of this unholy practice is recorded by Petto, and we may read in his "faithful Narrative" how the witch Abre Grinset, of Dunwich, Suffolk, confest in 1665 that "The Devil did appear in the form of a Pretty hansom Young Man first, and since Appeareth to her in the form of a blackish Gray Cat or Kitling, that it sucketh of a Tett [teat] (which Searchers since saw in the place She mentioned)."

In 1633 the Lancashire witch, Margaret Johnson, "alsoe saith, yt when her devill did come to sucke her pappe, hee usually came to her in ye liknes of a cat, sometymes of one colour, and sometymes on (*sic*) an other. And yt since this trouble befell her, her spirit hath left her, and shee never saw him since." (*Whitaker.*)

An account of a somewhat similar case in which a cat familiar sucked the blood of the mistress he served will be found in the chapter on Cat Genii. In this instance, the cat was not a true vampire, since he seems to have accepted the witch's blood as a gift or reward freely offered by her in return for special service,

* i.e. cat.

† i.e. rowan-tree. It was supposed to ward off all evil influences.

and to have been equally satisfied by the offering of a chicken. Thus we read that she " rewarded hym as before, wyth a chicken and a droppe of her bloud, which chicken he eate up cleane as he didde al the rest, and she cold fynde remaining neyther bones nor fethers."

The ever-present dominating aspect of vampirism is perverted sexuality. The erotic vampire seldom or never appears to the object of its passion in human form ; but to achieve its evil purpose, takes the shape of beast or bird, as did Pamphila in Apuleius (*Met.* III. 21). It haunts the victim night and day, and little by little draws out the very marrow from his bones. Deformed children, or monsters capable of unspeakable wickedness, result from the unholy union. Yet how avoid it ? How be certain in any given instance if the cat or dog that shows affection for a human being is an actual animal, or a devil in disguise ?

> " So Men (they say), by Hell's Delusions led,
> Have ta'en a Succubus to their bed."
>
> (*Cowley*, " The Mistress, Not Fair.")

This aspect of vampirism is emphasised in Oriental countries as the following Japanese story related by Hadland Davis well illustrates.

" The Prince of Hizen, an honoured member of the Nabéshima family, one evening, accompanied by his favourite lady, O Toyo, dallied in the garden until sunset, and never noticed when he and his companion withdrew within the palace walls that a large cat had followed them. The lovers parted for the night, and the cat followed O Toyo to her bedroom, where she was soon asleep. But at the midnight hour a sudden sense of fear awoke her, to see at her side an enormous cat in threatening poise. Before she could cry for help the brute sprang at her throat and strangled her. It then buried her body under the verandah, and itself assumed her form.

" So successful was the vampire cat's metamorphoses that the Prince guessed nothing of what had occurred, but remained the lover of the seeming O Toyo until the drain she made upon his vitality caused him serious illness. Doctors were called, but failed to diagnose his complaint, so as his sufferings were always intensified when night fell, it was decided that a hundred retainers should keep guard when he retired to rest. The watchers took their post, but just before ten struck were prostrated by sleep, and the vampire O Toyo came to prey on her victim as usual. Each night events followed the same course, and the Prince grew steadily worse. At last, when things had reached a desperate pass, a loyal young soldier, named Ito Soda, gave it as his opinion that the Prince was bewitched, and obtained leave to keep watch with the guard. At ten o'clock the usual drowsiness had overcome the hundred retainers, but Ito thrust his dagger into his thigh, and by the sharp pain he experienced contrived to keep himself awake. Whilst he watched the door opened, and in stole a beautiful woman who approached the Prince and seemed to try to bewitch him. But the brave unsleeping eyes of Ito prevented her evil spell from taking effect, and at last she retired frustrated. Once more the soldier kept watch with the same result. And now the Prince began to improve in health, and O Toyo kept away, and the guard no longer slumbered. These events convinced Ito that the beautiful being who entered at night, and passed as O Toyo, was really a ghoul. Accordingly he made plans to slay her that evening. The vampire showed fight, and seized a halbert as he tried to strike her with his dagger, but suddenly she threw away her weapon, and taking the form of a cat, sprang on to the roof, and succeeded in escaping to the mountains. There she was finally slain by hunters sent in chase of her by the Prince. Prince Hizen recovered his health, and Ito Soda was handsomely rewarded for his valour."*

The above story is characteristic of the Japanese vampire, which usually favours the cat form, and is credited with assuming the semblance of its victims after their demise to enable it to drain the life-forces of those who had been nearest and dearest to them. Possibly the superstition is connected with the curious idea that prevails in China, according to which the dead are empowered to arise for a short time, and do evil deeds, if at one and the same moment a dog is beneath the bed on which the corpse reposes, and a cat on the roof which covers it. Therefore cats and dogs are driven away from a house that contains a dead body.

A slightly modified form of the same superstition is found in Eastern Europe, where it is believed that an innocent man may become a vampire after his death if a cat or a bird accidentally cross his corpse before its burial.

It is clear from these examples that the explanation of the widespread dislike to the entry of a cat or other animal into a death chamber is the belief that the creature is a potential vampire, which may infect the corpse by its mere proximity. A bite is known to be fatal; but it is not indispensable to such a

* NOTE. According to the "Sunday Express" of July 14, 1929, there is a report from Japan, " that the vampire cat of Nabéshima is once more about its nightly business—bewitching the beautiful wives of the descendants of the old two-sworded fighting Samurai."

result when the vampire is in animal form ; so that the ordinary evidence of death caused by the attack of one of these monsters, viz. the mark of a bite in the back of the victim's neck, may be absent without impugning the hypothesis.

A striking example of what appears to be a genuine case of vampirism is related by Dr. Henry More.

" Johannes Cuntius, a citizen and alderman of Pentach, in Silesia, when about sixty years of age, died somewhat suddenly, as the result of a kick from his horse. At the moment of his death a black cat rushed into the room, jumped on to the bed, and scratched violently at his face. Both at the time of his death and that of his funeral a great tempest arose—the wind and snow ' made men's bodies quake and their teeth chatter in their heads.' The storm is said to have ceased with startling suddenness as the body was placed under the ground. Immediately after the burial, however, stories began to circulate of the appearance of a phantom which spoke to people in the voice of Cuntius. Remarkable tales were told of the consumption of milk from jugs and bowls, of milk being turned into blood, of old men being strangled, children taken out of cradles, altar-cloths being soiled with blood, and poultry killed and eaten. Eventually it was decided to disinter the body. It was found that all the bodies buried above that of Cuntius had become putrefied and rotten, but his skin was tender and florid, his joints by no means stiff, and when a staff was put between his fingers they closed around it and held it fast in their grasp. He could open and shut his eyes, and when a vein in his leg was punctured the blood sprang out as fresh as that of a living person. This happened after the body had been in the grave for about six months. Great difficulty was experienced when the body was cut up and dismembered, by the order of the authorities, by reason of the resistance offered ; but when the task was completed, and the remains consigned to the flames, the spectre ceased to molest the natives or interfere with their slumbers or health."

It is interesting to find that similar beliefs may still be traced in England. Thus Henderson relates how the Northumbrians at once put a cat to death if it crosses a human corpse. Nor is it solely among the uncultured that these ideas persist. To many of my readers it may come as something of a shock to discover that even among educated people such doctrines are not dead to-day. A Roman Catholic writer, Mr. Montague Summers, seriously upholds the actuality of incubi and succubi, and quotes " many and great names, men of science, men of learning, men of authority, men to whom the world yet looks up with admiration, nay, with reverence and love," to support his contention.

Happy are the sceptics, he says "that they do not, will not, realise the monstrous things that lie only just beneath the surface of our cracking civilisation."

BIBLIOGRAPHY

"A Faithful Narrative," p. 18. By Samuel Petto. Printed London, 1652.

"Antidote against Atheism." By Henry More, D.D. Pub. about 1600.

"Historical Essay." By Francis Hutchinson. Pub. London, 1718.

"History of Whalley," p. 216. By T. D. Whitaker. Pub. London, 1818.

"The History of Magic." By Joseph Ennemoser. Trans. by William Howitt. Pub. by Henry G. Bohn, London, 1854.

"Myths and Legends of Japan," p. 265. By F. Hadland Davis. Pub. by George G. Harrap & Co., London, 1920.

"The History of Witchcraft and Demonology." By Montague Summers. Pub. by Kegan Paul, Trench, Trübner & Co., London, 1926.

CHAPTER XXV

CAT GENII AND FAMILIARS

" These be the adept's doctrines—every element
Is peopled with its separate race of spirits.
The airy Sylphs on the blue ether float ;
Deep in the earthy cavern skulks the Gnome ;
The sea-green Naiad skims the ocean-billow,
And the fierce fire is yet a friendly home
To its peculiar sprite—the salamander."

(*Anon.*)

SPIRITUALISTIC sorcery is chiefly concerned with invocatory rites based upon the belief in what are known as Elemental spirits. From the very earliest times of which we have any record the existence of such intelligences has been credited. Ancient Assyrian incantations are addressed to these beings, and the belief of the Egyptians in their existence is evidenced by the 108th chapter of " The Book of the Dead," which is entitled " The Chapter of Knowing the Spirits of the West."

Even to-day the mysterious land of Egypt, like other countries that acknowledge the sway of Islam, is inhabited by untold multitudes of fairy beings known as Ginn. These spirits have much in common with the human species, for they know birth, maturity, decay, and death. They are of both sexes, and follow various occupations, some being slaves, and others free. In religion they conform to the creeds of men. But they differ, in that the normal span of their lives is about three hundred years; and in being usually invisible, but possessing the power to assume all sorts of weird and ghostly shapes which may resemble men, animals, or monsters. They seem to be closely connected in a sympathetic union with our race, for every human child is said to have its own special companion Ginn, who is born at the same hour. Throughout the Moslem world the art of invoking these beings is cultivated by a large number of people. Certain Moslem sorcerers are even said to have married female Ginn, and it is claimed that those whose occult lore enables them to command these spirits, can perform miracles through their instrumentality.

In confirmation of the above, we may quote Lane, who in his preface to his translation of "The Arabian Nights," says: "I have resided in a land where genii are still firmly believed to obey the summons of a magician or the owner of a talisman, and to act in occurrences of every day; and I have listened to stories of their deeds related as facts by persons of the highest respectability."

And the same renowned author and traveller, in his work on "Modern Egyptians," relates the following striking story of one of these familiars which manifested as a cat. He says: "The sheykh Khalee'l El-Meda'bighee, one of the most celebrated of the 'ool'ama of Egypt, and author of several works on various sciences, who died, at a very advanced age, during the period of my former visit to this country, used to relate the following anecdote. He had, said he, a favourite black cat, which always slept at the foot of his mosquito curtain. Once, at midnight, he heard a knocking at the door of his house; and his cat went and opened the hanging shutter of his window, and called, 'Who is there?' A voice replied, 'I am such a one' (mentioning a strange name), 'the gin'nee: open the door.' 'The lock,' said the sheykh's cat, 'has had the name (of God) pronounced upon it.' 'Then throw me down,' said the other, 'two cakes of bread.' 'The bread-basket,' answered the cat at the window, 'has had the name pronounced upon it.' 'Well,' said the stranger, 'at least give me a drink of water.' But he was answered that the water-jar had been secured in the same manner; and asked what he was to do, seeing that he was likely to die of hunger and thirst; the sheykh's cat told him to go to the door of the next house; and went there also himself, and opened the door, and soon after returned. Next morning the sheykh deviated from a habit which he had constantly observed: he gave, to the cat, half of the fatee'reh upon which he breakfasted, instead of a little morsel, which he was wont to give; and afterwards said, 'O my cat, thou knowest that I am a poor man : bring me then a little more gold' ; upon which words the cat immediately disappeared, and he saw it no more."

In Provence, as in Egypt, belief in genii is even yet extant. Branch Johnson writes that it is unwise for belated travellers on the Crau " to answer any greeting after sundown, lest it come from a Matagot or Matagon, one of those mysterious occupants of the fields and earth who, neither good enough to be angels nor bad enough to be devils, have become mischievous to human beings. . . . Usually they appear as cats," though sometimes in other forms, and " their chief characteristic is that they move with incredible rapidity from place to place, so that it is useless to attempt flight from them. Only by their blazing eyes may they be seen, or by a pale luminosity which emanates from their bodies ; and the traveller must cover his eyes and recite a *Paternoster* and, calling upon his Saints, hurry through the darkness to the safety of a lighted cottage."

In prehistoric Japan, as elsewhere, human sacrifice was a recognised institution, and spirits of the wilds were worshipped in fear, and claimed many victims. Thus a bow might miraculously appear on the roof of a man's house, to signify that his eldest maiden daughter must be sacrificed to the Deity of Wild Animals. And in compliance with the cruel demand, she would be buried alive to enable the monster to devour her flesh.

Hadland Davies relates one of the legends that preserve the memory of such ancient customs, and is especially interesting to us, since the evil spirit of the mountains who demanded human sacrifice was in feline form. To recount the tale as briefly as possible : " A certain bold knight once rested in a ruined temple among the mountains where he had been travelling alone. He was quickly asleep, but when midnight approached his repose was rudely disturbed. Close beside him a party of unearthly cats were dancing, and loudly and repeatedly shouting, ' Tell it not to Shippeitarō ! ' The mysterious hour of midnight fell, and the feline party disappeared, whilst our hero, who seems to have been of a most phlegmatic disposition, returned to dreamland. Next day he resumed his journey, presently arriving on the outskirts of a village, the inhabitants of which appeared to be in terrible trouble. The knight asked the cause of their distress, and learned that the unfortunate people must that very day deliver their annual tribute of the fairest maiden among them to the evil feline genii of the mountain. This being would drag her to its lair in the ruined temple where he had spent the night, and there devour her. On hearing this tale of woe the knight recalled his experience of the previous evening, and asked who

Shippeitarō might be. 'Why!' replied his hearer, 'he is a big, brave dog belonging to the headman of our Prince.' 'Ha!' thought the knight, 'he could disperse those phantom cats!' And he hastened off to secure his services. He was quickly successful, and returned with his canine friend. The cage was already prepared for the unfortunate victim, but Shippeitarō took her place in it, and the knight, helped by several youths, carried the litter to the temple. The young men were afraid to remain in such haunted precincts, so the knight and the dog kept lonely watch, until at midnight the phantom cats reappeared. This time an enormous tom-cat of ferocious mien accompanied them as leader, and sprang around the cage, uttering screams of anticipatory delight. Suddenly the knight flung open the door, and Shippeitarō sprang forth, and grabbed the great cat between his teeth. His master quickly drew forth his sword, and slew the monstrous brute. The lesser cats flew in panic, and Shippeitarō instantly dispersed them. So the evil mountain spirits no longer levied bloody toll on the village, and the valiant knight modestly bestowed all the praise on his canine helper Shippeitarō." It is probably the influence of such legends as this which accounts for the superstitious dread with which cats are regarded in Japan. The Nipponese cats seem to be considered under a curse, and live a pariah existence which is supposed to be aided by supernatural resources. They are credited—in common with badgers and foxes—with the power of bewitching human beings, and are hated and dreaded accordingly. Perhaps because of similar attributed powers, the Japanese cat is coupled with the serpent as one of the only two creatures who forebore to weep when Lord Buddha died.

The widespread sources of the domestic animal familiar so often met with in British witchcraft, will be apparent from such instances as those narrated above. The belief is of enormous antiquity, and, in its higher manifestations had out-grown most of such crude expressions as those we have just been considering, but like all ancient religions which the Christian Churches contacted, was debased and degraded to its original status by the misrepresentations of the votaries of the newer creed. The genii, jinn, fairies, hobgoblins, elves, and sprites, were all classed as devils, whilst the priests and priestesses of the dethroned gods were persecuted and maligned as the accomplices of Satan and malicious sorcerers. History has recorded the horrible cruelty by which Christianity, in defiance even of its own teachings, established its power and stamped out opposition.

In considering the following accounts of witches tried in Britain, we can scarcely emphasise sufficiently that they are derived from biased sources; and also that almost all the confessions were extracted by torture, so that however fairly and accurately they may be recorded, they cannot have much value as evidence. Witchcraft would undoubtedly assume a totally different aspect, if a sympathetic contemporary account were available, as unfortunately is not the case.

Let us glance at some of the contemporary records that furnish concrete examples of the familiar demon in cat form. One of these precious documents is quoted in the columns of the "Spiritual Magazine" of July, 1877, page 311, and relates how Dame Alice de la Poer was "delated" by her husband, John de la Poer, to Richard, Bishop of Ossory in the fourteenth century. Part of the charge against the unfortunate lady was "That the aforesaid Dame Alice was wont to, and in the constant habit of, sleeping in one and the same bed with a certain devil, whose name was Roland Fitz Artis, who might sometimes be seen in the shape of a black cat, and at other times in that of a mangy dog," etc.

An exceptionally detailed and interesting record of an attendant sprite or familiar cat is to hand in the case of Elizabeth Francis, who was tried at Chelmsford, in 1556. According to Cooper, Elizabeth "learned this arte of witchcraft of hyr grandmother, whose nam mother Eue. Item when shee taughte it her, she counseiled her to renounce God and His worde and to geue of her bloudde to Sathan (as she termed it), wyche she delyuered her in the lykenesse of a whyte spotted Catte, and taughte her to feede the sayde Catte with breade and mylke, and she dyd so, also she taughte her to cal it by the name of Sathan and to kepe it in a basket. Item that euery tyme that he did any thynge for her, she sayde that he required a drop of bloude, which she gaue him by prycking herselfe sometime in one place and then in an other. When shee had kept this Cat by the space of XV or XVI yeare, and as some saye (though vntruly) beinge wery of it, she came to one mother Waterhouse her neyghbour, she brought her this cat in her apron and taught her as she was instructed by her grandmother Eue, telling her that she must cal him Sathan, and geue him of her bloude and breade and milke as before.—Mother Waterhouse receyued this cat of this Frances wife in the order as is before sayde. She (to trye him what he coulde do) wyld him to kyll a hog of her owne, which he dyd, and she gaue him for his labour a chicken, which he fyrste required of her and a drop of her blod. And this she gaue him at all times when he dyd anythynge for her, by pricking her hand or face and putting the bloud to hys mouth wyche he sucked, and forthwith wold lye downe in hys pot againe wherein she kepte him. Another tym she rewarded hym as before, wyth a chicken and a droppe of her bloud, which chicken he eate vp cleane as he didde al the rest, and she cold fynde remaining neyther bones nor fethers. Also she said that when she wolde wyl him to do any thynge for her, she wolde say her Pater noster in laten. Item, this mother Waterhouse confessed that shee fyrst turned this Cat into a tode by this meanes, she kept the cat a great while in woll [wool] in a pot, and at length being moued by pouertie to occupie the woll, she praied in the name of the father and of the sonne and of the holy ghost that it wolde turne into a tode, and forthwith it was turned into a tode, and so kept it in the pot without woll."*

In 1579 two cases were tried at Windsor in which the Cat Familiar took a prominent position.

"Mother Deuell, dwellynge nigh the Ponde in Windesore, hath a Spirite in the shape of a Blacke Catte, and calleth it Gille, whereby she is aided in her Witchcrafte, and she daiely feedeth it with Milke, mingled with her owne bloud. Mother Margaret, dwellying in the Almeshouse at Windesore, dooeth feede a kitlyng or Feende by her named Ginnie with crummes of bread and her owne blood." (*Rehearsal.*)

In 1582, at St. Osyth, in Essex, Thomas Rabbet, aged eight, stated that his mother, Ursley Kemp, "hath foure seuerall spirites, the one called Tyffin, the other Tittey, the third Pigine, and the fourth Iacke: and being asked of what colours they were, saith that Tyttey is like a little grey cat, Tyffin is like a white lambe, Pygine is black like a toad, and Iacke is blacke like a cat. And hee saith, hee hath seen his mother at times to giue thē beere to drinke, and of a white Lofe or Cake to eate, and saith that in the night time the said sprites will come to his mother, and sucke blood of her vpon her armes and other places of her body."

In 1646, when the witches of Huntingdonshire were tried, Francis Moore confessed that "one goodwife Weed† gave her a white Cat, telling her, that if she would deny God, and affirme the same by her bloud, then whomsoever she cursed, and sent that Cat unto, they should dye shortly after. Whereupon the said Examinate saith that shee did deny God, and in affirmation thereof shee pricked her finger with a thorne, whence issued bloud, which the Cat presently licked, and the said good wife (*sic*) Weed named the Cat *Tissy*. And she further saith that she killed the said Cat about a yeare since." The above case is particularly interesting since it affords us a glimpse of the ritual employed by the cult. The denial of God must be understood as a specific denial of the Christian deity, since the witches appear

* "Witches at Chelmsford," p. 24–32. Philobiblon Soc., VIII.

† Elizabeth Weed of Great Catworth.

to have worshipped Janus or Diana, or their Egyptian prototypes, as we have noted in other chapters.

The blood-sucking cat familiars must not be confused with cat vampires. The witches taught and encouraged them to partake of the vital fluid in order to create a psychic copula. As we may see from the Hebrew scriptures, the blood was regarded as the very life and soul of its possessor; even after it was separated from the body, the personality enshrined within it persisted. Thus we read how Jehovah said to Cain after the murder of Abel, "The voice of thy brother's blood crieth unto me from the ground" (Gen. iv. 10). And it is again and again reiterated that the blood of animals slain for food must on no account be eaten. Such ideas were not confined to the Jewish race, but can be traced in almost every age and country. To drink the blood of another is to establish a mystical and close communion of the soul.

The witches desired full control of their familiar animals, so followed the ancient means.

> "I have heard old beldams
> Talk of familiars in the shape of mice,
> Rats, ferrets, weasels, and I wot not what,
> That have appear'd, and suck'd, some say, their blood"

is the testimony of the seventeenth-century dramatists, Ford and Dekker.

In 1618 two old women were hanged at Lincoln upon the charge of having bewitched the Earl of Rutland's children by means of a cat familiar. One of them confessed that she rubbed Lady Catherine's handkerchief upon her cat and bade it fly, and that the cat had thereupon cried "mew." She was hanged upon this evidence. The children died of what seems to have been low fever. But a monument raised to their memory in Bottesford Church, near Nottingham, bears an inscription stating that they died in infancy from wicked practices of sorcery. Apparently the Cat was the witch's familiar. Her mere association with the creature was sufficient to condemn the old woman as one who "used enchantments, and dealt with familiar spirits" (2 Kings xxi. 6).

The famous scholar and poet, Edward Fairfax, who flourished in the seventeenth century, and translated Tasso's "Godfrey of Bouillon" into such beautiful English that he is said to rank equally with Spenser as the father of modern English verse, was a firm believer in witchcraft as an evil and destructive force. According to his own account, written with obvious sincerity, his experiences made him "a woeful witness" to its reality.

Accordingly, in 1621, we find him prosecuting six women whom he alleged had bewitched his three daughters. Marvellous to relate, the accused were all acquitted when tried at York Assizes: and it is to this we owe our possession of the "Dæmonolgia," the volume written by Fairfax to justify his action. Much curious information may be found therein about the six witches "of whom five fall in my knowledge." Two of them possessed familiar spirits in cat form, whilst another owned a familiar obscure in kind, "a deformed thing with many feet, black of colour, rough with hair, the bigness of a cat, the name of it unknown." The daughter of this woman was one of the owners of the cat familiars, "her spirit, a white cat spotted with black and named Inges." A third woman who had been "reputed a witch for many years" was waited upon by "a spirit in the shape of a great black cat named Gibbe" for more than forty years. Of the three remaining witches, one is said to have had a bird as familiar, and the others apparently had none, But in their troubled dreams, the bewitched children saw a seventh woman who tormented them, and she possessed a spirit "in the likeness of a white cat," named Fillie, which had attended her for twenty years. The eldest girl, Helen Fairfax, used to fall into "deadly extasie" in which she had fearful visions of cats. One of these displayed human teeth "when it opened its mouth to blow on her." Another endeavoured to prevent the Bible being read, and the hand Helen used to beat it off was rendered useless. Her sister Elizabeth also suffered ghastly dreams, and the two fell into "a great extremity of sickness." And there we must leave them, for unfortunately the narrative is unfinished, or its end is lost.

George Giffard, minister of God's word at Malden, in 1603, in his "Dialogue concerning Witches and Witchcrafts," has handed down to us the story of a witch who employed a familiar in the form of a cat to destroy three hogs and a cow belonging to a farmer who had incurred her hatred. But "the man suspecting, burnt a pig alive, and as she sayd, her cat would never go thither any more."

It would be interesting could we follow the train of thought which moved the farmer to his horrid sacrifice, and learn if it were offered to Jehovah or to Satan, but Giffard does not relate. Neither does he condemn the fear-inspired action. Writing of another witch, an old Essex woman, who was tried in 1588, but whose name is not recorded, he informs us that she "confessed all: which was this in effect: that she had three spirits: one like a cat, which she called Lightfoot, another like a toad, which she called Lunch, the third like a weasill, which she called Makeshift. This Lightfoot, she said, one Mother Barlie of W. solde her aboue sixteene yeares agoe for an ouen cake, and told her the Cat would doe her good seruice, if she woulde, she might send her of her errand: this Cat was with her but a while, but the Weasill and the Toad came and offered their seruice: the Cat would kill kine, the Weasill would kill horses, the Toad would plague men in their bodies. . . . Another Mother W. 'sayd she had a spirit in the likenesse of a yellow dun cat.'" (*Giffard*, pp. 19–39.)

And again, Giffard confronts the incredulous with much general evidence.

"What say you to this? That the witches have their spirits, some hath one, some hath more, as two, three, four, or five. Some in one likeness and some in another, as like cats, weasils, toads, or mise, whom they nourish with milk or with a chicken, or by letting them suck now and then a drop of blood: whom they call when they be offended with any and send them to hurt them in their bodies, yea to kill them and to kill their cattell."

According to the abridger of the Criminal Record, an instance of such witchcraft occurred in August, 1661, when several witches were condemned and executed, among them being Margaret Hutcheson, against whom "it is lybelled," that she "threatened John Boost for calling her a witch: and within a few days thereafter, by throwing a piece of raw flesh into his house, which was burnt in the fire (after dogs and catts had refused to eat it) a disease seized on his cat, which made her to fight and sweat to death; that she threatened John Bell for contending with her husband, and immediately thereafter, three cats entered to his house, which were like to devour them, whereupon two of his children died, and his wife contracted a long disease."

Two unusual points seem to call for attention in this case: first, that dogs and cats refused to partake of the witch-tainted flesh, and, second, that a cat was the victim of the witch's malice; though cats were also the instruments whereby she carried out her fell designs.

It would be an easy task to give many more well-attested examples, proving how firmly established was the strange belief that the attendant spirits of necromancers were usually in feline form. But space compels us to be content with those we have already cited, and we must only allow ourselves to remark a few of the numerous allusions to the idea which may be found in contemporary literature, ere closing this chapter.

In Shakespeare's "Macbeth," which is said to have been penned about 1606, the three witches who figure so prominently are represented in conjunction with a tawny cat. One of them herself bore the name of Graymalkin, which is an old name for a cat, and when the three assembled in their gloomy cavern to prepare their evil enchantments against the king, the first witch commenced proceedings with what she evidently regarded as the portentous words:

"Thrice the brinded cat hath mew'd."

It seems probable that the ominous feline was her own familiar, who served her by its powers of second sight.

In the old play, "Love for Love" (1695), an allusion is made to the then prevalent belief that witches often suckled imps in animal form by means of supernumerary teats, which were said to secrete milk for their nourishment.

We find Angelica, in Act two, calling out in raillery to her Nurse and ancient Uncle: "Look to it, Nurse; I can bring Witness that you have a great unnatural teat under your Left Arm, and he another; and that you Suckle a young Devil in the shape of a Tabby-Cat by turns, I can."

Writing more than one hundred years later than Shakespeare, the poet Gay, in the fable of "The Old Woman and her Cats,"

THE OLD WOMAN AND HER CATS
From an early edition of "Gay's Fables."

has drawn for us a striking picture of the ideas that were generally accepted in his lifetime. The moral he would inculcate is:

"Who friendship with a knave hath made
Is judg'd a partner in the trade."

And around this theme the poem is composed; but for us its interest lies in the insight it affords to the belief so firmly held by our forebears that the mere ownership of cats proved an old woman to be a witch.

Gay describes "A wrinkled hag of wicked fame," who "mumbles forth her backward prayers, An untam'd scold of four-score years." But her reputation as a witch was not dependent on such trifles as these, but on her association with "a num'rous brood" of hungry cats.

> "Teaz'd with their cries her choler grew
> And thus she sputter'd. Hence ye crew.
> Fool that I was to entertain
> Such imps, such fiends, a hellish train!
> Had ye been never hous'd and nurst
> I, for a witch had n'er been curst.
> To you I owe, that crouds of boys
> Worry me with eternal noise;
> Straws laid across my pace retard,
> The horse-shoe's nail'd (each threshold's guard)
> The stunted broom the wenches hide,
> For fear that I should up and ride;
> They stick with pins my bleeding seat,
> And bid me show my secret teat."

The cats are represented as replying that they are equal sufferers by the partnership of which the old woman complains, since they might otherwise have lived in credit as "beasts of chace."

> "'Tis infamy to serve a hag;
> Cats are thought imps, her broom a nag;
> And boys against our lives combine,
> Because, 'tis said, your cats have nine."

BIBLIOGRAPHY

"Rehearsall both straung and true." Printed London, 1579.

"Discoverie of Witchcraft." By Reginald Scot. Printed London, 1584.

"Discourse of the subtill Practices of Devilles." By George Giffard. Printed London, 1587.

"Mystery of Witchcraft," p. 91. By Thomas Cooper. Pub. London, 1617.

"Witches of Huntingdon," pp. 1–12. By John Davenport. Pub. London, 1646.

" Dæmonologia." By Edward Fairfax. Written 1612. Pub. privately by the " Philobiblon Society," 1859.

" The Witch of Edmonton," Act II, Scene 1. By John Ford and Thomas Dekker. Printed about 1630.

" Fables by the late Mr. Gay," 4th edition. Printed for J. Ponson and J. Watts, London, 1733. First pub. 1726.

" An Account of the Manners and Customs of the Modern Egyptians," pp. 307–8. By Edward William Lane. Pub. by Nattali & Bond, London, 1835.

" The Arabian Nights' Entertainments." Trans. from the Arabic, by Edward William Lane. Pub. by Bliss, Sands & Foster, London.

" A Historical Account of the Belief in Witchcraft in Scotland." By Charles Kirkpatrick Sharpe, Esq. Pub. by Hamilton, Adams & Co., London, 1884.

" Myths and Legends of Japan," pp. 269–70, 342. By F. Hadland Davis. Pub. by George G. Harrap & Co., London.

" Folktales of Provence," p. 107. By W. Branch Johnson. Pub. by Chapman & Hall, London, 1927.

CHAPTER XXVI

CAT AS OMEN OF DEATH

IN the dawning hours of human consciousness, man, gazing with wondering awe on the strange world that surrounded him, saw in the lower animals manifestations of the Divine. The very inarticulateness of the brute voices seemed to him to constitute an oracle calling for reverend interpretation as the speech of The Unknown God. The hidden ways, and sudden appearances of beast or bird when least expected, were revelations of The Great Spirit's will. The Unembodied and Unmanifest could only apprise man of His Presence and Purpose through the bodied and manifest ; so the beauteous or terrible creatures were His honoured mediums and ministers.

Even in these days of Agnosia, when the sum of man's knowledge is that he knows nothing, oracles and omens have not entirely ceased, if we may accept the evidence of those who claim to have had first-hand experience of them. Science, although it has discredited so many ancient beliefs, and laid bare such innumerable falsehoods, has, on the other hand, by its discoveries of hitherto unknown laws, and investigations into psychic phenomena, rendered credible many ancient records that quite recently were considered to be mere legend or romance. No longer is it possible to regard the mysterious and occult as matter *pour rire.* But the gods and their prophets have ever spoken in parables, and do so still. Things which cannot be told in words—even if a common language exists between the communicator and the recipient—may be expressed by pictorial analogy, and for those who lack a common language, this is the only means of conveying ideas. Beings on another plane, whose conditions of life are totally different from our own, who normally are invisible and inaudible to us, may reasonably be supposed to use this simplest and most natural mode of communication when they would forewarn us of some future happening. The art of the Soothsayer teaches that nothing occurs accidentally, but that events and all nature stand in secret connection with each other. Even the passing forms of clouds, or the flight of birds, as well as the cries and movements of animals are fraught with meaning to him who comprehends the unity substanding apparent diversity.

Cicero explains the possibility of foretelling the future by asserting that prophecy does not concern itself with that which has no existence, but only with that which is not yet revealed; for everything exists although the time has not yet arrived to unfold it, "*sunt enim omnia, sed tempore ab sunt.*"

The Cat, because of her unique position in symbolism as the representative of Hecate, goddess of Death, is, as we might expect, a widely respected omen of approaching mortality. Her connection with the world of night and shadow, and her silent, unexpected appearances, emphasize this aspect, whilst her wonderful variation in colour and modes of expression, make her to be regarded as almost a language in herself.

Let us glance at some of the interpretations that occult lore has placed upon her actions, for it would have us see in certain of them, solemn warnings that the termination of mundane life for ourselves or others is near; and whether we believe or disbelieve in omens, the intense interest of such a subject must be admitted by us all.

The Italian naturalist, Ulisse Aldrovandi, who flourished in the sixteenth century, has recorded how when Stefano Cardano lay dying, a cat appeared unexpectedly before him, gave a loud cry, and vanished. He also tells us of a cat which scratched the breast of a woman, who, recognising in her assailant a supernatural being, died a few days later.

Christianity, of course, identified the warning feline apparitions so often seen by the dying, with the devil; and in Tuscany it was said that when a man desired death, Satan passed before his bed in the form of any animal except the lamb, but more particularly favoured that of a he-goat, a cock, or a cat.

In Germany, to the original belief that a black cat upon the bed of a sick man foretold his approaching death, Christian superstition added that if it was seen upon a grave, the feline signified that the departed was in the devil's power.

Professor Rochholtz records a German belief that two cats fighting each other is to a sick man an omen of approaching death. Gubernatis thinks that "the two cats are probably another form of the children's game in Piedmont and Tuscany, called the game of souls, in which the devil and the angel come to dispute for the soul. Of the two cats one is probably benignant and the other malignant; they represent perhaps night and twilight."

Both cat and mouse are sacred to the funereal St. Gertrude in Germany. Mice represent the souls of the departed, and suggest another analogy connecting the cat with the idea of death. St. Gertrude is usually represented as surrounded by their small forms. Sometimes she is the cat who slays them.

In Normandy it used to be believed that a tortoiseshell cat, if she climbed a tree, foretold death by accident, whilst if a black cat crossed a pedestrian's path in moonlight, it presaged death from an epidemic.

To dream of cats is considered as an ill omen. The learned Ephesian, Artemidorus, who wrote a "Treatise on Dreams" in the reign of Antoninus Puis, said that to dream one was badly scratched in fighting with a cat foreshadowed sickness and trouble.

Other writers say that to dream of a black cat at Christmas is an omen of a dangerous illness in the following year, whilst to dream of a cat with threatening eyes, or to play with a cat in a dream means one has fair-seeming, but false friends.

Modern stories of warning cats very often suggest that the messenger is of unearthly origin. It would seem as if the lowly familiar form of our household pet was selected for the grim office of Death's ambassador so that the information might be conveyed to the affected man as gently and unalarmingly as possible.

I have here brought together some representative cases. The first of these is related by Sir Walter Scott, who received the account of it from the medical man under whose observation it occurred. He says that if he were at liberty to name this gentleman "the rank which he holds in his profession, as well as his attainments in science and philosophy, form an undisputed claim to the most implicit credit." Among this doctor's patients was a well-known man of affairs, honoured for his "unusual steadiness, good sense, and integrity." Although at this period he was much confined to his sick room, and sometimes to bed, yet he still occasionally attended to business and applied his mind, "apparently with all its usual strength and energy, to the conduct of the important affairs entrusted to him." He displayed no symptoms of acute or alarming disease, but his "slowness of pulse, absence of appetite, difficulty of digestion, and constant depression of spirits, seemed to draw their origin from some hidden cause which the patient was determined to conceal." For long the physician vainly endeavoured to discover the source of the mysterious malady, but at last persuaded the sufferer to take him into his confidence. He then said that he knew himself to be dying under the oppression of a fatal disease which consumed his vital powers, and that his case was not a singular one, since a character in the famous novel of "Le Sage" was described as suffering similarly. He was haunted by an apparition so painful and abhorrent to him, that his reason could not combat the persecuting vision, and he had become a wasted victim to an imaginary disease. Its advances had been gradual, and at first were not even disagreeable. The visions had commenced about two or three years previously, when he found himself "from time to time embarrassed by the presence of a large cat, which came and disappeared," how, he could not exactly tell, till the truth was finally forced upon him, and he was "compelled to regard it as no domestic household cat, but as a bubble of the elements, which had no existence" save in his imagination. Still, being rather a friend to cats, he did not mind what he regarded as his imaginary attendant; but within a few months it disappeared, and its place was taken by the apparition of a gentleman-usher. This phantom after persisting a few months, also withdrew, and now a horrible one took their place—the apparition of a skeleton. "Alone, or in company," said the unfortunate victim, "the presence of this last phantom never quits me." The doctor argued in vain to help his patient overcome what he himself felt to be a mere hallucination. He resorted to other means of investigation and cure, but with no success. The patient sank into deeper and deeper dejection, and died in the same distress of mind in which he had spent the latter months of his life.

Whether we agree with the narrator, the actor, and the witness of the facts of this strange story, that its phantom characters were purely hallucinatory or not, the reason of their peculiar appearances remains a mystery, as does the apparent lack of any connecting link between the three. If actual, were they ghosts or elementals, vampires or demons? If appearances only, why such persistence? If symbols of death, why the changing figure? We must leave it to our reader to place his own interpretation on the enigma.

It is well known that certain families are warned by premonitionary symbols when the death of one of their members is imminent. Such signal apparitions are very varied in kind, but in some instances take the form of a phantom animal.

One of the many interesting examples in which a cat has been the foreteller of death is recorded in the "Proceedings of the S.P.R." (Vol. V, p. 156), by Mrs. E. L. Kearney. She tells us how in January, 1892, her grandfather lay ill, and one evening, as she descended the staircase after leaving his room, she saw in the passage a strange cat coming towards her. On perceiving her it ran to hide behind a door which divided the corridor into two, and was so arranged as to be always open. Mrs. Kearney immediately followed the strange animal into its retreat, but was much surprised to find it was not there, nor yet in the remainder of the apartment. The following day her grandfather died. This case gains in significance by being considered in connection with a similar happening in the same family. Mrs. Kearney's mother told her that on the eve of the day when her father died, she had likewise seen a cat which walked around the invalid's bed. Like her daugther, she had eagerly pursued the stranger, but had also found nothing.

Miss Bates, in her remarkable autobiography, tells of a curious incident which occurred at a dinner-party in a house where she was a guest. She had been admiring a pretty little slate-coloured kitten which was seated on the grand piano in the drawing-room, when the ladies were alone after dinner. After the gentlemen joined them, she was deep in conversation with her host, when she noticed a small *black* kitten run past her dress. Miss Bates, being very fond of cats, glanced up, and satisfied herself it was not the slate-coloured kitten which still retained its seat on the piano. Also the newcomer was black. But she thought no more of the matter until the guests had departed, and she and her hostess were retiring to bed. Then, as they went upstairs, her friend said, rather mysteriously: "I think something will happen to-night to you," and afterwards added, "Whilst you were talking to my husband this evening, I saw a black kitten run straight across your dress—just opposite to me." "Well, of course, I saw the kitten," Miss Bates replied, "but there is nothing very remarkable about a black kitten in the house." "*But,*" said her hostess, "*we have no black kitten* in the house or anywhere on the premises. Where did it go to? You never saw it again? No; it was not an ordinary kitten, and I did not suppose till this moment that anyone had seen it but myself." A few weeks after this incident Miss Bates heard of the death of a very dear friend of hers, and realised, "with a shock of pained surprise, that the final state of unconsciousness must have set in" on the very evening when she was enjoying herself at the dinner-party. "How terrible," she thought, "that no word or sign should have come to me." Then suddenly she remembered the kitten, and found it "impossible not to ask in the depths of my heart whether, perchance, the spirit of my faithful friend had been trying to send me some symbol of her approaching death."

Inkster Gilbertson, writing in the "Occult Review," relates a story told to him by Dr. Tindall, the President of the Christian Occult Society, of an experience of his own. "As a young man he lived with his parents in Bayswater. It was a bright day, and the door leading to the backyard having been left open a black cat suddenly rushed into the house, and darting about from side to side as if it were mad, ran through the hall and up the staircase to the first landing, where it climbed up to the window and tore the linen blind to pieces before making good its escape.

"The doctor had two aunts living together at Pimlico, his father's sisters, and five or ten minutes after the incident just recorded a cab from their house drove up to the door and a woman asked for the doctor's father. On seeing him she immediately blurted out: 'Your sister has fallen down dead.'

"The news was only too true, and the doctor has never forgotten the tragic occurrence, for his father did not recover from the shock it gave him and died within a year afterwards."

A very interesting case of a ghostly white kitten, whose appearance foretold disaster, is given in the "Journal of the S.P.R." for January, 1927. In this instance the cat was "seen many times over a period of thirteen years," and on several occasions by two persons at the same time, "one of whom called attention to it after it had been plainly perceived by the other. Sometimes the cat was apparently felt as well as seen. And "every such appearance of the 'white kitten' was shortly followed either by the death of a person related or the beginning of the fatal illness." Dr. W. F. Prince, who relates this case, says that a curious feature of it is that "years before the first hallucination of a 'white kitten,' such a kitten was owned by one of the afterward witnesses, and mysteriously disappeared, with a consequent rather poignant effect upon the emotions of this witness. If it could be supposed that in some unknown fashion there could come into her mind premonitions of the death of relatives, it might be that by some obscure mechanism, the subconscious would call up the image of the cat that had disappeared and probably died. But one of the witnesses was of a younger generation and had no recollection of the historical cat, and consequently no feelings whatever about it."

The basis of these strange beliefs and stories would seem to be the doctrine embodied in the teachings of almost all schools of religious philosophy; that everything below is in correspondence with the things above, and that visible objects have their spiritual counterparts in the invisible realm: also that beings ordinarily invisible to us may assume sensible form for the purpose of presenting a symbolic message to him who can interpret the code.

BIBLIOGRAPHY

"Opera Omnia." By Ulisse Aldrovandi. Printed 1599–1668.

"Letters on Demonology and Witchcraft," 2nd edition, pp. 26–32. By Sir Walter Scott. Pub. by John Murray, London, 1831.

"Zoological Mythology," Vol. II, p. 67. By Angelo Gubernatis. Pub. by Trübner & Co., London, 1872.

"Seen and Unseen," p. 124. By E. Katherine Bates. Pub. by Greening & Co., Ltd., London, 1908.

"Animal Ghosts," p. 50. By Elliott O'Donnell. Pub. by Wm. Rider & Son, Ltd., London, 1913.

"The Occult Review." Article by Inkster Gilbertson. Pub. by Wm. Rider & Son, Ltd., London.

"Les Manifestations Metapsychiques et les Animaux," p. 98. By Ernest Bozzano. Editions, Jean Meyer. Pub. Paris, 1926.

"Journal of the Society for Psychical Research." Pub. at the Society's Rooms, London, 1927.

CHAPTER XXVII

CLAIRVOYANT CATS

THE Egyptians named the Cat *Mau*, which signifies the Seer (from *mau*, to see), perhaps because they associated it with the symbol of the all-seeing Eye of Horus. But occult lore has always credited Puss with considerable powers of clairvoyance, and investigation of modern instances confirms the idea that she possesses this faculty in no small degree. In this chapter we propose to lay a few of the many recorded cases of her exercise of it before the reader, just remarking, ere we do so, that for the purpose of proving the possibility of psychic happenings, one case that has been clearly demonstrated is as conclusive evidence as a thousand cases would be. Those who deny the phenomena of clairvoyance have to go the length of saying that out of the numerous instances recorded by intelligent witnesses, or, in the case of human beings, actually experienced by the recorders themselves, there is not one which is not either a delusion or a deliberate fabrication. Such a position is not only manifestly absurd, but closes the gates of innumerable avenues of knowledge by denying the value of actual testimony. Where all is an unfathomable mystery, dogmatic materialism has no foundation on which to rest, and cannot for a moment be upheld by the truly philosophic.

The following is an interesting example of the violent fear of a cat in the presence of an evil ghostly manifestation. The Rev. J. G. Wood, so well known as a naturalist, gives the letter describing the case in his " Man and Beast," and it was afterwards investigated and corroborated by the S.P.R. (see their " Journal " for May, 1888). The writer of the letter was a lady who, with her mother, lived in an old house in Boulogne-sur-mer, and the experience she described took place about 1845. She says :

" It was during the winter of 18—— that one evening I happened to be sitting by the side of a cheerful fire in my bedroom, busily engaged in caressing a favourite cat—the illustrious Lady Catherine, now, alas ! no more. She lay in a pensive attitude and a winking state of drowsiness in my lap.

" Although my room might be without candles it was perfectly illuminated by the light of the fire.

" There were two doors—one behind me leading into an apartment which had been locked up for the winter, and another on the opposite side of the room, which communicated with the passage. Mamma had not left me many minutes, and the high-backed, old-fashioned arm-chair which she had occupied remained vacant at the opposite corner of the fireplace. Puss, who lay with her head upon my arm, became more and more sleepy, and I pondered on the propriety of preparing for bed. Of a sudden I became aware that something had affected my pet's equanimity. The purring ceased, and she exhibited rapidly increasing symptoms of uneasiness. I bent down and endeavoured to coax her into quietness, but she instantly struggled to her feet in my lap, and spitting vehemently, with back arched and tail swollen, she assumed a mingled attitude of terror and defiance.

" The change in her position obliged me to raise my head, and on looking up, to my inexpressible horror, I then perceived a little, hideous, wrinkled old hag occupied mamma's chair. Her hands were resting on her knees and her body was stooped forward so as to bring her face into close proximity with mine. Her eyes, piercingly fierce and shining with an overpowering lustre, were glaring at me through them. . . . Those eyes so wonderfully large, and in their expression so intensely wicked, entirely absorbed my senses and precluded my attention to detail. I should have screamed, but my breath was gone, while that terrible gaze so horribly fascinated me I could neither withdraw my eyes nor rise from my seat.

" I had meanwhile been trying to keep a tight hold on the cat, but she seemed resolutely determined not to stay in such an ugly neighbourhood, and after some most desperate efforts, at length succeeded in escaping from my grasp. Leaping over chairs and tables and all that came in her way, she repeatedly threw herself with frightful violence against the top panel of the door which communicated with the disused room. Then, returning in the same frantic manner, she furiously dashed against the door on the opposite side. My terror was now divided, and I looked by turns, now at the old woman whose great staring eyes were constantly fixed on me, and now at the cat who was becoming every instant more frantic. At last the dreadful idea that the animal had gone mad had the effect of restoring my breath, and I screamed loudly. Mamma ran in immediately, and the cat, on the door opening, literally sprang over her head, and for upwards of half an hour ran up and down stairs as if pursued. I turned to point out the object of my terror : it was gone. Under such circumstances the lapse of time is difficult to appreciate, but I should think that the apparition lasted about four or five minutes. Some time afterwards it transpired that a former proprietor of the house, a woman, had hanged herself in that very room."

A somewhat similar account of a cat's terror was published in the " Evening News " of October 5th, 1923, under the heading, " Queer Tales of the Uncanny." It is entitled, " What did the Cat See ? " The writer, H. G. Swindon, says :

" Returning home late one evening a week after my mother's death, I found the cat in a state of great agitation, trying to escape from one of the rooms. I picked her up and placed her in my mother's favourite arm-chair—a chair into which the cat always sprang when my mother vacated it. But now, to my surprise, she flew out of the chair and scratched both my hands badly.

" Three times I placed her in the chair, but each time she jumped out, and attempted to scratch me again, crying piteously. I searched the rooms thoroughly but could find no visible cause for the cat's agitation, so I let her through the door, whereupon she tore up the hall and hid herself in some part of the house. We have had the cat for nine years, and to us who know its great liking for my mother's chair, the cat's sudden aversion was most uncanny. Moreover, since that occasion the cat has never once got into that chair, nor will it remain in the chair if placed there.

" The cat will not even remain in the room with the chair ; if by chance she gets shut in when we go to bed she will scratch the door persistently until one of us goes down and lets her out, whereupon she will purr with pleasure. *Could the cat have seen something that was invisible to human eyes ?* "

An affirmative reply is certainly suggested by consideration of the preceding case, and we may further confirm it by comparison with the story that here follows, which was related by R. D. Mclean in a letter to the " Occult Review " of April, 1924. A friend of this writer " had seen the spirit of one of her deceased relations sitting in a chair in her room. Her cat came into the room, sprang on to the lap of this spirit, was much surprised to find the lap would not hold her, and fell on to the floor greatly dismayed."

R. D. McLean comments: "This would seem to show that animals have difficulty in distinguishing between physical and astral beings." This difficulty is not confined to animals. In the chapter on the Cat as Omen of Death will be found some cases in which human beings failed to distinguish between physical and astral cats.

The famous author, Edward Shanks, writing in "T.P.'s and Cassell's Weekly," on "The Ghost that I like best," relates the following case of clairvoyance in a cat. "My favourite ghost," he says, "is chosen by pure favouritism. It is not much of a ghost, but it is my own, or, at least, I have a long lease of it, which is nearly as good. The house in which I live consists of two old cottages thrown into one. The little room which I use as a study was once, so far as I can judge, the kitchen and sole living-room of the smaller cottage. One day, some fifty years ago, the labourer who lived here, oppressed, I daresay, by the too close presence of his wife and children, hanged himself from a beam in this room. So says village tradition; and there is to this day a large, firm nail in the beam, from which a man might very well hang himself. He might, that is to say if he were a dwarf or without legs: any other sort of man would find it difficult. And, for reasons which will appear, he cannot have been legless. This tradition once heard, vanished from my mind. But after some time it happened that I was working alone past midnight, all the others in the house being long asleep. Not quite alone, for my cat was there—a detestable cat, kept only for mousing, not at all the author's favourite cat who shares his study and his labours with him. Something, I do not know what, made me look round. There, directly beneath the suddenly sinister-looking nail, was the cat, walking up and down with all the motions and the pleased expression of a cat which is rubbing itself against somebody's legs. Up and down she went for several minutes, purring softly, while I sat looking over my shoulder, unable to move. Then I went to bed and left her there, and left all the lamps burning and all the doors open behind me. And yet, strangely, in the morning the pride of possession threw out the horror of the night. It was my ghost, my very own; not a freehold ghost, to be sure, but even a leasehold ghost is more than most people have. . . ."

In this story again the corroborative testimony of a human clairvoyant is lacking, and we have only the action of the cat to guide our judgment, but in the anecdote given below both factors are present. It is related by Miss Bates, who tells how having taken rooms in a newly established house for paying guests she quickly discovered her hostess to be "a convinced and very remarkable psychic." "Curious things happened during the meals—especially at dinner in the evening, when she often put down knife and fork and directed my attention to the far end of the handsome dining-room, where she was wont to see the ghost of her late husband. 'Look, dear Miss Bates! Surely you *must* see him—dear Henry, I mean. There he stands, beard and all, just between the sofa and the wall. I can see him as clearly as I see you!' I am bound to say I never did see 'dear Henry'; but the fine tabby cat certainly saw something in that corner, for it would rush most frantically to the sofa, jump on to one end, and sit staring at Henry (presumably) with its tail stuck out, and its fur rising up, glaring into the corner with a look of combined fear and fascination."

A more easily comprehended, because more material form of clairvoyance is that of feeling beforehand, and reacting to, magnetic or meteorological changes. Many animals, including Man, share this faculty in greater or lesser degree, but perhaps the Cat is particularly sensitive, and weather prophets in olden time would narrowly watch her demeanour when they sought to prognosticate Nature's varying moods.

I myself was instructed by the ancient guardian of my childhood's days to observe the actions of the nursery cat, and regard them as portents of unquestionable veracity that might be fearlessly followed. The little poem quoted below exactly describes the attitude of my own nurse in such matters:

> "Much mystic lore of various use she knew,
> Why coals seem coffins and why flames burn blue,
> If with her tail puss played in frolic mood,
> Herself pursuing, by herself pursued;
> 'See!' cried my Nurse, 'she bids for rain prepare,
> A storm, be sure is gathering in the air;'
> If near the fire the kitten's back was found,
> Frost was at hand, and snows hung hovering round,
> Her paw prophetic rais'd above her ear
> Foretold a visit for some friend was near."

It is almost universally believed that a cat is foretelling rain if it cleans itself behind its ears with a wet forepaw. And in Sicily, when the Rosary is recited for seafarers, the mewing of a cat foretells a tedious voyage.

An actual example of Pussy's sensitiveness to magnetic disturbances is stated to have occurred before the Messina earthquake. A merchant who resided in that town noticed his two cats scratching at the door of his room. As soon as he opened it they flew downstairs to the outer door and scratched there. He let them through, and followed them along the streets and into an open field. Even there their fears were not allayed, but they frantically tore and scratched at the grass. Soon after the first shock of the earthquake came, and the merchant's house, along with many others, thundered in ruins to the ground.

Such instances as we have detailed in this chapter of the clairvoyant powers possessed by cats might be multiplied almost indefinitely. Puss appears to have the freedom of two worlds and to be equally at home in either. Not only does Occult Lore credit Puss with being herself clairvoyant, but teaches that this faculty may be, as it were, torn from her by the violent and unscrupulous votary of Black Magic. We have seen how in the Ritual of the Taigherm, second sight is forced from the gods by means of tortured cats, but now we are about to consider how the same gift is obtained from the material body of the animal, or some portion of it, without there being any necessity to invoke supernatural aid.

Exact directions for obtaining clairvoyance in this manner may be found in the "Talmud" (treatise "Berakhoth," folio 6). After warning the aspirant that "If the eye could perceive the demons that people the universe, existence would be impossible. The demons are more numerous than we are: they surround us on all sides like trenches dug round vineyards," it proceeds to direct him how he may view the evil angels if yet determined so to do. "Let him who desires to see them take of the secundine of a black cat, which is of the first litter of a black cat, which was of the first litter of the mother; and having burnt the same in the fire, beat it to a powder, and put a little of it in his eyes, and then he at once perceives the demons."

Numerous variants of spells to achieve this purpose, in which a cat, or some portion of one is the sole or main ingredient, are described in occult literature. For instance, Francis Barret, in his elaborate occult treatise, "The Magus," under the heading, "Natural Magic," writes: "There are some *collyriums* which make us see the images of spirits in the air or elsewhere; which I can make of the gall of a man and the eyes of a black cat, and some other things."

The idea that the clairvoyance of the Cat is inherent in its material body or a portion thereof, and may be transferred to a human being along with that which contains it is even now persistent among certain primitive peoples. For example, the sorcerers of the Talansi of the Northern Territories of the Gold Coast wear round their necks the complete skin of a small black cat. They consult with spirits in order to guide those who come to them for counsel, and occupy an influential position both in religion and every-day life. The custom varies slightly with locality. Thus a correspondent of "Cat Gossip," writing from Bechuanaland, in 1927, describes a similar practice, saying: "Quite recently I noticed that the head-dress of a native witch-doctor, stated to be made from the skin of a 'wild-cat,' was grey

EGYPTIAN STATUETTE IN BRONZE, DATING FROM THE XVIII DYNASTY

Photo by Spink and Son. Block by "Cat Gossip."

and spotted like the coat of my 'Pariah-cat,' as I call him; the tail dangling behind, being very fluffy, and six-ringed."

Nor is it everywhere thought to be necessary to slay the cat to obtain participation in her powers. Until comparatively recent times in Britain an idea prevailed that the mere proximity of a tortoise-shell cat aided the development of second sight, and children were encouraged to play with them.

Even images of cats have been held potent to convey the gift, an idea probably derived from Egyptian influence, for, in the tombs of Beni-Hasan, figures of cats have been found with the mummies that they might warn the deceased of unseen evil in the other world. The bronze statuette illustrated dates from the XVIII Dynasty.

BIBLIOGRAPHY

"Man and Beast, their Here and Hereafter," Vol. II, pp. 339–343. By the Rev. J. G. Wood. Pub. by Dalby, Isbister & Co., London, 1874.

"Seen and Unseen," p. 114. By E. Katherine Bates. Pub. by Greening & Co., Ltd., London, 1908.

"T.P.'s and Cassell's Weekly." Edited by T. P. O'Connor. Dec. 8th 1923.

"The Occult Review." Edited by Ralph Shirley. Pub. by Rider & Son, London, April, 1924.

"Cat Gossip." Edited by H. C. Brooke. Pub. Taunton, March 30th and October 26th, 1927.

"The Natives of the Northern Territories of the Gold Coast." By A. W. Cardinall. Pub. by George Routledge & Son, London.

CHAPTER XXVIII

CATS AND TELEPATHY

THE faculty of Telepathy is closely allied to that of Clairvoyance, and, though usually latent, it is occasionally unmistakably manifested not only by man, but by many of his sub-human brethren. I am not referring in this chapter to the lower forms of Telepathy, which approximate so closely to instinct that it is difficult to distinguish where one ends and the other commences ; but to the attainment of a state of consciousness in which the material and spatial conditions that ordinarily limit our lives are transcended, and mind may communicate with mind without tangible media.

The Cat is prominent among those animals that share the potentialities of this faculty with man, and is, in some rare cases, so deeply in sympathy with a human being as to be able to establish telepathic relations with him. Needless to say this is a far more difficult matter than the establishment of similar relations between man and man, since no common language exists to facilitate the transmission of thought. The pure idea must be conveyed from brain to brain unclothed in a garment of words, and with sufficient distinctness to overcome the confusion that might so easily arise through the absolute difference of the angles from which such unsimilar beings as a man and a cat must view the same object.

But great as the obstacles are, cases are not wanting to prove that they can be overcome. Such a close telepathy was established between Dumas the Elder and his cat as to enable that gifted animal to determine whether or no his beloved master was returning home at his usual hour from the office where he worked during the day.

At this period of his life Dumas lived with his mother and the cat Mysouff in the Rue de l'Ouest, and acted as a clerk under Louis Philippe, Duc d'Orleans. The office was in the Rue St. Honore, half an hour's walk from Dumas' home, and every morning Mysouff accompanied his master as far as the Rue de Vaugirard, and every afternoon he went again to the same spot to meet and conduct him home, with affectionate welcome.

The extraordinary part of this performance was that if by chance any unforeseen circumstance caused Dumas to vary from his usual time of return, it was useless for his mother to open the door. Mysouff would not stir from his cushion. But when Dumas was faithful to his wonted hour, if she forgot to let Puss out, he would scratch the door until she released him. Therefore she called Mysouff her barometer; it was set fair when Dumas came home to dine, but stormy when he failed to appear.

Another equally remarkable example of the telepathy possible between man and cat is described by Ernest Bozzano, who experienced it at first hand. Below is his own account:

"There are certain days," he says, "when I tarry at my writing until a late hour, and I was thus absorbed by the subject of my work when I became literally possessed by the idea that my cat had need of me. I arose to seek her. After uselessly searching through the house, I went into the garden, and, as darkness obscured the scene, I called her. At last I heard a feeble mewing in the distance. I repeated my call, and the mewing answered me, but the cat did not come. I returned to fetch a lantern, and walked once more through the kitchen-garden towards a field whence it seemed to me the cries arose. After some search I found my cat in a hedge, caught in a trap set for rabbits with its slipknot encircling her neck. If she had struggled for her liberty, she must have been strangled. Happily she had had the intelligence not to stir, but instead, to send a message to her master asking for help. This action of the cat was not the first instance in which a telepathic communication was established between us. On certain occasions our impressions appeared to have misled us; we could find no valid reason for them. In vain we called her all over the garden. Then all at once, by a sort of mental photography, I have seen her imprisoned in a little empty chamber beneath the roof of the house, a place that was nearly always closed. The vision was true. The cat, I know not how, was shut in there. She had sent me a telepathic message to release her from prison."

The last case has a special interest, since it clearly shows that the means whereby thoughts are conveyed without words takes the form of a kind of mental picture-writing. This means of communication is probably far older than speech, but the remarkable point in Bozzano's narrative is that the cat's vision of herself and the garret so exactly coincided with his own that he instantly recognised it when it was presented to his mind's eye-

What a proof of almost human development of the animal's perceptive and mental powers.

Another very interesting personal experience is given us by Madame Camier, whose account was published in "The Revue Scientifique et Morale du Spiritualisme." The case is quoted by Bozzano, who comments that he considers both its incidents to be explained by telepathy, and not, as the narrator suggests, by Spiritualism. Madame Camier writes:

"I owned a very beautiful Angora cat with long white hair, shaded with grey, to the black that encircled her green eyes. She was sweet and affectionate in nature, and was much admired by everyone; but she had one fault, which was that every night she tried to slip out and take a walk. The courtyard of the house where I lived was divided into two by a railing; she used to escape by leaping over this. One night I came into the courtyard just in time to catch hold of her as she prepared to bound on to the fence. I had hardly grasped her in my arms, when I was astonished by perceiving another Angora cat in all points identical with mine, who leaped over the fence. At this time I knew nothing of the doctrines of Spiritualism; I looked on the other side of the fence for explanation of the strange matter, knowing well that there was no other cat like mine in the district; but on the other side I saw nothing. When, later, I was initiated into the new teaching, I understood that my cat was at that moment so dominated by the idea of flight, that her *périsprit* liberated itself with so much force as to appear substantial.

"After some time the poor creature fell ill, and I saw it was necessary to confide her to the care of a veterinary. The night when she died I felt—positively felt—my cat hang on with her claws to the coverlet, and mount on the bed as she had been in the habit of doing. The impression was so real that I instinctively held out my hand to assure myself that I was not deceived. The following morning I returned to the veterinary's house, where I learned that my cat had died during the night; her last thought had been for me."

From the instances in this chapter it would seem that the gulf which usually separates man from his less-evolved brother is not unbridgable, and that the law underlying the mysterious faculty of Telepathy, is the union of the many in the One. A single heart beats through all the varied manifestations of Life. And vibrant chords attuned in sympathy unite all sentient beings, so that communication is always possible between those who love.

BIBLIOGRAPHY

"La Revue Scientifique et Morale du Spiritualisme," p. 351. Article by Madame Camier. Pub. 1920.

"Les Manifestations Metapsychiques et les Animaux," p. 44. By Ernest Bozzano. Pub. Paris, 1926.

CHAPTER XXIX

THE CAT AS PHALLIC SYMBOL

IT seems probable that the Cat first became regarded as a Phallic Symbol because she was held to be the terrestial representative of the Sun and Moon, and therefore of the god or goddess ruling mundane generation and conception through the occult influences attributed to those orbs. The Cat's own fruitfulness may also have been taken into account, but appears to have been a secondary consideration in deciding her appropriateness.

So to understand the position occupied by Puss in this rôle, we must glance at the mythology of some of the solar and lunar deities she represented, and the tenets of the creeds built around them.

First let us remark that Phallic worship in its origination was the expression of the reverence felt by a simple and pure-minded people for the miracle of procreation, conception, and birth. Gazing with awe upon the mystery, they saw in it the visible, earthly emblem of the creative power of God. Not until later years when religion degenerated, and unholy rites crept in, was the ideal which had been the worship of Life Itself obscured and destroyed.

Although we are accustomed to-day to think of the moon, when personified, as feminine in gender, in many ancient religions it was represented by a masculine or hermaphrodite deity, and its association with a goddess was a development from the older idea.

We have already noted that the cat-headed goddess Bast is the feminine aspect of the creator-demiurge Ptah, the most ancient of all the gods. " The divine and primordial intelligence and wisdom," " He who is self-existent," the " Giver of Life." Ptah, as the primitive Egyptian conception of the personified sun, is said to have generated The Sacred Bull, Apis, the symbol of fecundity in Nature, by a ray of light. His name signifies " He who opens," and is suggestive of his dual functions as God of Life, and God of Death, the Opener of the dark prisons of the womb and of the tomb. Not only as the representative of the sun, but also because of its connection with Bast the cat was a secondary symbol of Ptah. In later Egyptian allegory, Osiris usurped the place of Ptah as the god of Life and reproduction, and, though a sun-god, was said to inhabit the Moon. Plutarch describes an Egyptian festival, entitled "The Ingress of Osiris into the Moon," which has a phallic significance. And in a Louvre papyrus referring to the supposed influence of the Moon on generation, we read: "Couplings and conceptions abound when he (Osiris-Lunus) is seen in Heaven on that day."

The foregoing considerations help us to understand an extraordinary penalty the Egyptians were wont to inflict on women they had condemned to death for adultery. These unfortunates were sewn up in a sack with a cat, and cast into the Nile. This barbarous custom seems to have appealed to the imaginations of primitive peoples, for it travelled far. There is a dark tradition attached to a deep sinister pool formed by the river that runs down Allmanagja (All Men's Rift) in Iceland. It is known as Drowning Pool, and it is said that there, as in Egypt, women criminals used to be tied up in a sack together with a live cat, and flung into its depths. The reason of the cruel ritual is supplied by Paul Megnin: "Chez les anciens peuples germaniques," he says, "le chat était pris pour symbole de l'adultère et en même temps de l'indépendance: chez les Scandinaves et les peuples du Nord de l'Europe il était l'emblème de l'amour; la déesse Faya était toujours représentée dans un char traîné par deux grands chats." "Raffinement de cruauté," is his comment, "du peut-être à cette idée orientale que de toutes les femelles d'animaux, la chatte est celle qui ressemble le plus à la femme par sa souplesse, ses câlineries, son inconstance, et ses fureurs."

Perhaps just because it was so far-flung, the cult of the God of Fertility did not perish with the passing of Ptah and Osiris. Among the Romans it took the form of the worship of Janus, the two-faced god of fruitfulness, reverently regarded by his worshippers as the oldest, most exalted, and holiest of all deities, who was the first to be remembered in every prayer and honoured at every sacrifice; who even took precedence of Jupiter. His name, which may be spelt Ianus, is the masculine equivalent of Jana, or Diana, and we early find this strangely assorted pair in close partnership as the solar and lunar deities who inspired the religion that survived almost to the present day in Witchcraft.

Janus appears to have been recognised by the Witch cult chiefly in virtue of his title and office as Club-bearer, or Janitor, which was his because of the Rod and Keys he carried as Guardian of the Ways and Opener of the Doors, functions that unmistakably point to his direct descent from Ptah. As god of Conception, and Measurer of Times, the beginnings of all things were sacred to him. And here the reason of his connection with Diana becomes apparent. For she, as Moon-goddess, was also a Keeper of Time, and her loving sympathy with the sufferings of her sex had made her the Goddess of Childbirth. She assisted women in their pregnancy, and preserved them from death when Janus opened the door of life to their babes. A strange occupation for the Virgin Huntress, but even the Gods are not immune from the vagaries of Fate! As the Lunar-phallic cult developed the feminine aspect of the Moon deity came into greater prominence, the more masculine solar symbol was almost lost sight of, and the primitive rites for ensuring fertility were presided over by priestesses rather than by priests. The symbolism of Nature as the Great Mother seems to have been responsible for this. It made a direct appeal to the simple minds of early peoples, and its sentiment ensured a welcome in their hearts. Consequently it survived through endless vicissitudes, and even in its decadence gave birth to an almost countless number of variations of its essential doctrines. In all these, the supremacy of the priestess, wise woman, or witch was now so firmly established as to remain unshaken. She was prophet, priest, healer, or slayer by virtue of the sacred occult knowledge her training and position bestowed on her. She stood as the doorway of communication between the spiritual and material worlds, and claimed the gifts of clairvoyance and clairaudience and raising the souls of the dead. She could supply the antidotes to the terror of night, the arrow that flieth by day, the pestilence that walketh in darkness and the destruction that wasteth at noonday. Demons obeyed her incantations, and disease or death followed her curse.

Diana had not disdained to take refuge in the moon as a Cat. The feline huntress of the night was her sacred symbol. Consequently we find it closely associated with her priestesses, and even regarded as embodying the goddess, or providing the medium by which her gifts were conveyed to her servants, though later it was degraded to the rank of a familiar spirit by Christian obscurantists.

The Church has so many charges to answer in regard to the creation and fostering of superstition that it is pleasant to discover she sometimes stood up against it, even though with less zeal than she manifested when defending its cause. Such a case is recorded by McPherson, who draws attention to "a strange belief" connected with birth "mentioned by Dr. Gregor and exemplified in cases which came before the Church Courts. It was believed that if a male cat chanced to jump over food and emitted semen, the one who partook of the food conceived cats. My informant," he continues, "has heard people in Glenlivet say they did not like a male cat to jump across the table when food was upon it. This belief crops up in various cases which came before the Presbyteries. On March 5th, 1654, Jean Simpson of Rothiemay confessed at a meeting of the Session that she and her mother went to Agnes Bain for herb medicine to stay the cats that were in her belly. Her case was referred to the Presbytery, before whom she appeared on the 22nd of the same month at Botarie. She admitted she said she had ' cats in her bellie.' In fact, she so firmly believed it that she went to the minister of Rothiemay and urged him to give her a recommendation to the physicians in Aberdeen. This he refused to do. Her mother in giving evidence said she thought it had indeed been cats and that her daughter had not been with child. But when Jean went to

CARVING ON A STALL IN ST. MARY'S MINSTER, ISLE OF THANET

the minister of King-Edward ' To get a potion from him to kill the cats,' he refused, saying it was a child and not cats. It is evident this belief about cats prevailed amongst the Underworld. It would be fostered by the witches who professed to sell curative potions. At Elgin, in 1571, a trial occurred which reveals the same conception. Janet Kar was convicted of wronging Megot Nachty, in saying ' maky maie yow ceist ane barrall of makis furth of the weym yow castis bot kitlyngis (kittens) and nocht childerying.' Almost a century later, the same belief was paraded by a witch. In 1661 delation was given in by Archibald Forsyth in Elgin against Margaret Murray, witch in Elgin, accusing her of bewitching his wife who was in great pain till Margaret came to her. The witch said in the presence of many honest women that it was cats that were in her womb. So that she was never well thereafter, but died in the birth of the child. The witch in this case and Jean Simpson in Rothiemay, each for her own ends, fostered this belief."

Though we claim to have transcended such crude ideas, it is still possible to trace in contemporary customs the belief in the phallic significance of the Cat ; and the desire that Diana should by its means give an outward token of her intention to bless and fructify the marriage union. Thus we are informed by French folklore that a strange white cat mewing on a doorstep foretells a speedy marriage ; in Southern England the possession of a black cat is held to ensure that the daughters of the house will wed, and in the Midlands a black cat is a luck-bringing wedding gift.

The "Morning Post" of August 18th, 1927, under the title of "A Procession of Omens," gave the following story from the letter of "a Surrey reader" who had it from a married friend. "On her wedding day there was a black cat on the steps of the church. There was another at the hotel door, a third in the hall, a fourth in the reception room where the guests met for the wedding breakfast, a fifth by the taxi in which the newly married pair drove away, and a sixth at the station from which they left for their honeymoon."

Miss Primrose Grace, the granddaughter of the famous cricketer, seems to have believed in such omens, for she was attended by a black cat at her marriage ; and a photograph of the bride and bridesmaids, which appeared in the "Daily Mail" of April 29th, 1926, showed Puss prominent in the foreground of the picture. Similarly Miss Phyllis Bletsoe had a black cat presented to her for luck when she was married, and the "Daily Express" of September 17th, 1930, represents her holding the mascot in her arms.

Another belief is that if a cat sneezes within the bride's hearing on her wedding-day, or its eve, good luck will come to her, but should a maiden tread on a cat's tail, she must give up all hope of marriage within that year.

There used to be a superstition at Scarborough among the sailors' wives that to keep black cats in their homes was to ensure the safety of their husbands at sea ; but it was considered unlucky for the same sailors to embark with two* black cats on board. The explanation may be found on p. 60.

Possibly it is the prevalence of such superstitions among sailors that accounts for their being found in widely separated portions of the earth. Among the Telugu Indians, for example, we find Puss associated with wedding customs. These people consider marriage with a third wife to be unlucky. But, for the enthusiastic lover, there is a way of securing his heart's desire without

* Two is a feminine number.

evil consequences. And it is Puss who helps him out! He weds a cat *pro forma*, and places the symbol of marriage—which is a yellow dyed string—around its neck: after which ceremony he may fearlessly take a third woman in a fourth wedding.

But man is an ungrateful being, and the service exacted from Puss is ill-repaid by the Teluguan. He sees in cats a dainty dish, and uses them as food. His conscience does not seem quite clear about the matter, however, for if one who sees him carrying a cat reproaches him for his cruel purpose, he will always make the excuse that the cat is required to contract a third marriage.

Such isolated relics are all that now remain to connect the Cat as a Phallic Symbol with the life of to-day, but they have their significance for those who read them in the light of bygone creeds, so are not irrelevant here.

BIBLIOGRAPHY

"Ovid's Metamorphoses," Vol. I, Book V, p. 180. Trans. by the most Eminent Hands. Printed for T. Davies and Others. London, 1773.

"Extracts from the Presbytery Book of Strathbogie," p. 247. Edited by John Stuart. Pub. Aberdeen, 1843.

"Rothiemay Kirk Session Records," Vol. I, p. 95.

"Notes on the Folklore of the North-east of Scotland," p. 124. By Walter Gregor. Pub. London, 1881.

"Notre Ami le Chat," p. 47. Par Paul Mégnin. Pub. by J. Rothschild, Paris, 1899.

"Lean's Collectanea," Vol. I, p. 394. Pub. by J. W. Arrowsmith, Bristol, 1902.

"The Records of Elgin (New Spalding Club)," Vol. I, p. 127; Vol. II, p. 300. By William Cramont. Pub. Aberdeen, 1903–7.

"Folk Phases of Four Counties." By Northall.

"The Philosophy of Witchcraft," p. 90. By Ian Fergusson. Pub. by George G. Harrap & Co., London, 1924.

"Cat Gossip," Vol. II, p. 159. Edited by H. C. Brooke. Pub. Taunton.

"Primitive Beliefs in the North-east of Scotland," p. 112. By J. M. McPherson, B.D. Pub. by Longmans, Green & Co., London, 1929.

CHAPTER XXX

THE CAT AS CHARM AND TALISMAN

IT will be recalled by readers of northern mythology that the rope which proved strong enough to bind the terrible wolf Fenris after he had snapped as nothing the most powerful chains that the Asas were able to manufacture was made of such things as the footfalls of cats: things which because they have no existence cannot be destroyed. Immemorial tradition has preserved and handed on to us many of the charms and talismans employed by primitive peoples, which, together with spells and incantations, were composed of similar immaterialities—sometimes blended with more substantial matter—according to magical formula. The dim beliefs in similars and charms that preceded the ideas of animal or man-shaped deities did not perish when the latter were introduced, but persisted side by side with them, and long survived the faiths that gave them birth. Ancient ritual when divorced from religion degenerated to its original status, or, hand in hand with the faith that had raised it from the level of fetichism, it was branded as Satanism and Black Magic by the creed of an alien conqueror, and so persecuted that the scattered fragments which alone remain have lost almost all significance. Things now done "for luck" were once done for religion. The old footpaths still attract newcomers to tread their devious ways, led perhaps by a half-conscious fear that unless they are followed some misfortune may result.

An innate consciousness of the unseen and supernatural world is experienced by man even to-day, when so many material calls distract his outer consciousness. Still he feels the urge to pierce its inner secrets, to guard against its perils, or to enlist its aid in adventure. And the honoured position formerly held by the Cat as symbol of Sun and Moon, Day and Night, Good and Evil, Being and Not-being, makes this animal even yet regarded as a most potent force in Occultism of every description.

The reason why a black cat is always employed for purposes of Black Magic is explained in the ancient hexameter quoted by Eusebius (*Præp. Evan.* iv. 9), "dark victims to the powers of darkness, light to the powers of light," he counselled. We may add that the gods of a superseded creed are invariably regarded as the powers of darkness by the exponents of their successors, and are relegated to an underground existence. As we have seen in other chapters, this is the explanation of Satanism, Witchcraft, and many secret rituals. The cat that walks in darkness is an appropriate symbol of the hidden faith, and accompanies it through all vicissitudes.

Nor is the creature necessarily regarded as a victim.

Since Christian dualism had assigned to Satan the position of God of worldly prosperity, the mere possession of his favourite

AN EGYPTIAN CAT OF TO-DAY
Felis ocreata.
Block by "Cat Gossip."

animal symbol, a black cat, was thought of as a means whereby he might be approached, and by favour shown to it as his representative induced to confer some of the many gifts at his disposal on its owner. Even sincere Christians were often by no means averse to putting into practice the advice of their Lord to make friends of the mammon of unrighteousness, when it appeared that there was something to be gained by it. We may see the lingering remains of this belief among all classes of the population to-day, in the numerous black cats named "Satan," and images of black cats carried by the superstitious; all so many flags of truce held out to the Lord of the World.

> "Them that ever mind the world to win
> Must have a black cat, a howling dog and a crowing hen,"

is an ancient saw. And another is preserved for our instruction by Sir John Denham, a seventeenth-century poet of some reputation.

> " Kiss the black cat,
> And that'll make ye fat :
> Kiss ye the white one
> And that'll make ye lean."

It seems probable that " fat " and " lean " are here intended to be understood in a metaphorical sense, for there is a widespread superstition, which is specially marked in many of the Western Counties, that white cats bring ill-fortune, perhaps as symbolising " Our Lady of Sorrows."

Even so some think that any cat is better than none, and that if a house be deserted by cats there will always be illness in it.

The Cat, from its power of seeing in the dark, and because it represented the Moon that illumined the night, was naturally

YOUNG MALAYAN KINK-TAILED CAT
Photo. Professor Boden Kloss, Singapore Museum.
Block by " Cat Gossip."

regarded as potent to heal blindness of all kinds, and to confer the gift of second sight which the all-seeing Moon possessed.

The naturalist Topsell, who flourished in the seventeenth century, has left us minute direction for using the head of a black cat to remedy loss of eyesight. The colour of the animal presumably represented the darkness that enveloped the patient, and was an important item in the prescription.

" For the pain and blindness in the eye, by reason of any skins, webs, or nails, this is an approved medecine : take the head of a black cat, which hath not a spot of another colour in it, and burn it to powder in an earthern pot, leaded or glazed within ; then take this powder, and, through a quill, blow it thrice a day into thy eye ; and if in the night any heat do thereby annoy thee, take two leaves of an oke, wet in cold water, and bind them to the eye, and so shall all pain flie away, and blindness depart, although it hath oppressed thee a whole year : and this medecine is approved by many physicians both elder and later."

Professional charmers still flourish in Cornwall and make a serious business of their art, which, as of old, utilises the magic qualities of the black cat. The "Daily Mail" reporter of the Congress of the Folk-Lore Society, which was held on September 24th, 1928, remarked that "In the presence of some of these one instinctively feels magic and mystery in the air." Miss B. C. Spooner, who had tramped many miles along lonely moorland roads in Cornwall to collect fragments of folklore, told the Congress of a charm to cure a sty in the eye. "Stroke the eye, from the nose out, with the tail of a black cat, saying with a stroke to each line, 'I poke thee, I don't poke thee, I toke the queff that's under the 'ee. Oh, qualyway. Oh, qualyway.'"

A similar remedy was quoted in the "Sunday Express" shortly before the Congress. In this case merely a hair from the tip of a black cat's tail was required, but this had to be plucked when the new moon arose in a cloudless sky, and the number nine so closely associated with the mystic lore of the cat is introduced, since it must be drawn across the swollen eyelid nine times.

The belief that the Cat has the power to confer true vision on the mentally blinded is referred to in the Scottish proverb, "Cast the Cat over him." The advice is now proffered when extravagant tales impossible of belief are told, and the suggestion is that the teller is raving. Anciently, if a man were delirious with fever, the remedy was held to be the practical application of the proverb.

A fuller illustration of the Cat's supposed potentiality to give second sight may be found in the account of the Taigherm, which I have included in the chapter on The Cat as Sacrifice.

An old woman of my acquaintance, whose vocation it is to "lay out" the bodies of the departed, warned me to be very careful never to allow a cat to enter the room in which a corpse is lying. She declared that if a cat gained access to a dead body, it would tear out the eyeballs and eat them ; and she said she had seen this happen on more than one occasion.

We may here find the origin of the Scotch superstition recorded by Pennant, according to which a cat must be mercilessly destroyed if it enters a room in which there is a corpse.

The reason given is that the first person over whom the cat jumps afterwards will be stricken with blindness ; and it seems probable from the above that sympathetic magic is feared.

Such magic is employed by the Southern Slavonian when he wishes to steal undetected. In this case the formula is to burn a blind cat, and throw a pinch of its ashes over the man he would defraud. When he has done this, Krauss tells us, he can take what he likes from the stall for the deluded owner will be none the wiser, having become as blind as the cat with whose ashes he has been sprinkled. The thief may even ask: "Did I pay for it?" for the unfortunate merchant will certainly answer, "Yes."

For such purposes the brains of a black cat were another favourite weapon of witchcraft much in demand when manufacturing charms and talismans.

Ben Jonson has illustrated the dubious methods employed in obtaining the coveted spell-worker.

> "I from the jaws of a gardener's bitch
> Did snatch these bones, and then leaped the ditch,
> Yet I went back to the house again,
> Killed the black cat, and here's the brain."

Not only charms but counter-charms were manufactured from the potently magical black cat. At the period when "Tyburn's Triple Tree," "which had neither bark nor branch, yet bore fruit all the year round," flourished, the ghastly superstitions of the "Hand of Glory," and its companion, the "Dead Man's Candle," gained popular credence. The Hand of Glory was the right hand of an executed murderer, severed from the wrist during an eclipse of the moon; whilst the candle, which was set between the fingers of the bleached hand, was made with a wick of dead man's hair from the fat of the murderer, or, if we may trust Ingoldsby,

> "With the grease and the fat
> Of a black Tom Cat,"

and was supposed to have the power of paralysing the faculties of those upon whom its light fell.

> "Wherever that terrible light shall burn,
> Vainly the sleeper may toss and turn;
> His leaden eyes shall he n'er unclose
> So long as that magical taper glows,
> Life and treasure shall he command
> Who knoweth the charm of the glorious Hand!"

The counter-charm which could cause the light to expire, was the odour of a black cat's gall.

Whilst it cannot be denied that black cats predominate as amulets, and lucky charms, they do not entirely oust all other colours.

There is an old Buddhist superstition that the possession of a light cat ensures that silver will always be in the house, and that gold will always be where there is a dark-coloured cat.

According to Conway, a tri-coloured cat is a certain protection against the house where it lives being destroyed by fire, whilst in Ireland and Scotland it is still believed that a tortoise-shell cat brings good fortune, and it is considered as a good omen if such a cat settles in a home.

Finally, a cat with double claws, if found, is said to be a most potent bringer of good fortune and ought to be very carefully guarded and preserved.

Probably because of her connection with the Moon, the Cat is considered to be an effectual charm for procuring rain in many countries, if the prescribed ritual is followed, and I quote below some of the instances collected by Mr. Frazer. In Southern Celebes the people endeavour to make rain by tying a cat in a sedan chair and carrying it thrice round the thirsty fields, whilst they drench it with water from bamboo squirts. When the poor animal begins to miaul, they say: "O Lord, let rain fall on us."

In Malay when rain is desired, a woman places an inverted earthenware pan on her head, and then, setting it on the ground, she fills it with water and bathes an unfortunate cat in it until the creature is nearly drowned. It is believed that heavy rain will certainly follow the performance of this charm.

Mr. Skeat, who describes it, says that the inverted pan signifies the vault of heaven. A common method of producing rain in Java is to bathe a cat, or sometimes two cats, which should be male and female. Occasionally they are carried in procession with music. Even in Batavia children may sometimes be seen going about with a cat to make rain. They duck their victim in a pool and then release it.

To produce rain in Sumatra, the village women, dressed in light clothing, assemble by the river, wade into it, and splash one another. They bring with them a black cat, which is thrown into the stream and forced to swim about there. It is finally allowed to escape to the bank pursued by splashing from the women. In this case the colour of the cat is an ingredient of the charm. The black will sympathetically darken the sky with rain clouds. This principle is yet more thoroughly applied at Kota Gadang, in Sumatra. Here there is a stone, which by an effort of strong imagination may be thought to bear a faint and far-off resemblance to a cat. Naturally, therefore, it possesses the property of drawing down water from the sky, since the actual black cat can do so. Therefore it is occasionally smeared with the blood of fowls, rubbed and incensed, whilst a charm is uttered over it. The Chinese believe firmly that the cat is an insurance of good luck to its owner. A vivid picture of the misfortune this belief entails on poor Puss may be found in "The Soul of China." There we read how : " Inside half the shops a cat, collared and chained, dragged and tugged and mewed—rather weird-looking pussies most of them, for the older the cat the greater the luck it brings in old-age-venerating China. And the cat is the animate (and not voiceless) luck-bringer of China—almost sharing pride of place with the Hearth God himself in every Chinese village home. For the Hearth God is the Hearth God, sacred to home life, unmindful of grosser business affairs. Dogs roam at large throughout China, but cats must live on the chain. Dogs run loose in China—and why not, since a Chinese dog will only bite foreigners and beggars, but cats are almost always collared and chained. For the luck may go out with the cat, and unlike the cat, not come back. And since the older and uglier the cat is, the greater and surer the luck it brings, while kittens may be allowed some natural freedom of limb and of play, cats of more dignified and more responsible years rarely are allowed any at all. But centuries of such usage have not reconciled the Chinese cat in the least, and they make up for their monstrous curtailment of prowl by a fiendish and perpetual freedom of screech. They yowl all the time, in one great, shrill, discordant unison of indignant protest."

Even in China every cat is not the harbinger of good fortune, however, for according to Doolittle, the Chinese are the only people in the world who dislike the approach of a black cat, which to them is an omen of sickness or of poverty.

Having now gained some small idea of the importance of the cat in amulet and charm, we shall not be surprised to find that those who exploited her powers in magic white or black, sometimes had to resort to charm, in order to obtain cats in the numbers required for their purposes.

The "Conjurer's Magazine," published in 1791, gives an example of such a charm to draw cats together and fascinate them. " In the new moon gather the herb Nepe (*Nepeta cataria*, or cat-mint ?) and dry it in the heat of the sun ; gather vervain in the hour 8, and only expose it to the air while the moon is under the earth. Hang these together in a net in a convenient place, and when one of them has scented it her cry will soon call those about within hearing ; and they will rant and run about, leaping and capering to get at the net, which must be hung or placed so that they cannot accomplish it, or they will tear it in pieces." Near Bristol is a "field of Cats," so called from a large number of the animals having been drawn together there by this contrivance.

Again, because of her importance as an amulet, the Cat must be persuaded to accompany the family of her adoption when they move house, and a charm that will overcome her dislike of changing quarters must be put into operation.

The practice of buttering a cat's paws to induce her to settle in a new house is a charm widely practised among all classes to-day. An old Scotch writer throws new light on the subtle sympathy said to exist between cats and kings by the following interesting comparison :

" But do ye ken the freet of yon doing wi' the oil on the palms of the hand ? It's my opinion that it's an ancient charm to keep the new king in the kingdom : for there's no surer way to make a cat stay at hame than to creesh her paws in like manner."

From which it appears our forefathers believed that cat and king were equally enthralled by the power of one potent charm !

BIBLIOGRAPHY

" Masque of Queens." By Benjamin Jonson. Printed about 1600.

" Historie of Foure-Footed Beastes." By Ed. Topsell. Fol : Printed 1607.

" Tour in Scotland." By Thomas Pennant. Pub. 1771–5.

" The Penny Post," Vol. XXVIII, p. 248. Pub. by James Parker & Co., London, 1878.

" Legends of the Gods." By E. A. Wallis Budge, M.A., etc. Pub. by Kegan Paul, Trench, Trübner & Co., London, 1912.

" Amulets," pp. 39, 42. By W. M. Flinders Petrie, D.C.L., LL.D., etc. Pub. by Constable & Co., London, 1914.

" Guy Mannering," p. 31. By Sir Walter Scott. Pub. by Marcus Ward & Co., London, 1878.

" The Ingoldsby Legends." (" The Hand of Glory "), p. 30. By Thomas Ingoldsby. Pub. by F. Warne & Co., London.

" Myths and Legends of Japan," p. 265. By F. Hadland Davis. Pub. by George G. Harrap & Co., London, 1920.

" The Soul of China." By Louise Jordan Miln.

CHAPTER XXXI

THE SYMBOLOGY OF CAT AND MOUSE

WE have seen in other chapters that the Cat is the emblem of both Sun and Moon, and also of the many deities who personified these glorious luminaries. We will now consider the association of the Cat with its traditional victim, the rat, or mouse, as it is represented in solar and lunar mythology.

In its exoteric significance, the mouse symbolises the grey clouds that the Cat of the Sun or Moon disperses with the darting paws of its radiance; or, in sportive mood, now concealed, and now pouncing forth, allows a delusion of freedom ere it consume them.

But esoterically, the mouse, or rat, or bird (for the glyphs are interchangeable), is the human soul,* whether it be the grey ghost that haunts the night, or the still embodied psyche. This is illustrated by Baring Gould, who, writing in 1872, said: "Offerings to rats and mice are still prevalent among the peasantry in certain parts of Germany, if we may credit Grimm and Wolf." He goes on to explain that "Rats and mice have generally been considered sacred animals," and that "among the Scandinavian and Teutonic peoples they were regarded as the souls of the dead."

Many legendary stories that reflect this belief survive in Teutonic mythology. The following from Prastorius is a typical

* See p. 192

example. At Saafeld, in Thuringia, once lived a maidservant who, whilst her friends were shelling nuts, fell asleep. As she did so, those beside her observed a small red mouse creep out of her mouth, and run through the open window. A man, who was of the party, shook the sleeping girl, but finding this failed to arouse her, he carried her unconscious form to another place. Soon after the mouse returned to where the girl had been, and darted hither and thither as if trying to find her. But when it could not discover her whereabouts, it vanished, and, at the same moment, the girl expired.

Esoterically considered, the Cat, most present when it seems most absent, relentless in purpose, unerring in aim, seeing in darkness, is certainly a remarkably fine ideograph of the Great Hunter. I cannot refrain from sharing with my readers the pleasure given me by a poem of Humbert Wolfe which beautifully portrays the thought of the ancient symbologists. He writes:

"God does not hunt the soul on even flat pads like a hound, but pounces like a cat. Not he deliberate, as a slow star beams gradually, but where the tumults are of the angry sun, he chooses from the crowd one soul and strikes it, as a flying cloud is suddenly struck to an encrimsoned pause beneath the steel-blue splendour of the claws of the great cat of the sun. He cannot bear to leave the smallest of the birds of the air to fly across his radiant path unriven with white unruffled feathers, but springs through heaven with one vast bound and shining as he springs to shreds of beauty tears the clouds' white wings."

A myth of the Troad accounts for the worship of Apollo Smintheus by fabling that this god rid the city of Smintha from the mice which infested it (Ovid, Met. xii, 585). The name Smintheus has been adopted by zoologists as the designation of a variety of small rodent, and Lang has suggested that the god's title might be justly rendered "Mouse Apollo," or "Apollo, Lord of Mice." A variation of this myth relates that Apollo delivered Phrygia from a plague of rats. How the god performed the feat we are not told, but Baring Gould has supplied the key to the meaning of the fable. His suggestion is that Apollo charmed away the rodents with his lyre, even as the Pied Piper enticed the rats of Hamelin with his unearthly music. For the music of the Sun-god or Piper is the irresistible call of Death, and the mountain into which those souls who hear the mystic strains are led, is the grave. The proverb reminds us how the mountain in labour produced a mouse. (*Parturiunt montes, nascitur ridiculus mus.*) From death's dark womb issue the grey mouse shades, or ghosts to wander in the twilight of the Astral world. They are chased by the Cat Moon, the feeble reflection of the sun, through the illusions of the night, until, at last the Cat of the Sun arises. He comes not as the ragged Piper now, but in His glory and power. He pounces upon, and absorbs into Himself the separate souls who so long eluded Him. The dawn is red with blood, for only by sacrifice of the little separate selves can the transmutation be achieved. But where the end is so great, who would quarrel with the means ?

An echo of this symbolism may be discovered in the story of Puss-in-Boots. When the ogre of death was induced by the Cat of

THREE RATS HANGING AN UNTROUBLED-LOOKING CAT

From a pew carving in Great Malvern Abbey. Stall No. 3, *fourth block.*

Ra, the God of Light and Life, to appear as a mouse, or as the self which ensouled the dread form, he could no longer offer effective resistance to the passionate desire of the God for his absorption, but was devoured, even as was Metis by Zeus.

Quite another version of the Cat and Mouse allegory is presented to us by an old French writer on heraldry. The story relates how at the creation of the world, Sun and Moon vied with one another in peopling the new sphere with animals. The blazing generous Sun produced a majestic lion, noble and full of fire like himself. The Moon saw the other gods lost in admiration at so beautiful a creature, and, determined not to be outdone, caused a Cat to spring from the earth. But the obvious inferiority in dignity, and beauty of the smaller feline caused ridicule on the part of the gods, and indignation on the part of the Sun, who, annoyed by the Moon's futile attempt to rival his powers, created a mouse, as symbol of his contempt. Still unwilling to admit defeat, the Moon produced a monkey. But this, the most farcical of all animals, caused immoderate merriment. The Moon became angered by the mockery her efforts provoked, and in a final effort to be avenged on the Sun, placed an eternal hatred between the monkey and the lion, and the cat and the mouse.

In the above legend we find Moon and Cat alike considered as objects of contempt, or, at best, as poor reflections of the Sun and his creative abilities, though very different ideas inspired the great religions. Primitive man looking on the waning moon thought of it as actually wasting or being eaten away. Thus the Dacotas believe that when the moon is full a crowd of mice commence nibbling at its side until it is consumed, whilst the natives of the Northern Territories of the Gold Coast explain a lunar eclipse by saying that a cat is eating the moon. According to their theory the sun returns over the same road at night as he traversed during the day, and the moon having lost her road gets in his way, whereupon, he commences to eat her. The natives loyally come to her aid, and by slowly clapping their hands beg the solar cat to release her.

BIBLIOGRAPHY

"Zoological Mythology," Vol. II, p. 60. By Angelo Gubernatis. Pub. by Trübner & Co., London, 1872.

"Curious Myths of the Middle Ages," pp. 417, 435. By Baring Gould. Pub. by Rivingtons, London, 1872.

"Custom and Myth," p. 103. By Andrew Lang. Pub. London, 1884.

"Among the Indians of Guiana," p. 351. By Macculloch. Pub. 1883.

"The Natives of the Northern Territories of the Gold Coast," p. 23. By A. W. Cardinall. Pub. by Routledge & Sons, London.

"Notre Ami le Chat." By P. Mégnin. Pub. by J. Rothschild, Paris, 1899.

CHAPTER XXXII

THE CAT IN HERALDRY

THE thoughtful reader, recalling that the manifested Cosmos, and everything within it is in some sense a revelation of at least an aspect of the Divine Unmanifested, will realise that every true symbol in its highest and deepest interpretation represents this mystic relationship.

The symbolism employed by ancient sages is not a thing of arbitrary invention, but the language which is our only means of apprehending and approaching the Indescribable and Incomprehensible. As Carlyle has beautifully phrased it :

" In a symbol there is concealment and yet revelation, silence and speech acting together, some embodiment and revelation of the Infinite, made to blend itself with the finite, to stand visible, and, as it were, attainable there."

" As above, so below." Man is " the microcosm of the macrocosm," unknown and unknowable, even as his Creator. Heraldry is the human and personal application of the language of symbolism. The chosen emblem is as the very shadow that pursues the hero, the mirror which reflects his form, the mask or shield covering his inner self from the slings and arrows of a hostile world. It is so identified with him as to be actually confused with himself, and his descendants proudly adopt and so perpetuate its form.

> " Was not all the knowledge
> Of the Egyptians writ in mystic symbols ?
> Speak not the Scriptures oft in parables ?
> Are not the choicest fables of the poets,
> That were the fountains and first springs of wisdom,
> Wrapp'd in perplexed allegories ? "
>
> (*Ben Jonson.*)

So ancient is the device of heraldry, that many conflicting opinions have arisen as to the actual antiquity and origin of heraldic designs. Some authorities declare they are older than civilisation itself ; others would trace the source of these family distinctions to the phonetic alphabets of ancient India and China; some have found their beginnings in the national banners and titular and patronymic shields of the ancient Egyptians, or in the crests and cognominal ovals of ancient Mexico. But these, and other theories are not so conflicting as a first glance suggests, if we but think of heraldry as a part of that great system of symbolical teaching which prevailed among the nations of antiquity before the invention of letters.

All ancient historians and authors ascribe to their heroes certain symbols. Diodorus Siculus gives to Jupiter a sceptre, to

STANDARD OF THE ANCIENT ROMANS
From "Vraye et parfaite Science des armoiries." Palliot.

Hercules a lion, to Macedon a wolf, to the Persians an archer; and we all know how the Roman eagle became a term synonymous with Rome itself from 752 B.C. until the fall of the empire. There is no recorded instance of any nation, tribe, or state that has not used some species of symbolical representation. The Cat, though comparatively rarely, takes its place with distinction among the remarkable collection of creatures portrayed in heraldry.

The old French genealogist, Pierre Palliot, mentioned that the Romans often made use of the Cat's form, when designing their banners and ensigns. An allusion to the Roman goddess of Liberty was probably intended, for this deity was represented with a Cat lying at her feet, and holding in one hand a cup, and in the other a broken sceptre.

The company of soldiery, *Ordinis Augusti*, who marched under a colonel of infantry, bore a green cat on white or silver ground. Another company, the *Felices Seniories*, displayed half a Cat, red, upon a pink shield. A third feline shield was borne by the Alpine troops, and displayed a Cat with one eye and one ear visible.

The Suevi, the Vandals, and the Alani all bore sable cats, because the animal symbolised liberty. The Dutch chose the Cat as their ensign for the same reason. They noted that the

CREST OF BAILEY, BRINGHAM, CROMPE, GRANT, GORDON, MACPHERSON, M'BEAN, M'INTOSH, MACINTOSH, AND SUTHERLAND

passionate love of liberty the Cat displays, and will contend so fiercely for, made it the appropriate emblem of their small but gallant nation, which had had so long a struggle to attain independence.

The Royal Arms of Great Britain are remarkable for the fact that they are without English supporters. James I supplanted the Tudor dragon by the unicorn ; but what interests us is the three leopards, two of which come from Normandy and the third from Guienne. The leopards which the Normans transmitted to us were probably originally cats. The first French Republic added the Cat to its banner, and followed the Roman tradition by placing it at the side of the Statue of Liberty. Prudhon, the

Republican artist, designed an interesting allegory of the Constitution, in which Wisdom, personified by Minerva, was depicted with Law and Liberty. Behind Law were children leading a lion and a lamb coupled together, whilst Liberty was known by the cat sitting at her feet. The reign of the Cat terminated with that of the Republic. From being the symbol of Liberty it degenerated to represent perfidy. The frontispiece of an old volume, entitled "Les Crimes de Papes," showed a cat at the feet of the Pope, to symbolise treason and hypocrisy. After this, the cat, when displayed at all, almost ceased to be the emblem of noble houses, and became that of shopkeepers and merchants, the Cat in Boots, for example, becoming a favourite trademark of the bootmakers' guild.

We get an interesting explanation of how the heraldic Cat

CREST OF AMARY AND DAWSON

descended to this level in the Harleian MSS. We are there told that certain tradesmen "having been domestic sarvants to some nobleman, thay leaving ther masters saruis toke to themselves for ther signes ye crest, bag (i.e. badge), or ye arms of ther Lord." Hence we find the Cat was displayed by ex-servants of "ye Lord Euers, Cat of Mount and Leper (Leopard), Marquis of Worster and ye Lord Buckhurst."

The wild cat, also known as the musion, was the emblem of the Burgundians, and Clotilde of Burgundy, who married Clovis, King of the Franks in 493, bore on gold, a sable cat killing a rat. The crest of the Dawsons seems reminiscent of that of Clotilde, for it is described as "a tabby cat's head, gardant, erased, in mouth a rat, ppr. Their motto being *Vitæ via virtus*. The arms of an imprisoned cat are said to have been granted by Childebert, King of France from 511 to 558, to a knight, who made prisoner

Gundemar of Burgundy, during the war between France and the Burgundians.

The tradition recalls an amusing dialogue in Ferne's " Glory of Generositie " :

" *Paradis,* the herald : ' Therefore, I pray you, begin and tell your sovereign what coat armour this knight beareth ? '

" *Torquatus,* a knight : ' Methinks he beareth sable, a musion passant gardant or, oppressed with a fret gules of eight parts, nayles argent.'

" *Columel,* a ploughman : ' Jezu, Zir ! call you this arms ? Now by my vaye, c'had thought arms should not have been of such trifling things. Why, this is even the cat in the milk-house

CREST OF GILLIES, GILLIS, LITTON, LOWRIE, LOWRY, M'INTOSH, MACKINTOSH M'PHERSON, PENNINGTON, RAE, RICHARD, AND RICKART

window. Full ill will her dayri thrive giffe she put zutche a vermin beast in trust to keep it.' "

A curious and interesting feature in heraldry is what have been called " punning arms," from the idea that the arms were brought into being as a pun on their possessor's name. But, as we have noted, a far more probable explanation is that anciently the name of every person or place had a symbolic meaning.

We have many examples of such a practice in English heraldry, as e.g. Archer, three arrows ; Hunter, three greyhounds and a bugle horn ; butler, three wine tankards, and the cat has afforded the symbolist or punster a ready target for his ingenuity which he has not failed to avail himself of.

The County of Caithness is supposed to have derived its name from Teutonic settlers of the race of the Catti, and to have been originally titled Catti-Ness. Needless to say, such an opportunity for making a pun was not neglected by the ancient heralds, and most of the now scattered families of the old Clan Chattan adopted the Mountain Cat as their crest. The Earl of Sutherland, who in olden days was the paramount chief of this clan, was known as *Mohr ar chat,* i.e. the Great Cat. The motto of the Mackintosh family is " Touch not the cat, but a glove." The word " but " is here used in its original meaning of " beout," i.e. " without," so that the true reading is " Touch not the Clan Chattan, or Mountain Cat without a glaive." The crest is " cat-a-mountain, salient, guardant proper " ; supporters two cats proper.

The same words are the adopted motto of Grant of Ballindal-

BADGE OF THE CATESBY FAMILY
From the stained glass in Lapworth Church, Warwickshire.
(*Art Journal*)

loch, and are explained by the second motto, *ensé et an'imo.* In French : *On ne prend pas tel chat sans moufles.*

The badge of the Catesby family is a spotted cat, as pictured on the stained glass in Lapworth Church, Warwickshire, and Catesby is the hero enigmatically referred to as " the cat," in the well-known line :

" The cat, the rat, and Lovel our dog."

The Cat-a-mountain, or wild cat, was for a long time preserved in Rockingham Forest, the country of Catesby. But it was the head of the Cat tribe, the lion, that Catesby bore on his shield.

Other examples of this punning heraldry are afforded by Keats of Gloucester and Berks, represented by a mountain cat, passant, and Keat with a demi-cat, gardant, or Cattley whose bearing is a demi-cat, rampant, gardant, supporting an anchor, or Caterall of Cheshire, who shows on a chapeau az. turned up., erm., a cat, passant, ppr.

Abroad the punster has been equally attracted by the name of our feline friend. For example, the old German house of Katzen bore a silver cat holding a house on an azure field. The Neapolitan lord of the House of Della Gatta also displayed a silver cat on an azure field, and the Limousin family, La Chetardie, bore two silver cats, one above the other on azure.

A suggestive example of how it may sometimes have happened that Puss attained to the honour of being the heraldic representative of a family by her intrinsic merits is recorded in "Watson's Annals." We may read therein that Elizabeth Hurd and her husband were among Penn's early colonists in Philadelphia, and, whilst they toiled to build for themselves a dwelling, sheltered in a cave on the river bank. They were working together to erect a chimney, when Hurd somewhat sharply called out to his wife: "Thou had'st better think of dinner!" Elizabeth knew that bread and cheese were the sole contents of the larder, but, meekly accepting the dictum of her lord, she walked back to the cave, wondering sadly how to feed her hungry partner. As she went she met her cat returning from hunting with a large rabbit in his mouth. Elizabeth thankfully took from him the spoil, and was thereby enabled to greet the half-famished man with a well-cooked, nourishing meal. She told him how it had been provided. It seemed to the poor settlers like a gift from heaven, and they wept with reverential joy. Nor did they ever forget the help they had received in their hour of need. When, after many years of prosperity, Elizabeth Hurd passed on, she left to her grand-niece, Mrs. Morris, a silver tureen engraved with a cat carrying a rabbit in its mouth.

BIBLIOGRAPHY

"La Vraye et Parfaite Science des Armoiries." By Pierre Palliot. Pub. 1660.

"The Art Journal," p. 3. Pub. by George Virtue, London, 1854.

"Cat Gossip," Vol. III, No. 72, and Vol. IV, No. 129. Edited by H. C. Brooke. Pub. at Taunton.

"Fairbairn's Crests." Revised by Laurence Butters. Pub. by Bickers & Son, London.

"Historic Worcestershire." By W. Salt Brassington, F.S.A. Pub. by Midland Educational Co., Ltd., Birmingham, 1894.

"Plays and Poems." "The Alchemist," Act II, Scene 1. By Ben Jonson. Pub. by George Routledge & Sons, London, 1885.

"Notre Ami le Chat." Par Paul Mégnin. Pub. by J. Rothschild, Paris, 1899.

CHAPTER XXXIII

THE CAT'S NINE LIVES

" What wouldst thou have with me ?
Good king of cats, nothing but one
of your nine lives."
("Romeo and Juliet," III, 1.)

THE constant recurrence of certain numbers in sacred and occult literature forces itself upon the attention of even the most casual and superficial reader, and it is obvious that these numbers represent something more than arithmetical symbols. Indeed, in some cases their esoteric significance is so obtrusive that they cease to retain any numerical value. Where the Cat is concerned this remark especially applies to the numbers 3 and 9 which are closely linked with feline symbology. We have seen in other chapters how the Cat was employed by the exponents of ancient religions to typify each of the Three Persons of the Deific Trinity, so need not enlarge further here on its sacred association with the number three, but will pass on to its connection with the number nine, which, as the Trinity of Trinities, was considered to be the most sacred digit of all.

In the Egyptian pantheon three companies of nine gods each, were fully developed by the period of the Vth Dynasty, and because of their protecting love for the cat, may have originated the thought that she had nine lives. The gods who compose the first group are Tem, Shu, Tefnut, Qeb, Nut, Osiris, Isis, Set, and Nepthys. The gods of the Little Company are quite minor deities, whilst the Third Company is seldom named, and the titles of its gods are unknown. Certain texts when referring to the gods repeat the sign for god eighteen times to indicate a double group of nine, or the entire company of the greater and lesser cycles of the gods. Probably this idea that all divinities could be enumerated in nines was the reason why nine was dedicated to both Sun and Moon, and the Cat that symbolised them, by nations that had contacted Egyptian thought. Apollo, as the god of light was said to be the producer of the nine months of which the original or lunar year consisted, and we find him surrounded by the nine Muses, whom Virgil describes as his sisters (Ecl. vi. 66), and who presided over literature, science, and art.

> " Daughters of Jove ! that on Olympus shine,
> Ye all-beholding, all-recording nine."
>
> (Pope's Iliad, XIV, 599–600.)

Diana, both as sister of Apollo, and in her own character as moon-goddess, was intimately connected with the Cat, and the number nine. The importance of both these symbols in the Dianic cult is emphasised by a line in Quarles' " Litany," describing the witches as

> " Two-legged cats with thrice nine lives."

The poet would seem to be thinking of one of those ritual dances we have elsewhere pictured, in which the Daughters of Diana, masked and robed as cats, in honour of the lunar deity, may have sought to represent the Three Companies of Egyptian gods, and become identified in mystic communion with the " thrice nine lives " of those divinities through the exaltation induced by their ordered movements.

In the account given by Pomponius Mela of the nine priestesses of the Island of Sark, we find a most interesting link between the originally sacred votaries of the celestial deities, who used their occult powers to heal and bless, and those degraded Daughters of Diana, the later witches, whose gifts are said to have been prostituted to evil and destructive purposes ; or at best employed for such questionable feats as transforming themselves into animal shapes and raising tempests.

Mela tells us that : " Sena being situate in the Britishe Sea, against the countrie of the Osis-Myes, is renowned with the Oracle of the God of the Galles, whose Vowesses in number nine, are hallowed to continuall Virginitie. They call them Gallicens, and are of opinion that through the singular wisdom wherewith they are endued, they rayse the seas and winds with their charmes, and transforme themselves into what Beastes they will, and heale such diseases as to others are incurable, and knowe thinges to come and prophesie of them, but not unto any other than such as sayle thither for the nonce, and come of set purpose to demaund Counsell of them."

It will be interesting to compare the Gallicens with the nine Telchini of Rhodes, the Sons of Poseidon, who forged the trident of Neptune, and fought in the armies of Dionysos mounted on sea-horses. For in this early conception we find the origin of that baseness of ideal to which the Daughters of Diana in later times appear to have descended. Like the Gallicens, the Telchini were able to assume whatever form they pleased (Diod., v.

55), and, perhaps partly on this account, were denounced as deluders, sorcerers, and demons by the common people. But they went beyond such practices. Their glance, the evil eye, was fatal to him on whom it fell (Ovid, Met. i. 7). They mingled Stygian water with sulphur, in order to destroy animals and plants, and they were able to command hail, rain, or snow. According to some accounts they quitted Rhodes, after foretelling a great flood, and scattered into various countries. But others say that Apollo, to whom the island was sacred, drove them from it, and that they afterwards wandered to and fro on the seas as if possessed by madness (Crabb).

Turning to Northern Europe, we find the Saxon goddess Hel, the dark aspect of Freya, whose cat-drawn chariot we have described in another chapter, was also closely connected with the number nine. We may read in the Edda how Odin gave her power over the nine worlds, or, according to another version, over the ninth world, and that it took nine nights' ride through gloomy valleys to reach the river Giöl, and the gold-covered bridge by which it was spanned.

An example of the use of the number nine in ritual " conjuring of cats " by the later witches is recorded by Pitcairn as having been practised by a Coven at Seaton. " Eftir thay had drukkin togidder a certane space," he says, " thay, in thair devillische maner, tuik ane katt, and drew the samyn nyne tymes throw the said Beigis cruik ; and thaireftir come with all thair speed to Seaton-Thorne, be-north the zet. . . . And thay thaireftir past altogidder, with the Devill, to the irne zet [iron gate] of Seatoun, quhair of new thay tuik ane cat, and drew the samyn nyne tymes throw the said Irne-zett. And immediatlie thaireftir, came to the barne foiranent George Feudaris dur, quhair thay christened the said catt, and callit hir Margaret. And thaireftir come all bak agane to the Deane-fute, quhair first thai convenit, and cuist the kat to the Devill."

This account of the " christening " of the cat suggests that the witches' cult was not uninfluenced by the newer creed. But be this as it may, the ancient, almost world-wide numerical symbolism, so closely associated with the sacred feline, was adopted by the Christian Churches, and incorporated into their ritual.

Nona hora, or noon, the ninth hour, corresponding with our three in the afternoon, through the ecclesiastical custom of saying *Nones*, which is the office for the ninth hour, at twelve o'clock, has acquired the meaning of midday, the hour specially sacred to the Sun-god, who is then at the zenith of his power and glory. Obviously it is sacred to all who see in the sun the symbol of the Supreme. Also it is critical, for it marks the turning-point.

The sun must now commence his descent into the grave. The ninth hour was the hour of Christ's death. Christ, the Sun of Righteousness, who, in early Christian symbolism, like his Egyptian prototypes, Osiris and Horus, was represented by the sacred Cat, to emphasise that he was the new-born, rising Sun, the light of the world.

BIBLIOGRAPHY

"The Rare and Singuler Work of Pomponius Mela, that excellent and worthy Cosmographer," Book III, Chapter VI. Trans. into English by Arthur Golding, Gentleman, London, 1590.

"Universal Historical Dictionary." By George Crabb, A.M. Printed for Baldwin & Cradock, London, 1833.

"Criminal Trials," Vol. II, p. 542. By Robert Pitcairn. Pub. Edinburgh, 1833.

"Plutarch's Lives," p. 52. Trans. from the original Greek, by John Langhorne, D.D., and William Langhorne, A.M. Pub. by Routledge & Sons, London, 1879.

"The Pantheon," p. 286. By Andrew Tooke, A.M. Printed in London.

"Asgard and the Gods." Adapted from Dr. W. Wagner, by M. W. Macdowall. Pub. by Swan, Sonnenschein, Le Bas & Lowrey, 1886.

"The Secret Doctrine," 2nd edition, Vol. II, p. 552. By H. P. Blavatsky. Pub. by the Theosophical Publishing Company, Ltd., London, 1888.

CHAPTER XXXIV

THE CAT'S NOMENCLATURE

IT is an axiom among certain circles of occultists that names contain within themselves tremendous power to affect their owners for good or evil. This is partly explained by the connection of the letters expressing them with what is claimed to be the Science of Numerology. As I have treated of the latter in its relation to the Cat in a separate chapter, we need not examine it here. But the name is more than can be expressed by number. It is the symbol of the Self: the word that is an integral portion of the being who bears it; a vital mysterious link between the personality and those who would approach thereto. Like a portrait, or image, or actual portion of the owner's body (such as nail-clippings, etc.), it is claimed that it may be a potent instrument in the hand of black or white magician to injure or bless; so intimately is it connected with the soul of him to whom it belongs. Therefore it will assist us to understand the subject of our study more completely if we glance at some of the many names by which the Cat has been known to man, and try to trace them to their origins.

The first appearance of the domesticated Cat in Egypt is said by some authorities to have been approximately 2500 B.C., and an effigy dating about two centuries later, which was discovered at Beni Hassan, reveals that it was known by the name *Mait*, the feminine form of *Mau*, a word supposed to have been derived from the sound of mewing. The Chinese did not domesticate the Cat until about A.D. 200–400, but a similar thought seems to have inspired their name for it, which was *Mao*, or *Miu*. The Cat's call is expressive of herself, and it has been suggested that the French synonyms of Minette, Minousse, Mimi, etc., and the German Miez, or Mieze-Katze, are also imitations of its sound.

Another source of many names bestowed upon the Cat is her salient characteristic of hunting, and this is responsible for her Sanskrit title of *Mârgaras*, the proper meaning of which is hunter, investigator, he who pursues the *mârgas*, or track. Gubernatis suggestively says that we may think of the hunter as the one who follows the margin or track; or, alternatively, as he who hunts and slays the *mrigas*, or forest animal. The Moon —the celestial Cat—elsewhere personified as Diana the Huntress, is called in Sanskrit *mrigarâĝas*, or king of the forest animals, and, as kings are wont, it sometimes protects and sometimes devours its subjects. The Cat-Moon may be conceived of as eating the grey mice of night, or as protecting the weak by her radiant light. It is easy to confuse the word *mârgaras* with the word *mârĝâras*, the Hindu name for cat, which signifies the cleanser ; for both words describe aspects of the Cat. The white cat is identified with the Moon who is the cleanser of the night, and disperses its darkness by her searching light, pointing the way with her marginal finger, and shielding innocent animals from their foes. But the black cat represents the dark night, and as such is the destroyer and engulfer of all that has form. In this complicated symbolism we must regard the track or *mârgas* as the clean part of the land, as the margin is the clean part of a book, so that it is related to the cleansing cat, as well as to the hunting feline. The German *Marder* (for " Margery the Cat ") is derived from the Sanskrit *Mârgaras*, and like that word signifies the Slayer. The tiger-cat of South America is appropriately named the Margay. But in Italy, by false etymology, *Mardar* is associated with St. Martha, who like the Cat is an embodiment of the domestic virtues.

The Latin name of the Cat, *Felis*, or *Feles*, is thought by some etymologists to have been derived from the root *fe*, signifying to produce or bear young, and to have reference to the fruitfulness which made the Cat the appropriate emblem of all the Great-Mother goddesses. But this origin is disputed, and it has been argued alternatively that the Romans bestowed the title *felis* on the Cat, and other animals, including the weasel, which " fell " to, or " felled " mice. The Anglo-Saxon, Celtic and Danish variations of " fell " mean " eager for slain," " to cause to fall," " to strike down and destroy relentlessly," and suggest the wild untamable feline that fitly represents Sekhmet, the personification of the destructive solar force.

The French name for the wild cat, the *Haret*, seems confirmatory of this view. It appears to be cognate with our word " harry," from the Anglo-Saxon *here*, an army, and to imply pillage, plunder, and destruction, such as are associated with war.

The following words denoting cat appear to be all derived from an Aryan root *ghad*, meaning to grasp, or catch, as the cat seizes her prey.

Greek *Catta*, Latin *Cattus*, French *Chat*, Italian *Gatto*, Old English *Gattus*, Spanish and Portuguese *Gato*, Polish *Kot*, Russian

Kots, German *Katze, Katti, Ket;* Welsh and Cornish *Kath*, Basque *Catua*, Armenian *Gatz*, and Arabic *Kittah*

The word " Puss " is also of obscure derivation, and much ingenuity has been expended in attempting to discover its source. The most attractive suggestion is that it comes from the Egyptian *Posht*, or *Pasht*, i.e. the goddess Bast, and there seems nothing strained or improbable in this explanation. The Turkish and Afghan *Pis-chik* (little *Pis*), the Aryan *Pusag*, and Persian *Push-nak*, with the Arabic *Bussah*, may be also connected with Bes, the spouse of Bast, since to him, as to his bride, the cat is sacred.

Another tempting derivation of Puss is from the Latin *Pusus*, a little boy, or *Pusa*, a little girl; the word appears in the children's game of " Puss-in-the-Corner," and is often employed as a pet name for a child or young woman. It is easy to see how it may have come into use to call that most human of pets, the household cat.

With this possibility we may compare the Hindustani " Phis, Phis " (fish, fish) used in calling a cat. Puss is a term suggesting cajolery and flattery; " Phis " speaks of an offering. Both terms are redolent of the deference due to the sacred animal. But a third idea is less respectful, and supposes that Puss was originally an imitative word representing the sound made by the cat when spitting. This seems to be negatived by the fact that in Shakespeare's time Puss was the common name for the hare or rabbit, and it would be interesting to discover if the rodents were named after the feline, or derived the title from a common or an independent source.

The Old English name for a Tom-cat was a Gib, or Gibbe-cat (hard g), and the term persisted in common use in Northern England and Scotland until recent times, and even now has not completely died out. The name seems to have been specially applied to an old male cat whose gravity approached to melancholy. Thus Shakespeare makes Falstaff declare: " I am as melancholy as a gib-cat " (" Henry IV," Act I, Sc. II). A light is cast on the significance of the phrase by Fennell, who, in his " Natural History of Quadrupeds," written in 1843, says: " Most of the former [he-cats] that are kept are emasculated, in which state, always accompanied with a subdued and melancholy appearance, they are called *Gilberts*, or Gib-cats."

The uncanny gloom of these cats caused them to be connected with witchcraft, and Marston describes " A hag whose eies shoot poison—that has become an ould witch, and is now turning into a gib-cat." (" The Fawne," IV.)

The name seems to have been a familiar abbreviation of Gilbert, and of old High German origin. It was at first used as a proper name for an individual cat, like the modern English "Tom," but finally became regarded as a generic term. An example of its use in the former sense may be found in Poole, who says:

> "Ere Gib, our cat, could lick her ear."
> ("Edward I.")

It has been suggested that Tibert, the name of the cat in "Reynard the Fox," may have been the old French equivalent of Gilbert. It is a variation of Tybalt, a form of Theobald, and, like Gilbert, was a popular name for a cat. Chaucer, in his "Romance of the Rose," renders "*Thibert le Cas,*" by "Gibbe, our cat" (I. 6204). Tybalt is called "King of cats" in "Romeo and Juliet."

However, it would seem that a Tib-cat was the feminine counterpart of Gib-cat. On the other hand, a Tabby cat was so called from the black and white watered silks which came originally from El Tabbiana, near Bagdad, but the word acquired the meaning of female cat, as distinguished from Tom-cat.

A somewhat different aspect of the Cat is brought into prominence by the interpretation Gubernatis places on certain of her names. For instance, the Sanskrit word *Naktaĉârin*, which is applied indiscriminately as an epithet of both cat and thief. He points out that whilst ants, mice, moles, and serpents "love to stay hidden, and to keep their secrets concealed, the ichneumon, the weasel, and the cat generally come out of their hiding places, and chase away whoever is concealed, carrying from the hiding places whatever they can. They are both themselves thieves, and hunt other thieves." He adds that the Sanskrit word *Nakulus* signifies the ichneumon, which makes common cause with Puss in the destruction of mice, scorpions, and serpents. Its derivation he considers to be from the root *nac, nak=necare*, so that *nakulus* designates "the destroyer of nocturnal mice," a name equally applicable to the Cat. He adds that the mouse, *mûsh, mûshas,* or *mushakas* (Sanskrit, mush, steal), is the thief, the ravisher, and one in significance with the rat (*a rapiendo*). The "Mouser" is, like *nakulus*, the destroyer of mice. So we see that the Cat's strange, paradoxical nature has caused her to coil herself in a circle again. She is not only the thief that cometh in the night, cloaked and hidden by its gloom; she is also the Destroyer of Thieves, the representative of the solar and lunar Eyes of Deity, before Whom "all things are naked" (Heb. iv., 13), the Exposer, the Revealer, the stark, bare Truth who has divested herself of every rag of concealment, and is the inevitable Foe of all who walk in darkness. Philo's advice to consult "the mirror of the names " for hidden meanings is a key that unlocks many doors.

BIBLIOGRAPHY

" Zoological Mythology," Vol. II, pp. 42 *et seq.* By Angelo de Gubernatis. Pub. by Trübner & Co., London, 1872.

" The Century Dictionary." Prepared under supervision of William Dwight Whitney, Ph.D., LL.D. Pub. by " The Times," London

" Dictionary of the Derivations of the English Language." Pub. by William Collins, Sons & Co., London.

" De Vita Contemplativa." Ascribed to Philo. Circa A.D. 20.

CHAPTER XXXV

MANX LEGENDS

THE origin of the race of tailless cats which inhabit the Isle of Man is a mystery that has never found a satisfactory explanation. But legend persistently associates shipwreck with the coming of the Manx cat to its island home. According to one account the breed came over in the Spanish Armada, and was propagated by cats that escaped from two ships wrecked off Spanish Point, near Port Erin. An old Manx newspaper asserts that in 1808 an "East County ship was

TYPICAL MANX CAT
Mr. H. C. Brooke's Champion Bouhaki.
Block by " Cat Gossip."

wrecked on Jurby Point, and a rumpy cat swam ashore." Another tradition, saved from oblivion by the Rev. W. B. Clarke, states that a Baltic ship wrecked between Castle Rushen and the Calf was responsible for the introduction of the Manx cat to the island. As the vessel drew close to the shore two or three tailless cats leaped from the bowsprit, and were taken by the wreckers, and these were the first of the kind ever seen in Man. All these legends are confessedly of recent date, and are but another way of saying that the origin of the breed is unknown, and is derived from a foreign source.

The learned explorer, Auguste Pavie, considered that the Annamite cats may have been connected with the Manx. The former were of graceful shape, small in size, and had yellow eyes and naturally short tails. They were introduced into Burma during an invasion, and may have been imported into the East Indies from Britain by English trading expeditions in the eighteenth century. Siam and Malaya also seem to be possible sources of the Manx.

The cats of the Malayan Archipelago are noted for their peculiarly kinked, knotted, clubbed or otherwise malformed tails. The reason for this condition is unknown, but it is a state which has endured for a long period of time, reference being made to it as far back as 1783 by William Marsden, F.R.S., late Secretary to the President and Council of Sumatra, who wrote in his "History of Sumatra," "All their tails imperfect and knobbed at the end."

A native legend relates that a certain Princess bathing in a lake in the Palace grounds strung her rings on the tail, at that time straight, of her pet cat. Alas, the cat dropped her tail, and the rings slipped into the water. On the next occasion the Princess knotted the cat's tail, so that the rings remain in place, and since then all the native cats have kinked tails.

It must be rather difficult for the traveller to distinguish between naturally and artificially tailless cats. Mr. Frazer informs us that all cats in Bismark Archipelago, off the north coast of New Guinea, walk about with stumpy tails. But Nature is not responsible for the shortcomings of their caudal appendages. The natives of that land regard a cat as a dainty dish, and the less scrupulous among them are sometimes tempted to seize the cat of their neighbour when they are short of a meal. This temptation is removed by docking Puss of a portion of her tail and hiding it. If after this operation the cat is stolen and eaten, the owner can avenge the crime by burying the severed piece with certain spells in the earth. This will cause the thief to fall ill. So no one dares to steal a cat with a stumpy tail.

Whilst staying at Newlyn, in Cornwall, many years ago, I noticed a large number of cats with short tails which I supposed to be derived from Manx stock. But I was assured by a resident that they had been docked by their owners. He ascribed the reason to the native cruelty of the Cornish peasantry, whom he intensely disliked. It seems more probable that superstition was responsible for the practice, but though my personal experiences taught me to think of the people of Cornwall as invariably kind, at that time I did not know enough to look deeper for a cause.

From the ancient Welsh legend, given below, it would appear that Manx cats were known in Cornwall at an early date, and that it was from thence the Isle of Man derived the breed. They were evidently sacred animals, since they are fabled to have been the offspring of a goddess, or at least of the religious system that honoured her. According to Davies, "about eight hundred years before Christ the ancient Britons worshipped an 'unknown God under the Phœnician name "Hwch"' (Sow), and the number of place-names within this parish (of Dinas Ffaraon) connected with 'Hwch' and 'Moch' ('Pigs'), such as Llwyn yr Hwch, Dinas Moch, Cae'r Moch, etc., makes it reasonable to assume that the above-named religion was the religion of the district."

The legend informs us that Dallwaran Dallben, who lived in the vale of Dallwyr, in Cornwall, owned a sow named Henwen, and its keeper was Coll ab Collfrewi. "The sow was big with young, and as it had been prophesied that the Isle of Britain would be injured by her progeny, Arthur collected the forces of the country and went forth to destroy it. The sow in the meantime, being about to farrow, proceeded as far as the promontory of Penwedig, or Land's End, in Cornwall, where she put to sea. She next landed at Aber Tarogi, in Gwent, Coll having hold of her bristles and following wherever she wandered, whether by land or sea. At Wheatfield, in Gwent, she laid three grains of wheat and three bees; hence Gwent has been famous ever since for the best wheat and honey. From Gwent she went to Dyfed, where she laid a grain of barley and a pig; and from that time the barley and swine of Dyfed are proverbial. After this she proceeded to Arvon, and in Lleyn she laid a grain of rye, since which time the best rye is produced in Lleyn and Eifionydd. Proceeding thence to the cliff of Cyferthwch, in Snowdon, she laid the cub of a wolf and an eaglet—these were the wolf of Menwaed, and the eagle of Brynach, which in aftertimes became so famous. From hence the sow went to the black stone, in Arvon, under which she laid a kitten, which Coll threw into the Menai. The sons of Palug, in Mona, took it up, and nursed it up, to their own injury. This became the celebrated Palug cat, one of the three chief molesters of Mona."

Coll ab Collfrewi was described as being the nephew and disciple of Rhuddlwm Gawr, or the Bony Red Giant, possibly a Phœnician merchant whose religious system was allegorised as a sow. Davies, from whom we have quoted above, deals at some length with sow worship should our reader want to learn more of it.

The oldest origin of all attributed to the Manx is that it was the last of all the animals to enter the Ark, and that its delay caused Noah to lose his temper and impatiently slam the door on its tail. The following verse by Jane Crosby amusingly relates the story:

" Said the Cat, and he was Manx,
  Oh, Captain Noah, wait !
I'll catch the mice to give you thanks
  And pay for being late !
So the cat got in, but oh,
His tail was a bit too slow ! "

Another version of the Noah myth says :

" Noah, sailing o'er the seas
  Ran fast aground on Ararat,
His dog then made a spring and took
  The tail from off a pretty cat :
Puss through the window quick did fly,
  And bravely through the waters swam
Nor ever stopped till high and dry,
  She landed on the Calf of Man.
Thus tailless Puss earned Mona's thanks
  And ever after was called Manx."

Miss Mona Douglas, speaking to the Jubilee Congress of the Folk-Lore Society in London, in 1928, of animals in Manx folklore, said there was a local belief that the cats of the Isle of Man had a king of their own. " This king lives the life of an ordinary house-cat during the day, but at night he assumes his regal powers and travels the lanes in fiery state. Woe betide the householder with whom he lives if he has been unkind to his royal guest, for the king of the Manx cats may take terrible vengeance." Miss Douglas added that " Cats are believed to be on intimate terms with the fairies, and with all the inhabitants of the invisible world. . . . If a cat is put out of doors when the family retires, the fairies let it in again during the night."

BIBLIOGRAPHY

" Mythology and Rites of the British Druids." By Edward Davies. Pub. London, 1809.

" Bedd Gelert, Its Facts, Fairies, and Folklore," p. 208. By D. E. Jenkins. Pub. by Llewelyn Jenkins, Portmadock, 1899.

" The Daily News and Westminster Gazette." Sept. 25th, 1928.

" Animals," p. 242. Jan., 1926.

" The Golden Bough." By J. G. Frazer. Pub. by Macmillan & Co. London, 1907.

L'ENVOI

WE have traced the Cat through endless vicissitudes, through a glorious and a terrible past. What a burden her small and shapely shoulders have been called upon to bear in the religious evolution of mankind. It is hard to realise the extraordinary fate that has been hers when we glance at the friendly, familiar figure of the household cat to-day. Could poet in wildest dreams have dared unfold a romance of Destiny to equal the veridical facts of her association with man ? We think not. The fate that made her the symbol of Life and Death, of Day and Night, of Sun and Moon, of Deity and Devil, to-day but furtively plays around her like a child half ashamed of its association with, yet still attracted to, a once-loved toy. Yet so strangely capricious is Destiny that none may foresee what the future will bring forth. Some sudden gleaming light may burst upon the shadowed form of Puss, causing us to pause again in awestruck admiration of her mystery ; or she may silently leave our sides and wander far in the mysterious darkness of the Night, swallowed up by its immensity and lost for ever to human consciousness.

FAREWELL

INDEX

G

H

I

J

K

L